Praise for *The Quest for Global Dominance*

"The reality of thinking and being global in mindset should be a no-brainer for all of us. But for those who believe that such is not the case, this book puts to rest any romantic or unrealistic views that we can sit back and bask in our prosperity. So it's back to work on figuring out how to win globally, not locally or nationally, that will get you in the Hall of Fame for Business Leaders worldwide. You will find yourself referring often to *The Quest for Global Dominance* as you chart your course forward."
> —William F. Achtmeyer, chairman and managing partner,
> the Parthenon Group

"*The Quest for Global Dominance* is the best source of insight available for executives who want their companies to win in the face of global competition. It provides sound framework, practical advice, and dozens of helpful examples from companies around the world. For any company, from startup ventures to world leaders, this book tells managers what they must do in order to gain and keep a competitive advantage when rivals can come from anywhere and competition in an industry transcends borders."
> —Philip Anderson, INSEAD Alumni Fund Chaired
> Professor of Entrepreneurship, INSEAD

"A must-read for executives who expect to harness the accelerating trend of globalization. The authors make a compelling case for an accelerating rate of change based upon broad-based support for free trade, the increased economic power of developing nations, and the pervasive impact of enabling technology."
> —Alexander M. Cutler, chairman and chief executive officer,
> Eaton Corporation

"This book is not only visionary, but also very practical in thinking about globalization. It makes a compelling case for why globalization has to be at the very forefront of your plan to be able to build a foundation for a lasting business."
> —Desh Deshpande, chairman, Sycamore Networks

"A terrific book that effectively melds theories with successful practices of global companies and global strategy with the importance of organizational mindset and culture. Through an exceptional number of relevant, current, and real examples, the authors address the full range of issues, challenges, and opportunities that companies and practitioners face. This is a very readable, insightful, and compelling tool for building global competitive advantage."
> —Peter Dolan, former CEO, Bristol-Myers Squibb

"A terrific set of ideas on building a winning global firm with fresh insights into particularly crucial topics like global teams and launching born-global businesses. This is important and must-reading for savvy executives and students around the world."

> —Kathleen M. Eisenhardt, Ascherman Professor of Strategy, Stanford University, and codirector, Stanford Technology Ventures Program

"Rich with up-to-date examples, but also built on rigorous research, this book is a must for executives who are intent on going global."

> —Donald C. Hambrick, Smeal Chaired Professor of Management, Smeal College of Business, Penn State University

"This book provides fundamental inputs for managers who are leading modern global corporations within the new age. Above all, I am impressed with the focus on building a global knowledge ecology within these modern corporations. Globality truly becomes relevant and meaningful when seen in the light of knowledge development, taking us from learning within smaller individual 'silos' or 'kingdoms' to learning and knowledge accumulation in a global context. Overall, this is a great book and a must for the modern leader of the global firm."

> —Peter Lorange, president, IMD International, Lausanne, Switzerland

"In today's 'flat' world, no company can remain immune to the forces of globalization. *The Quest for Global Dominance* explains how companies can not only face up to these forces but proactively exploit them. It emphasizes the importance of cultivating a global mindset, describes how to design an optimal global architecture, explains how to build a global knowledge machine while avoiding many of the pathologies and pitfalls, and shows how to transplant the corporate DNA across countries. The authors present their ideas clearly and support them with contemporary case studies. *The Quest for Global Dominance* is a superb and timely book, full of fresh ideas, that deserves to be widely read and that must be on the shelf of every practicing manager."

> —Costas Markides, Robert P. Bauman Professor of Strategic Leadership and chairman, Strategic and International Management Department, London Business School

"The velocity of change in the global arena has significantly accelerated. *The Quest for Global Dominance* provides the strategic imperatives to succeed in a global business."

> —John Menzer, vice chairman and chief administrative officer, Wal-Mart Stores, Inc.

"Globalization is undoubtedly a key imperative for business leaders the world over. The authors bring rich experience, a keen eye for detail, and strong conceptual abilities to their investigation of this phenomenon. *The Quest for Global Dominance* not only presents incisive and in-depth analysis but also inspires real-world, implementable solutions to the challenges faced by practitioners of management in today's global village."
— N. R. Narayana Murthy, chairman and chief mentor, Infosys Technologies Limited

"*The Quest for Global Dominance* presents the impact which globalization is having on countries, companies, and leaders in a fresh and superbly documented way. Above all, it raises the strategic implication of this in a fashion that should allow leaders to consider how to leverage their global presence and capability into a more successful leadership enterprise."
— John E. Pepper, chairman of the board, the Walt Disney Company

"The authors of this book 'get it.' Based on the last 10 years, the next 20 will see continuing change and convergence of markets (globalization) and rapid evolution of business models (both globalization and virtualization). Managers must deal with these trends to survive and master them to flourish. The authors' advice is sound and timely, and we would all do well to heed it."
— Donald K. Peterson, former chairman and CEO, Avaya Inc.

"In a world of new opportunities and major challenges, *The Quest for Global Dominance* comes at the right time for those who not only want to stay in the game but also have the will to become an important actor in the massive transformation to occur. Global dominance is a must for industries and services, and this book explains why and what you should do to become a global leader in a specific segment. It's a fascinating book, easy to read, and very useful to those willing to be global."
— Didier Pineau-Valencienne, former president, Schneider S.A.

"Few topics continue to engage the attention of business leaders over centuries as the subject of how to of 'global domination.' From the ancient silk routes to the glory days of conflict between the Dutch, Spanish, Portuguese, and British fleets to control the trade routes, the preoccupation has been one of finding and holding on to the 'choke points' of the global system. The context of competition for a disproportionate global influence has changed over the centuries, but the basic managerial motive has not. Managers in multinational firms today face a new variant of this age-old battle for global domination. This book addresses the contemporary context within which this struggle is waged and the arsenal of tools that one has to master to win. The authors provide a very interesting blend of existing knowledge and new research to provide a new gestalt on globalization. By providing in one, very readable book the intellectual trail of where we are from, where we are, and where we are headed, the authors have captured for the busy executive an invaluable intellectual companion. It will force many to rethink their business strategies, personal managerial styles, and most importantly their capacity to leverage the most elusive of all resources—knowledge and emotional commitment of people around the world."

> —C. K. Prahalad, Paul and Ruth McCracken Distinguished University Professor, the University of Michigan Business School

"The authors of this book are among the masters on the subject of global strategy. In this book, they have succeeded in putting forth tight logic and leading-edge thinking in a manner that is highly practical. If you were to read only one book this year on how to assess and develop a global strategy for your business, this would be it."

> —John A. Quelch, senior associate dean and Lincon Filene Professor, Harvard Business School

"I found *The Quest for Global Dominance* to be an outstanding guide to building global presence and effectiveness based on the real, often painful, experiences of some best-practice companies and a few theoretical underpinnings. It helped put words and a framework around some of the experiences and learnings in my own international career. I often found myself nodding in agreement and saying how I would have loved to have read this before my first expat assignment. It goes well beyond merely stating the imperative— it explains how to make the transition from international/multinational models to true globalization. The book is particularly helpful in giving practical advice on managing the complex human dimensions of global businesses and global teams."

> —Peter F. Volanakis, president and chief operating officer, Corning Inc.

The Quest for Global Dominance

Transforming Global Presence into Global Competitive Advantage

Second Edition

Anil K. Gupta
Vijay Govindarajan
Haiyan Wang

Foreword by Jeffrey E. Garten

JOSSEY-BASS
A Wiley Company
San Francisco

Published by Jossey-Bass
A Wiley Imprint
989 Market Street, San Francisco, CA 94103-1741—www.josseybass.com

Readers should be aware that Internet Web sites offered as citations and/or sources for further information may have changed or disappeared between the time this was written and when it is read.

Limit of Liability/Disclaimer of Warranty: While the publisher and author have used their best efforts in preparing this book, they make no representations or warranties with respect to the accuracy or completeness of the contents of this book and specifically disclaim any implied warranties of merchantability or fitness for a particular purpose. No warranty may be created or extended by sales representatives or written sales materials. The advice and strategies contained herein may not be suitable for your situation. You should consult with a professional where appropriate. Neither the publisher nor author shall be liable for any loss of profit or any other commercial damages, including but not limited to special, incidental, consequential, or other damages.

Jossey-Bass books and products are available through most bookstores. To contact Jossey-Bass directly call our Customer Care Department within the U.S. at 800-956-7739, outside the U.S. at 317-572-3986, or fax 317-572-4002.

Jossey-Bass also publishes its books in a variety of electronic formats. Some content that appears in print may not be available in electronic books.

Library of Congress Cataloging-in-Publication Data

Gupta, Anil K.
  The quest for global dominance : transforming global presence into global competitive advantage / Anil K. Gupta, Vijay Govindarajan, Haiyan Wang; foreword by Jeffrey E. Garten.— 2nd ed.
      p. cm.
  Rev. ed. of: The quest for global dominance / Vijay Govindarajan, Anil K. Gupta. c2001.
  Includes bibliographical references and index.
  ISBN 978-0-470-19440-9 (cloth)
  1. International business enterprises—Management. 2. Industrial management.
  3. Organizational effectiveness 4. Comparative advantage (International trade)
  5. Globalization—Economic aspects. 6. Competition, International. I. Govindarajan,
  Vijay. II. Wang, Haiyan. III. Govindarajan, Vijay. The quest for global dominance. IV. Title.
  HD62.4.G68 2008
  658'.049—dc22

                                                                                          2008000872

Printed in the United States of America
SECOND EDITION
HB Printing 10 9 8 7 6 5 4 3 2

Contents

Foreword

When the first edition of *The Quest for Global Dominance* was published, I recognized it as a major breakthrough in thinking about globalization and in helping business leaders develop invaluable insights about what they needed to do to win in the global marketplace. In plain but engaging language, the authors managed to pack in both a broad conceptual framework as well as critical strategic imperatives for those leaders who would make the globalization of their operations an invaluable asset rather than a complex albatross. I was particularly struck by the way the authors integrated both local and global factors in their analysis and also their keen awareness of the importance of intangible human assets in the success of any global strategy. The information was right on point, the case studies illuminating.

It did not occur to me that a second edition could do more than update the voluminous and important information contained in the original version. However, after I read it I could see that it has done that and much more.

In this new edition, you will find not only updates, not only many new examples, and not only a more confident analysis. There are three entirely new chapters. One analyzes the globalization of Wal-Mart logically and objectively and captures not only the lessons of success but also what can be learned from some serious setbacks. In another totally new chapter, the authors focus on the globalization of young companies, breaking new ground in understanding that these days a company may be born as a global operation and very quickly become successful and even challenge bigger firms that have been in the game for a long time. They also point out that early globalization can be a double-edged sword and that a young company that globalizes early in its life must build the necessary organizational capabilities to deal with added complexity and coordination needs. The insights here are valuable not just to companies that are start-ups or in their relatively early stages. The fact is that bigger and more established companies also need to understand the nature of new competition in the twenty-first century. And third, there is entirely new material on how to think about China and India. For all that has been written about these two countries, *The Quest for Global Dominance* provides information that is not only fresh but deeply strategic. This chapter alone is essential reading for any business leader interested in peering into the world as it is evolving, and it alone is worth the price of admission.

Most global business leaders today know that the market is no longer only a national one. But even the best and the most experienced of them are humbled by the challenges of creating the right kind of organization; acquiring, retaining, and motivating a global workforce; entering new markets in the most effective way; using global assets to foster innovation; and not being held back by the added complexities of operating in different markets with their local idiosyncrasies, their powerfully different cultures, and their different laws and regulations. This book manages to address all of these questions, effectively and without needless complications.

This book is important to a wide audience. It is essential to business leaders no matter what their focus—finance, technology, marketing, strategic planning, human resources. It is definitely a must-read-and-study for students interested in business and in globalization more generally. I'd also recommend it to regulators who want to understand what business leaders are likely to be doing and thinking in the years ahead.

The Quest for Global Dominance remains the best by far in its arena—the most comprehensive, the most insightful, the most readable, and simply the most important in the growing genre of what companies need to know as they expand their international horizons.

New Haven, Connecticut   Jeffrey E. Garten
January 2008

Jeffrey E. Garten is Juan Trippe Professor of International Trade, Finance, and Business and former dean of the Yale School of Management. Previously he was managing director of the Blackstone Group and U.S. Undersecretary of Commerce for International Trade.

Preface

The twin forces of ideological change and technology revolution are making globalization one of the most important strategic and organizational issues facing companies today. With every passing day, it is becoming more obvious that managers must view every industry as a global industry and every business as a knowledge business. As worldwide presence becomes an imperative rather than a choice, an increasing number of companies must confront the essential question: *How do we engineer and exploit the ongoing globalization of our industry?* Our central purpose in writing this book has been to help managers address this question.

Origin and Focus of the Book

Rooted in rigorous research and yet written in a manner that makes the conceptual ideas contained herein highly actionable, this book reflects our intellectual heritage and deep-seated beliefs. Two of us, Anil and Vijay (who also coauthored the first edition), met as doctoral students at Harvard Business School. We consider ourselves rather fortunate in that we soaked in the best set of values that HBS offers—to work on the managerially important problems, to be intellectually rigorous, and to strive to advance the state of theory as well as the state of practice. We were lucky too that some of our key mentors—people such as Chris Argyris, Alfred Chandler, William W. Cooper, Paul Lawrence, Jay Lorsch, and Michael Porter—walked the talk rather brilliantly and thus made it all that much easier for us to conclude that this is the kind of intellectual life that we also wanted to lead. These shared core beliefs and a deep friendship made it only natural that we should want to work with each other. Right from the start, when we coauthored our first paper in 1978, we realized that we had phenomenal synergy. We often thought along similar lines and yet, when we disagreed, each of us was stubborn enough not to give in too easily. This stubbornness ensured that we would push ourselves even harder in our analysis and understanding of the phenomena being examined. We would like to believe that, in every case, the outcome was always a better insight and stronger supporting arguments.

We are delighted that Haiyan has joined Anil and Vijay as a coauthor in developing this second edition. Over the six to seven years since the publication of the first edition, the rise of China and India has emerged as perhaps the single most transformational force in the global economy. Accordingly, we concluded that the new edition must include an analysis of how companies can leverage the market and resource opportunities offered by China and India in their quest for global dominance. Having Haiyan as a coauthor has helped enormously in this endeavor. She grew up in China, has degrees from elite universities in China and the United States, and has over ten years' experience working as an executive, consultant, and entrepreneur in cross-border contexts. Her practical insights about how to succeed in China, how to leverage both China and India, and her tireless energy have been a major asset in developing this revised edition.

Building on the heritage of scholarly work by people such as Chris Bartlett, Richard Caves, Yves Doz, Sumantra Ghoshal, Charles Kindleberger, C. K. Prahalad, Michael Porter, Ray Vernon, and many others over the last twenty years, we have studied more than two hundred global corporations through a variety of research methods: large-scale surveys, case studies, and in-depth discussions with executives. We have also served as advisers and consultants to dozens of companies in the United States, Europe, China, and India in their efforts to review, redesign, and recreate their global strategies and organizations. Building on this knowledge base, we provide in this book a roadmap for smart globalization.

We identify and focus on four tasks essential for any company to emerge and stay as the globally dominant player within its industry. *One*, people must ensure that their company leads the industry in identifying market opportunities worldwide and in pursuing these opportunities by establishing the necessary presence in all key markets. In some cases, these opportunities entail creating a new industry—as illustrated by Yahoo!, which pioneered the Internet portal market in many parts of Asia and Europe. In other cases, these opportunities might manifest in the form of transforming an existing industry as illustrated by Cemex, whose global expansion has catalyzed a restructuring of the worldwide cement industry. *Two*, people must work relentlessly to convert global presence into global competitive advantage. Presence in the strategically important markets gives you the right to play the game. However, it says nothing about whether and how you will actually win the game. Doing so requires identifying and exploiting the opportunities for value creation that global presence offers. *Three*, people must cultivate a global mindset. They must view cultural and geographic diversity as opportunities to exploit and must be prepared to adopt successful practices and good ideas wherever they come from. The global economic landscape is changing much faster than most people realize. The winning corporations of tomorrow will be those which look at the world not only through American, European, or Japanese lenses but also through Chinese, Indian, Russian, Brazilian, and Mexican ones. *Four*, in developing their global strategies, people must take full account of the rapid growth of emerging markets, in particular the rise of China and India. China and India are the only two countries in the world that simultaneously constitute four realities: mega-markets for almost every product and service, platforms to dramatically reduce the company's global cost structure, platforms to significantly boost the company's global technology and innovation base, and springboards for the emergence of new fearsome global competitors. Given the game-changing nature of these realities, whether or not you have solid China and India strategies will rapidly become a crucial factor in determining whether or not your company is even a survivor ten years from now.

The book is organized as follows. Chapter One examines plat-form questions such as what is globalization, what is driving it, why it is here to stay, and what it means for companies and managers. Chapter Two presents an organizing framework and set of concep-tual ideas to guide firms in approaching the strategic challenge of casting their business lines overseas and establishing global pres-ence. In Chapter Three, we utilize this conceptual framework to an-alyze and derive lessons from the myriad of decisions that Wal-Mart made in the process of its global expansion starting in 1991. Chap-ter Four focuses on the strategic challenge of converting global pres-ence into global competitive advantage. In particular, this chapter identifies and analyzes the six distinct opportunities for the creation of global competitive advantage: adapting to local markets, captur-ing economies of global scale, capturing economies of global scope, optimizing the choice of locations for activities and resources, lever-aging knowledge across subsidiaries, and playing the global chess game. In Chapter Five, we shift from content to process issues and address the following issues: why mindset matters, what is a global mindset, what is the value of a global mindset, and what companies can do to cultivate a global mindset. Chapter Six continues the focus on process and addresses the challenge of converting the global corporation into an effective knowledge machine. In this chapter, we propose that building an appropriate social ecology is a crucial requirement for effective knowledge management, we ex-plicitly uncover the pathologies and pitfalls which prevent compa-nies from realizing the full potential of knowledge management, and we present a general framework for building the necessary so-cial ecology for effective knowledge management. Chapter Seven focuses on the dynamics of creating and managing high-performing global business teams by addressing two key issues: why global busi-ness teams can fail and what steps can be taken to make such teams more effective and efficient. Chapter Eight looks at a relatively new phenomenon—globalization of the young venture. As barriers to cross-border trade and investment come down and as people be-come more aware of customers, suppliers, and talent in foreign lands, an increasing number of young ventures are starting to go global early in their lives. A growing subset is even "born global" right from day one. We argue, however, that even though the enabling conditions for globalizing the young venture are becoming more friendly, early globalization is a double-edged sword, full of not only promises but also perils. Building on this analysis, we address important questions, such as when a young venture should consider early globalization and how the venture can build the needed organizational capabilities to succeed at it. Chapter Nine, the final chapter, analyzes the rise of China and India, what is propelling this rise, the similarities and differences between China and India, what challenges companies might face in leveraging these two economies, and the common mistakes that lead companies into developing suboptimal strategies for China and India. Building on this analysis, the chapter offers guidelines to companies regarding how they can get their China and India strategies right.

As may be obvious, the architecture of the book reflects two design criteria. One, we wanted the book to be broad in its coverage of issues relating to creating and exploiting global presence. Thus the book focuses about equally on key "content" issues (such as choice of markets, entry strategies, and impact of the rise of China and India) as well as on key "process" issues (such as cultivating a global mindset, creating knowledge networks, managing global business teams, and globalizing the young venture). Two, we wanted each chapter to focus on a specific action-oriented issue (such as building global presence, cultivating a global mindset, or dynamics of global business teams). Our hope is that this approach would make the contents of the book reasonably comprehensive and yet highly accessible and usable for the readers. They can read the entire book at one stretch or go directly to a particular chapter that holds immediate relevance.

In writing this book, we hope that you will share our enthusiasm for the rich subject of transforming global presence into global competitive advantage. We would value your comments and thoughts about the book. Please feel free to contact: Anil K. Gupta (Smith

School of Business, University of Maryland, College Park, MD 20742; tel: 301-405-2221; fax: 301-314-8787; agupta@rhsmith.umd.edu); Vijay Govindarajan (Tuck School of Business, Dartmouth College, Hanover, NH 03755; tel: 603-646-2156; fax: 603-646-1308; vg@dart mouth.edu); or Haiyan Wang (China India Institute, 8000 Overhill Road, Bethesda, MD 20814; tel: 301-318-5836; fax: 301-576-8575; hwang@chinaindiainstitute.com).

January 2008

Anil K. Gupta
College Park, Maryland

Vijay Govindarajan
Hanover, New Hampshire

Haiyan Wang
Bethesda, Maryland

Acknowledgments

No one lives and works alone, and no work is ever perfect. We are well aware that this book, like every other book that has ever been written, is a work-in-progress. While we are solely responsible for any weaknesses and limitations that might be reflected in these pages, we are deeply grateful to our many colleagues and friends who have helped shape our ideas over the last decade and nurtured and assisted us in bringing this book to fruition. In particular, we wish to acknowledge Milton Bennett, Prashanth Boccassam, Vincent Duriau, Peter Hazelhurst, Mike Knetter, Ed Locke, Lee Preston, Jorma Saarikorpi, Tapani Savisalo, Craig Schneier, Paresh Shah, Anant Sundaram, and Chris Trimble who read and gave us feedback on specific chapters. We also acknowledge the enthusiasm that many of our academic colleagues (including Shyam Chidamber, Tina Dacin, Charles Snow, Mark Wellman, Srilata Zaheer, and Jeffrey Garten) displayed for the first edition. We are grateful to them for using the book in their MBA and executive courses on global strategy, and for encouraging us to develop this second edition.

This book would not have been possible without the cooperation of many global corporations and their executives who generously gave their time and shared their insights. We owe them a substantial debt of gratitude.

Our sincere thanks to Judy Marwell who skillfully edited the manuscript for the first edition. We also thank Kathe Sweeney and Susan Williams, senior editors at Jossey-Bass, Cedric Crocker, our publisher, and Rob Brandt, editorial projects manager at Jossey-Bass, for their enthusiasm, commitment, and help with this project.

Anil Gupta received funding support for work on this book from the Center for International Business Education and Research, the Robert H. Smith School of Business at the University of Maryland, College Park. He also acknowledges the warm hospitality of Kathleen Eisenhardt and other colleagues at Stanford University, where he served as a visiting faculty during 2000 and brought the first edition to completion.

Vijay Govindarajan received funding support for this project from the William F. Achtmeyer Center for Global Leadership, the Tuck School of Business at Dartmouth College. He gratefully acknowledges the generosity of Bill Achtmeyer, a personal friend and role model.

Haiyan Wang acknowledges the enthusiasm, support, and friendship of her brother David Wang and sister-in-law Mei Xu for encouraging her to take on this project and join Anil and Vijay as a coauthor.

The Quest for Global Dominance

1

Rising Up to the Global Challenge

> The world is your oyster. Do you have the right fork?
> —*Thomas A. Stewart*[1]

What do we mean when we say that we live in an increasingly global world? If you are a Silicon Valley entrepreneur, it means that unless your business plan includes doing R&D in a low-cost, high-talent location, such as India, China, or Eastern Europe, you have almost no chance of being taken seriously by any venture capitalist. If you are Larry Page and Sergei Brin, the cofounders of Google, it means that you see your company as a born global player that will pursue customers everywhere almost from day one. If you are the CEO of Black & Decker, it means that you track the strategies of not only your long-established competitors such as Makita and Bosch but also new and aggressive entrepreneurial firms such as the Hong Kong–based Techtronic Industries. If you are the chairman of Nippon Steel, it means that you wake up every morning conscious of the possibility that your company may be an acquisition target for the global steel giant ArcelorMittal headquartered in Luxembourg but with steel operations on virtually every continent. If you are the CEO of Nokia, it means that the most important strategic question that you face may well be not how you will defend your market share in the United States and Europe, but how you will capture the attention and wallets of the next billion cell phone users in emerging markets, such as China, India, Indonesia, Brazil, Mexico, and Russia. If you are the finance minister of India, it means that you regard the ongoing integration of the country's economy with the rest of the world as fundamental to the realization of your homeland's potential as an economic superpower. And, last but not least, if you are a recent MBA and a junior manager at Procter & Gamble, you vow never to forget that you do not have a prayer of making it into the top ranks of the company unless you combine superb on-the-job performance with extensive international experience.

The twin forces of ideological change and technology revolution are making globalization one of the most important issues facing companies today. The makeover from state-dominated, isolated economies to market-driven, globally integrated economies is proceeding relentlessly in all corners of the world, be it Brazil, China, France, India, Russia, or South Africa. Accelerating developments in the information and transportation technologies are making real-time coordination of far-flung activities not only more feasible but also more reliable and efficient. In addition, we can now witness a rapid rise in the emergence of born global companies, such as Skype, Joost, and Facebook. The rise of born global companies is further transforming the worldwide economic landscape.

In this emerging era, every industry should be considered a global industry and every business a knowledge business. Today, globalization is no longer an option but a strategic imperative for all but the smallest corporations. This is as true of firms in such industries as cement, construction, and health care, which have traditionally been quite local, as it is of firms in such industries as semiconductors, pharmaceuticals, and automobiles, which globalized many decades ago. The only relevant question today is: Is your company a leader or a laggard in engineering and exploiting the ongoing globalization of your industry? The central premise of this book is that, no matter what the industry, only those companies that successfully lead the global revolution within their industry arenas will emerge as the winners in the battles for global dominance.

Over the last twenty years, we have studied over two hundred global corporations through a variety of research methods: large-scale surveys, case studies, and in-depth discussions with executives. We have also served as advisers and consultants to dozens of companies in their efforts to review, redesign, and recreate their global strategies and organizations. Building on this knowledge base, we provide herein a road map for smart globalization. We identify and focus on four tasks essential for any company to emerge and stay as the globally dominant player within its industry:

- *People must ensure that their company leads the industry in identifying market opportunities worldwide and in pursuing these opportunities by establishing the necessary presence in all key markets.* In some cases, these opportunities entail creating a new industry—as illustrated by Yahoo!, which pioneered the Internet portal market in many parts of Asia and Europe. In other cases, these opportunities might manifest in the form of transforming an existing industry as illustrated by CEMEX, whose global expansion has catalyzed a restructuring of the worldwide cement industry.

- *People must work relentlessly to convert global presence into global competitive advantage.* Presence in the strategically important markets gives you the right to play the game. However, it says nothing about whether and how you will actually win the game—doing so requires identifying and exploiting the opportunities for value creation that global presence offers. Converting global presence into global competitive advantage requires managers to address several important questions. How do you convert global scale into "economies" of global scale? How do you convert global scope into "economies" of global scope? How do you engage in just the right level of local adaptation? How do you optimize the choice of locations for different activities? How do you foster knowledge sharing across locations? And how do you leverage your positions in various locations around the world to compete on a globally coordinated rather than disjointed basis?

- *People must cultivate a global mindset.* They must view cultural and geographic diversity as opportunities to exploit and must be prepared to adopt successful practices and good ideas wherever they come from. The global economic landscape is changing much faster than most people realize. The winning corporations of tomorrow will be those that look at the world not only through American, European, or Japanese lenses but also through Chinese, Indian, Russian, Brazilian, and Mexican ones.

 • *In developing their global strategies, people must take full account of the rapid growth of emerging markets, in particular the rise of China and India.* China and India are the only two countries in the world that simultaneously constitute four realities: mega-markets for almost every product and service, platforms to dramatically reduce the company's global cost structure, platforms to significantly boost the company's global technology and innovation base, and springboards for the emergence of new fearsome global competitors. Given the game-changing nature of these realities, whether or not you have solid strategies for China and India will rapidly become a growing factor in determining whether or not your company is even a survivor ten years from now.

We begin the journey by examining some of the fundamental questions: What is globalization? What is driving globalization? And what do these trends imply for companies and for managers?[2]

What Is Globalization?

At one extreme, imagine a world that is a collection of economic islands connected, if at all, by highly unreliable and expensive bridges or ferries. At the other extreme, imagine the world as an integrated system where the fortunes of the various peoples inhabiting the planet are highly intertwined. The sneakers that you wear were manufactured in Indonesia. Your mutual fund company invests a part of your savings in companies listed on the Hong Kong Stock Exchange. The software that you just downloaded from the Web was developed in India. And the company that you work for routinely exchanges technologies and management ideas with its subsidiary operations in Japan and Germany. If you agree that, over the last fifty years, the world around you has undergone a transformation from something like the first scenario to something like the second one, then we would say that the worldwide economy is indeed undergoing a process of globalization. More succinctly stated, *globalization refers to growing economic interdependence among countries as reflected in increasing cross-border flows of three types of entities: goods and services, capital, and know-how.* The term globalization can relate to any of several levels of aggregation: the entire world, a specific country, a specific industry, a specific company, or even a specific line of business or functional activity within the company.

At a worldwide level, globalization refers to the aggregate level of economic interdependence among the various countries. Is the world truly becoming more global? Yes. As evidence, consider the following trends. In 2006, trade in goods and services stood at 31 percent of world GDP, up from 23 percent in 1999 and under 10 percent in 1970. Annual flows of foreign direct investment grew from 1.0 percent of world GDP in 1990 to 2.2 percent of world GDP by 2005. Trends in cross-border transactions in bonds and equities are even more dramatic. In 1970, such transactions as a ratio of GDP stood at less than 5 percent for the United States, Germany, and Japan. By 2005, they had grown to over 200 percent.[3] The pace of globalization continues unabated—as evidenced by the fact that the total deal value of cross-border mergers and acquisitions grew from $22 billion in 1990 to $58 billion in 2000 to $135 billion in 2005.[4]

The fact that the world economy is becoming more global does not in the least imply that all countries, all industries, or all companies are becoming globally integrated at the same rate. For a variety of historical, political, sociological, and even geographic reasons, diversity is and will remain one of the defining characteristics of humanity. Thus it is important to examine what this concept means at the level of a specific country, a specific industry, or a specific company.

At the level of a specific country, globalization refers to the extent of the interlinkages between that particular country's economy and the rest of the world. Historical and political reasons have caused some countries, such as Cuba, to remain quite isolated. Others, such as China, India, Russia, Brazil, and Mexico, have made great strides toward global integration—albeit at different speeds. Some of the key outcome indicators that can be used to measure the globalization of any country's economy are exports and imports as a ratio of GDP, inward and outward flows of both foreign direct investment and portfolio investment, and inward and outward flows of royalty payments associated with technology transfer.

Table 1.1 compares the global integration of China and India along some of the indicators at three points in time: 1980, 1997, and 2005. As this table indicates, starting from a roughly similar degree of economic isolation in 1980, China's economy has globalized at a much faster rate than has India's economy. The data also indicate that, over the last decade, India has begun to narrow some of the gaps.

At the level of a specific industry, globalization refers to the degree to which, within that industry, a company's competitive position in one country is interdependent with its competitive position in another country. Alternatively stated, the more global an industry, the greater the competitive advantage that a player within that industry can derive from leveraging technology, manufacturing prowess, brand names, and capital across countries. The greater the degree of such interdependence, the greater will be the extent to which the industry is dominated by the same set of global players who face each other in almost every market and coordinate their strategic actions across countries. The wireless handset industry, so far dominated globally by Nokia, Samsung, Motorola, and Sony-Ericsson, and the soft drinks industry, dominated globally by Coca-Cola, Pepsi-Cola, and Cadbury-Schweppes, are two examples of highly global industries. In contrast, the construction and the hospital industries, populated by hundreds of domestic companies all over the world, represent two good examples of industries still in the very early stages of globalization.

Some of the key outcome indicators of the globalization of an industry are the extent of cross-border trade within the industry as a ratio of total worldwide production, the extent of cross-border

Table 1.1. Global Integration: China Versus India

	China			India		
	1980	1997	2005	1980	1997	2005
Exports of goods and services as percentage of GDP	6	20	38	7	12	21
External debt as percentage of GDP	2.2	15.6[a]	11.2[b]	12.0	25.0[a]	15.6[b]
Inward flows of foreign direct investment as percentage of GDP	1.7	4.9[a]	3.6	0.1	0.7[a]	0.8

[a] Data pertain to 1996
[b] Data pertain to 2004
Source: Abstracted from World Bank, *World Development Reports 1998, 1999,* and *2007.*

investment as a ratio of total capital invested in that industry, and the proportion of industry revenue accounted for by players competing in all major regions of the world. For illustrative purposes, consider the ratio of cross-border trade to worldwide production. On this measure, relative to an index of 1.0 for all manufacturing industries, the mid-1990s figures for the computer industry were 2.2, for the auto industry 1.6, and for the pharmaceutical industry 0.7.[5] These figures indicate that, in terms of cross-border flow of goods and services, the computer industry was more global than the auto industry, which was more global than the pharmaceutical industry.

What Is a Global Company?

Ask ten different executives "What is a global company?" and, more likely than not, you will get ten different answers. Some might argue that a global company is one that is pursuing customers in all major economies, in particular the Americas, Europe, and Asia. Others might argue that you are not really global unless you put down roots in every major market in the form of producing locally what you sell locally. Yet others might suggest that the real test of globalization lies instead in whether your business unit headquarters are globally dispersed, whether your top management team consists of individuals from different nationalities, and so forth.

There are two problems with each of these perspectives regarding the nature of a global company. First, each definition overlooks the fact that globality is a multidimensional phenomenon and, like the proverbial elephant, can never be understood fully from just one perspective—be it market presence, production bases, composition of the top management team, or any other. Second, each definition overlooks the fact that globality is a continuous variable along a spectrum from low to high rather than a categorical binary variable with only two extreme values (global and nonglobal).

As depicted in Figure 1.1, we believe that the concept of "corporate globality" should be viewed as a four-dimensional construct based on the premise that an enterprise can be more or less global along each of four major characteristics: globalization of market presence, globalization of supply chain, globalization of capital base, and globalization of corporate mindset.

The first dimension, globalization of market presence, refers to the extent to which the company is targeting customers in all major markets for its industry throughout the world. Even within the same industry, globalization of market presence can range from relatively low to very high. For example, in 2006, Wal-Mart generated 22 percent of its total revenues from outside the United States. In contrast, Target and Sears generated 100 percent of their revenues from within the United States and none whatsoever from foreign markets.

The second dimension, globalization of supply chain, refers to the extent to which the company is accessing the most optimal locations for the performance of various activities in its supply chain. It is entirely possible for a company to have fairly local or regional market presence and yet a highly globalized value chain or vice versa. For example, in 1999, as a key element of the turnaround strategy for British retailer Marks & Spencer, CEO Peter Salsbury announced plans to set up a global supply chain for apparel goods with manufacturing hubs in Portugal, Morocco, and Sri Lanka.[6]

Figure 1.1. Assessing Corporate Globality

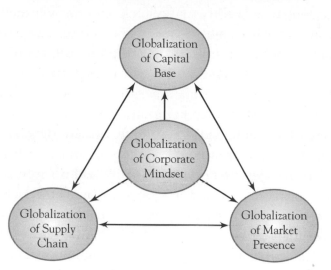

Caterpillar Inc. represents another good example of a company with a global supply chain. In 2007, Caterpillar delivered products to customers in nearly two hundred countries, operated manufacturing centers in twenty-four countries (ninety-eight locations), and had research and design technical centers in nine countries (twenty locations). Thus Caterpillar's supply chain represented a complex global network of sourcing units, manufacturing centers, parts distribution centers, logistics centers, marketing offices, dealers, and customer locations.[7]

The third dimension, globalization of capital base, refers to the extent to which the company is tapping into the most optimal sources of capital on a worldwide basis. Baidu, China's leading Internet search and online advertising company, represents a good example of how it is entirely possible for a company to be quite "local" along the dimensions of market presence and supply chain and yet have a highly globalized capital base. Baidu's market base and operations are centered primarily in China. Yet in August 2005, the company chose to get itself listed on the U.S.-based NASDAQ. A listing on the NASDAQ can potentially yield many benefits for

Baidu: access to a broader base of investors, greater international visibility, enhanced ability to use stock options for attracting top talent, and enhanced ability to make stock-based acquisitions.

Last but not least, the fourth dimension, globalization of corporate mindset, refers to the extent to which the corporation as a collectivity reflects an understanding of diversity across cultures and markets coupled with an ability to integrate across this diversity. The state of any enterprise's corporate mindset depends on the mindsets of the individuals who lead the enterprise as well as the organization that determines how these individuals interact, what information is collected, how it is processed, and how decisions are made. General Electric serves as a good example of a company with an increasingly global mindset. All GE businesses are managed through a global line-of-business structure; investment opportunities are identified and assessed on a global basis; corporate leaders are pushing hard to globalize "the intellect of the company"; and although the company has a strong worldwide corporate culture, the composition of the leadership itself is becoming increasingly diverse in terms of nationalities.[8]

What Is Driving Globalization?

Irrespective of the level of aggregation—the entire world, an individual country, a specific industry, or a particular company—globalization occurs because specific managers in specific companies make decisions that result in increased cross-border flows of capital, goods, or know-how. Two intertwined considerations are driving managers to make such decisions on an increasing basis: one, globalization is becoming increasingly feasible; two, globalization is becoming increasingly desirable. The following trends explain why.

First, an ever-increasing number of countries are embracing the free-market ideology. The policy shift from a planning to a market mentality is well known and has been well documented.[9] Suffice it to say that, since the end of World War II, the gale winds of market forces have continued to gather momentum—starting from the developed economies (Table 1.2), moving on first to South Korea, Taiwan, Hong Kong, and Singapore, then to the other countries of Southeast Asia, and finally sweeping up other major economies, such as China, India, Latin America, Central and Eastern Europe including Russia, and parts of Africa. Table 1.3 provides evidence of ongoing liberalization in investment regimes across a whole horde of countries.

As a consequence of economic liberalization, free trade already has become or is rapidly becoming a reality within regional blocks, such as the EU, NAFTA, ASEAN, and Mercosur. Furthermore, the World Trade Organization continues to chip away at the remaining barriers to the free flow of capital, goods, services, and technology

Table 1.2. Average Tariff Rates on Manufactured Products (Weighted Average; Percentage of Value)

Country	1913	1950	1990
France	21	18	5.9
Germany	20	26	5.9
United Kingdom	—	23	5.9
Italy	18	25	5.9
Japan	30	—	5.3
United States	44	14	4.8

Source: Abstracted from UNCTAD, *World Investment Report 1994.*

Table 1.3. Liberalization in Investment Regimes

	1994	1998	2005
Total number of countries that changed their investment regimes	49	60	93
Total number of regulatory changes	110	145	205
Changes in the direction of liberalization or promotion	108	136	164
Changes in the direction of control	2	9	41

Source: Abstracted from UNCTAD, *World Investment Reports 1999* and *2006.*

among countries and regional blocks. The financial crisis that en-
gulfed much of East Asia, Latin America, as well as Russia during
1997–1999 accelerated the pace of structural reforms and the further integration of many countries in these regions into the global
economy. As illustrated by Renault's acquisition of a controlling
stake in Nissan and Tata Motors' acquisition of Daewoo's commercial vehicles business, countries such as Japan, South Korea, Thailand, Brazil, and Argentina have considerably eased the restrictions
on foreign ownership of domestic assets and companies.[10] In short,
barriers to trade and investment among countries continue to decline rapidly and are making globalization increasingly more feasible and less expensive.

Second, technological advances continue their onward march.
Table 1.4 depicts the sharp decline in the costs of air transportation,
telecommunication, and computers since 1950. The decline in
transportation costs has radically shrunk the cost of shipping goods
across countries. During the two decades from 1980 to 2000, real
sea freight costs fell by over 75 percent. In the case of computers
and communications, the steep decline in costs has continued unabated since 1990. Aside from radical cost decline, the last two
decades have also witnessed the emergence and widespread adoption of technologies such as videoconferencing, mobile telephony,
voice-over-IP, e-mail, groupware (for example, Lotus Notes), and
the Internet. These developments in information technology have
dramatically reduced the "operative distance" between companies,
their customers, and their suppliers and made coordination of far-
flung operations not only more feasible but also more reliable and
efficient.

Third, the economic center of gravity is shifting from the developed to the developing countries. Assuming certain infrastructural
conditions, economic liberalization promotes competition, increases
efficiency, fuels innovation, attracts new capital investment, and
generally bears fruit in the form of faster economic growth. Not surprisingly, the embrace of market mechanisms has allowed the developing economies of the world to start catching up with the advanced

**Table 1.4. Declining Costs of Air Transportation,
Telecommunications, and Computers
(in 1990 U.S. Dollars Unless Otherwise Indicated)**

Year	Average Air Transportation Revenue per Passenger Mile	Cost of a Three-Minute Call from New York to London	U.S. Department of Commerce Computer Price Deflator (1990 = 1000)
1950	0.30	53.20	—
1960	0.24	45.86	125,000
1970	0.16	31.58	19,474
1980	0.10	4.80	3,620
1990	0.11	3.32	1,000

Source: Abstracted from International Monetary Fund, *World Economic Outlook 1997;* and Richard J. Herring and Robert E. Litan, *Financial Regulation in the Global Economy,* Washington, D.C.: Brookings Institution, 1995, p. 14.

economies. International organizations such as the IMF already count Korea, Taiwan, Hong Kong, and Singapore—some of the world's poorest countries in the 1950s—among the advanced economies. Other, even larger economies are on their way to advancement, the most notable cases being China and India.

In its now famous BRIC Report issued in 2003, Goldman Sachs analyzed the fifty-year growth prospects for the four largest emerging economies (Brazil, Russia, India, and China) and contrasted them with the growth prospects for the six major industrialized economies (United States, Japan, Germany, United Kingdom, France, and Italy). The report predicted that China's GDP would overtake that of the United States by around 2040, that India's GDP would be 80 percent as large as that of the United States by 2050, and that the GDPs of Brazil and Russia would be larger than those of Germany, United Kingdom, France, and Italy and almost as large as that of Japan by 2050.[11] During the four years from 2003 to 2006, the actual growth rates of the BRIC economies have been far ahead of Goldman Sachs's predictions. Recent updates by Goldman Sachs predict that China may become the world's largest economy by around 2030–35 and India the world's second largest by around 2040–45.[12] To sum up, the probability appears high that, within the next thirty to forty years, the size of the market for most products and services within each of the rising giants, China and India, may be larger than that of the United States or the European Union.

Table 1.5 provides comparative data on the growth rates of the advanced versus the developing economies since 1989 along with projections through 2008. Indeed, the world's economic center of gravity is shifting. The advanced economies are relatively mature and, for most industries, offer modest prospects for growth. In contrast, many developing economies are experiencing much faster growth in virtually every industry ranging from toothpaste and lightbulbs to home appliances, cars, computers, Internet services, and, not surprisingly, even fine wine. Thus any company today that seeks to grow—be it ABB, Samsung, Sony, Coca-Cola, General Electric, Microsoft, Wal-Mart, or Google—has little choice but to go where the growth is. For the vast majority of the world's leading corporations, such growth is rarely just in the home market.

Table 1.5. Comparative Data on Economic Growth Rates of Different Groups of Countries (Annual Percentage Change in Real GDP)

	1989–1998	1999–2008	Projected 2006–2007	Projected 2007–2008
Advanced economies[a]	2.7	2.6	2.5	2.7
Developing economies[b]	3.8	6.4	7.5	7.1
World total	3.2	4.4	4.9	4.9

[a]30 countries; for the complete list, see *World Economic Outlook April 2007*, International Monetary Fund.

[b]143 countries; for the complete list, see *World Economic Outlook April 2007*, International Monetary Fund.

Source: Abstracted from International Monetary Fund, *World Economic Outlook April 2007*.

Finally, the opening of borders to trade, investment, and technology transfers is rarely a one-way street. Although this opens up new and much larger market opportunities for companies, it also opens up their home markets to competition from abroad. In other words, economic liberalization brings about not only access to a much larger market but also more intense competition. As a consequence, it fuels the ongoing race among competitors to seek a first-mover advantage in serving globalizing customers, capturing economies of global scale, exploiting the cost-reducing or quality-enhancing potential of optimal locations, and tapping technological advancements wherever they may occur. The net result of this competitive dynamic is that the quest for economies of global scale and scope has become a self-feeding frenzy—be it in automobiles, aluminum, pharmaceuticals, tires, retailing, or Internet commerce. As the business historian Louis Galambos observed, "Global oligopolies are as inevitable as the sunrise."[13]

Why Globalization Is Here to Stay

It is important to remember that, notwithstanding the increasing obviousness of today's "global village," this is not the first time that we have witnessed the emergence of globalization.[14] Relatively unfettered trade, capital flows, and migration of people across national borders were very much a reality in many parts of the world during the period from the mid-nineteenth century to World War I. Barriers around national borders began to go up in 1914 and it was only in 1970 that the ratio of exports to world output again caught up with the figure for 1913.

There are, however, major quantitative and qualitative differences between the globalization of today and that of a hundred years ago. Average tariff rates are much lower now than at any time in the last two hundred years. And, relative to world GDP, the volumes of international trade, foreign direct investment, portfolio investment, and technology flows are much greater than ever. In the late nineteenth century, the term globalization would have been interpreted largely in terms of international trade and the flows of private capital from a few rich families to finance the building of railroads and other infrastructure in the new world. It also would have referred to economic integration among a relatively small number of wealthy countries. In contrast, the globalization of today encompasses every corner of the earth, is financed by the savings and retirement funds of billions of people, and is far more multidimensional and deeper than ever before. The present-day global enterprise—with interlinked value chain activities dispersed across the world—was virtually unknown and might well have been unthinkable in the late nineteenth century.

We like to use the terms "simple" versus "complex" globalization to distinguish today's globalization from that of yesterday. As depicted in Figure 1.2, much of yesterday's globalization could be viewed largely in terms of cross-border trade in either raw materials (think cotton or iron ore) or finished goods (think textiles or cars)—that is, goods at the two extreme ends of the value chain. In contrast, driven by the rapidly growing power of digital technologies as well as rapid declines in country risks, today's globalization is characterized by geographic dispersion of the company's value chain activities, the goal being to locate each activity (or sub-activity) in the most optimal location. As a result, a large and rapidly growing proportion of present-day cross-border trade consists of intermediate goods and services—that is, components and services located in the middle of the value chain.

As a good illustration of present-day "complex" globalization, consider the case of Li & Fung, a Hong Kong–based company that supplies over two thousand customers with both soft and hard goods from a network of eight thousand to ten thousand suppliers spread over forty countries. As a recent case study on the company observed, fulfilling an apparel order from a U.S. retailer could mean that the fabric may be woven in China, the fastenings may be sourced from South Korea, and the actual sewing may be done in Guatemala.[15] In short, in the case of even an everyday product, such as a shirt or a

Figure 1.2. "Simple" Versus "Complex" Globalization

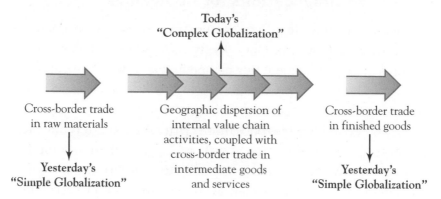

dress, different activities in the value chain are dispersed over several countries, creating a situation wherein trade in intermediate goods and services may well exceed the final trade in finished goods. Complex globalization of this kind would have been impossible without the power of present-day digital technologies.

It is a certainty that digital technologies will continue to make ours an increasingly connected world. Nonetheless, the emerging digital era is likely to be at best a mixed blessing for the global enterprise and for those responsible for leading it. On one hand, in a digital world you will have radically enhanced access to a wider base of potential customers and resources worldwide. On the other hand, this will also be true for your current competitors—and a whole range of potential competitors as well. Moreover, in the digital age, corporations will operate in a more transparent environment that will enable and foster greater comparison shopping by customers, faster imitation by competitors, and demands for enhanced accountability by investors. As Daniel Yergin observed, "The global shareholder is going to be an ever-tougher taskmaster. It's mathematically impossible for every company to be No. 1 or 2 in its market and for every fund manager to be in the upper quartile. As performance becomes more transparent, and information more accessible, the pressures [on companies] will only increase. There will be no rest, no matter how great the weariness."[16]

Implications for Companies

By definition, all strategic action represents a dialogue between the company and its environment. Every company must adapt to the changes in its environment that are inevitable. Yet there are choices. First, you can choose whether to be a first mover or a laggard in anticipating these changes and turning them into competitive advantage. Second, and perhaps more critically, you often have the power to shape the direction as well as the pace of environmental changes in ways that are more favorable to your own firm.

There are several fundamental changes in the global economic landscape that we regard as inevitable. *First, the economic map of the world will change more radically in the next twenty years than it has in the last twenty.* Given the commitment of the leaders in China and India to a widening and deepening of economic reforms, these two countries are likely to remain the most important economic stories. Notwithstanding China's rapid growth since 1979 and India's since 1991, these two economies have begun to acquire bulk only during the last few years. Because of the magic of compounding, continuation of high growth rates over the next two decades would have significantly greater material effect on the world's economic topography with each new year. In any case, China and India will be just two of the many important economic stories. Major countries such as Russia, Brazil, and Mexico have embraced economic reforms and begun the process of global integration only within the last twenty years. As these economies continue to gather momentum, they will increasingly become major contributors to the creation of new wealth on this planet. Thus it is a reasonable bet that in twenty years the economic center of gravity would not be merely shifting toward the developing countries, it may lie squarely in the middle of what we currently regard as the developing countries.

Second, the regional composition of the world's five hundred to one thousand largest corporations will be radically different in twenty years from what it is today. As a consequence, intra-industry competition will become significantly more intense. The *Financial Times* year

2000 list of the world's five hundred largest companies, based on market capitalization, included only three companies from India and (excluding seven companies based in Hong Kong) none from China.[17] Barely seven years later, the *Financial Times* year 2007 list included eight companies from China and eight from India.[18] Given the increasing bulk of these two economies (China and India), we deem it unthinkable that, in the year 2025, the composition of the world's largest five hundred to a thousand companies will look anything like what it does today. It is not inconceivable that, by 2025, well over one hundred of the world's five hundred largest companies may be headquartered in China or India.

Unlike the emergence of global competitors from Japan and South Korea during 1970–2000 (think Toyota, Sony, and Samsung), the more recent emergence of new global champions from China and India is already showing signs of taking place at a much faster and more fearsome pace. Virtually all Japanese and Korean giants grew organically. In contrast, the globalization of Indian and Chinese companies is likely to be much more acquisition-driven (look at Lenovo's acquisition of IBM's PC business and Tata Steel's acquisition of the Anglo-Dutch Corus). Capital markets, both public and private, are significantly more global today than they were two decades ago. Also, Chinese and Indian companies now have easy access to global investment banks (such as Morgan Stanley, Goldman Sachs, and Citigroup) as well as global consulting firms (such as McKinsey, BCG, and Bain) who are eager to help. The large size of Chinese and Indian economies also makes it more feasible for many domestic companies from these two countries to accumulate global scale before venturing abroad. It is important too that many of them are still being run by aggressive first generation entrepreneurs who are comfortable moving at great speed. Established MNCs from the developed countries overlook the threat from these new dragons and tigers at great peril.

To the list of budding powerhouses from China and India, one must also add rapidly growing players from other big emerging economies such as Russia (look at Severstal in steel), Brazil (look at

Embraer in commercial airplanes), and Mexico (look at CEMEX in cement). In short, if you think that, having witnessed the emergence of global players from Japan and South Korea over the last twenty years, you understand what intense competition really means, watch out. Compared to the world of 2025, this may have been just a warm-up.

Third, the ongoing technology revolution will make real-time coordination of globally dispersed operations routine. International telecommunications prices have already fallen by over 75 percent over the last ten years. According to many predictions, cost and price declines over the next ten years are likely to be even steeper. Combine these trends with mobile and broadband telecommunications (voice, video, and Internet) and it is inevitable that real-time coordination with globally dispersed customers, suppliers, and across the company's own subsidiaries will become commonplace over the next twenty years. One major outcome of these trends will be a further increase in the intensity of global competition and an even more desperate search for the best locations for the execution of discrete activities in the company's value chain.

Assuming that these trends are inevitable, we believe that the following questions merit serious consideration for inclusion in the strategic agenda of any medium-sized or large company today:

- *What must be (versus what is) the extent of your market presence in the world's major markets, particularly the major emerging markets, for your products and services? How should you build the necessary global presence?* Rapid economic growth around the world, particularly in the emerging economies, will continue to create huge demand for virtually everything—be it shoes, cement, fast food, refrigerators, computer software, insurance, or management consulting services. Explicitly or implicitly, your decisions and actions will help decide the important question of who will supply the products and services to meet this demand—your company, your current competitors, or new entrants? Given the largely borderless nature of the Internet, many start-ups in the high-technology sector are now realizing that they have little choice but to globalize at Internet speed—lest some other player preempt them, perhaps by imitating their business model, and occupy the global market space. For such companies, the evolutionary trajectory may well need to be something along the following lines: start-up in year one, entry into another major region in year two, and full-scale globalization by year three or four.

• *What must be (versus what is) the extent to which you capture the cost-reducing and quality-enhancing potential of optimal locations around the world for the execution of various activities in your company's value chain? How should you reduce the existing suboptimalities?* Countries dif-fer in cost structures, in ways of looking at the world, and in the pool of talent and ideas being generated on an ongoing basis. Capturing the comparative advantages of countries effectively and efficiently can create significant competitive advantage for your company. Wit-ness the case of Nike, which must constantly scout for the lowest-cost manufacturing locations, and Microsoft, which must constantly scout for the best software talent wherever it may reside. Similarly, you have no choice but to look at the world not merely as a market to exploit but also as a potential gold mine to reduce your cost struc-ture, recruit needed talent, and tap for new ideas.

• *What must be (versus what is) the effectiveness with which you are able to exploit global presence and turn it into true global competitive advantage—as opposed to global mediocrity or even global mess? How should you eliminate the existing shortcomings?* As we suggested earlier, global presence does not automatically translate into global com-petitive advantage. In fact, without systematic analysis, purposeful thinking, and careful orchestration, widespread global presence can easily degenerate into managerial distraction, resource duplication, and inefficiency. Thus you must constantly examine whether you are indeed doing the hard work needed to transform global presence into global competitive advantage.

• *Is the mindset of your company's top management, indeed every employee, sufficiently global? As the world around you changes and new opportunities open up in various corners of the world, is your company gen-erally a leader or a laggard in identifying and exploiting these opportunities?*

How should you create the needed global mindset? Managers, like all people, are the products of their origins and past experiences. It matters where you were born, what cultural environment you grew up in, where you live, whom you interact with, what media you are exposed to, and what you see and hear with your eyes and ears as you go about your daily business. Being human, each one of us individually is and will remain at least somewhat parochial. However, collectively, in the form of an enterprise such as Cisco, IBM, Sony, or ABB, we do have the possibility of creating a truly global mindset that treats the entire world as its home, that is sensitive to important events in any corner of the world, and that has the wisdom to differentiate between value-creating, value-destroying, and value-neutral opportunities. You must constantly ask whether your company has that type of a global mindset today and take developmental action, as needed.

Conclusion

We conclude this chapter by focusing on the implications of globalization for individual managers. We predict that knowledge, skills, and experience regarding how to navigate the company in a global environment will become increasingly a core requirement for promotion to leadership positions. We also believe that the need for global knowledge and skills will rapidly become crucial not just at senior levels in the company, but at all levels and in all units. A systems analyst in Stockholm may interact on a daily basis with software programmers in India. An R&D team may work on a collaborative development project spread across the United States, Japan, and Switzerland. A plant manager in Detroit may have crucial dependencies on auto parts suppliers in China, Mexico, Brazil, and Germany. A sales representative based in Atlanta may be an integral member of a global account management team serving the customers' needs across multiple locations on a coordinated basis.

Thus, totally aside from promotion to senior ranks, merely succeeding in one's local job will increasingly depend on skills at managing across national and cultural borders. Look at the career backgrounds of the CEOs of two of America's largest companies—Procter & Gamble and PepsiCo. Alan Lafley, Procter & Gamble's CEO, spent several years in the 1990s running the company's Far East and later Asia operations before returning to the United States and eventually rising to the top post. Indra Nooyi, PepsiCo's CEO, was born in India and moved to the United States in the early 1980s as a graduate student. Both leaders bring to their jobs in-depth capabilities and experience in both general management as well as globalization. It is a certainty that such a picture will increasingly become the norm rather than the exception for the corporate leaders of tomorrow.

To sum up, notwithstanding the huge changes that we have witnessed in the last two decades, the extent and pace of change in the next two decades will almost certainly be much greater. In our view, the inevitability of these changes implies that companies and managers today face a relatively simple, but important, choice: get on board or get left behind.

2

Building Global Presence

There is a race and a lot of people are qualified for
the race. But to go global, you need to be early
enough. Generally in new countries you need to
be the first in for the first win. When you arrive as
number three or four, it is too late.
—Daniel Bernard, Chairman (1993–2005), Carrefour[1]

The starting point in the quest for global dominance is to build global market presence. The framework and set of conceptual ideas presented in this chapter can guide firms in approaching the strategic challenge of casting their business lines overseas and establishing global presence. How should the firm choose which of its multiple product lines to use as the initial launch vehicle for the global market? What factors make some markets more strategic than others? What should companies consider in determining the right mode of entry? How should the enterprise transplant the corporate DNA as it enters new markets? What approaches should the company use to win the local battle? And how rapidly should a company expand globally? Addressing these six issues—choice of products, choice of strategic markets, mode of entry, transplanting the corporate DNA, winning the local battle, and speed of global expansion—helps firms go about building global presence in a systematic manner.[2]

Choice of Products for
Launching Globalization

When any multiproduct firm decides to go abroad, it must also decide whether it should globalize its entire portfolio simultaneously or whether it should use a subset of product lines as the launching pad for initial globalization. Consider the case of Marriott Corporation, which was essentially a domestic company until the early 1990s.[3] The company had two principal lines of business: lodging and contract services. Within the lodging sector, four of the major product lines were full-service hotels and resorts (Marriott brand), midprice hotels (Courtyard brand), budget hotels (Fairfield Inn brand), and extended stay hotels (Residence Inn brand). The contract services sector consisted of the following three product lines: Marriott Management Services, Host/Travel Plazas, and Marriott Senior Living Services (retirement communities). As the company embarked on its globalization venture, it had to confront the question of which one or more of these product lines should serve as the starting point for its globalization efforts. How should Marriott address this question?

Global expansion forces companies to develop at least three types of capabilities: knowledge about foreign markets, skills at managing people in foreign locations, and skills at managing foreign subsidiaries. Without these capabilities, firms are likely to remain strangers in a strange land, with global expansion posing a high risk. Globalizing the entire portfolio of products at once compounds these risks dramatically. Often it is wiser to choose only one or a small number of product lines as the initial launch vehicle for globalization. The choice of launch vehicle should adhere to the twin goals of maximizing the returns while minimizing the risks associated with early globalization moves. For the corporation, these initial moves represent experiments with high learning potential and it is important that these experiments succeed: success builds psychological confidence, credibility within the corporation, and last but not least, cash flow to fuel further rapid globalization.

Figure 2.1 presents a conceptual framework to identify those products, business units, or lines of business that might be preferred candidates for early globalization. Using this framework, each line of business in the company's portfolio should be evaluated along two dimensions: one pertaining to potential returns (that is, expected payoffs) and the other to potential risks (that is, required degree of local adaptation).

The first dimension focuses on the magnitude of globalization's payoffs. These payoffs tend to be higher when the globalization imperatives (see box) are stronger.[4] In the case of Marriott Corporation, these imperatives clearly are much stronger for full-service lodging, whose primary customers are globe-trotting executives, than they are for the retirement community business. In the full-service lodging business, a worldwide presence can create significant value by using a centralized reservation system, developing and diffusing globally consistent service concepts, and leveraging a well-known brand name on whose high quality and service customers can rely. In contrast, none of these factors is pivotal in the retirement community business—thereby rendering the imperatives for globalization much less urgent.

Figure 2.1. A Framework for Choice of Products

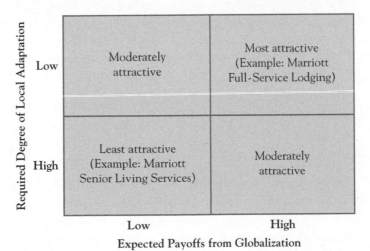

The Imperatives to Globalize

There are five imperatives that drive any firm to pursue global expansion. Because of differences in industry structure and the firm's strategic position, the intensity of these factors can be expected to differ across firms and, for the same firm, over time.

The growth imperative. For many industries, developed country markets are quite mature. Thus the growth imperative generally requires companies to look to emerging markets for fresh opportunities. Consider a supposedly mature industry such as paper. Per capita paper consumption in developed markets, such as North America and Western Europe, is around six hundred pounds. In contrast, per capita consumption of paper in China and India is a tiny fraction of this amount.[5] If you are a leading paper manufacturer, can you really afford not to build market presence in places like China or India? We doubt it. If per capita paper consumption in both China and India increased by just one pound over the next five years, demand would increase by 2.4 billion pounds, an amount that can keep five state-of-the-art paper mills running at peak capacity.

The efficiency imperative. Whenever there are one or more activities in the value chain (R&D, production, and so on) where the minimum efficient scale exceeds the sales volume feasible within one country, a company with global presence will have the potential to create a cost advantage relative to a domestic player within that industry. Mercedes-Benz illustrates this principle. Historically, Mercedes-Benz concentrated its research and manufacturing operations in Germany but derived its revenues from the entire global market. Given the highly scale-sensitive nature of the auto industry, it is clear that Mercedes-Benz's ability to compete in Europe, or even Germany, has for long depended not just on its market position in Europe (or Germany) but also worldwide.

The knowledge imperative. No two countries, even close neighbors such as Canada and the United States, are completely alike. Therefore, when a company expands its presence to more than one country, it must adapt some features of its products and processes to the local environment. This adaptation requires the creation of local know-how. Some of this know-how may be too idiosyncratic to be relevant outside the particular local market. However, in many cases, local product or process innovations emerge as world-leading innovations and thus have the potential to generate global advantage. For instance, GE India's innovations in making CT scanners simpler, more transportable, and cheaper, and P&G Indonesia's innovations in reducing the cost structure for cough syrup, would appear to enjoy wide-ranging applicability.

Globalization of customers. This phrase refers to customers who are global corporations (such as soft-drink companies served by advertising agencies) as well as those who are globally mobile (corporate executives served by American Express or global travelers served by hotel chains such as Sheraton). When the customers of a domestic company start to globalize, the firm must keep pace with them. These customers may strongly prefer worldwide consistency and coordination in the sourcing of products and services. They may also prefer to deal with a small number of supply partners on a long-term basis. Furthermore, allowing customers to deal with different suppliers in other countries puts a company at risk of losing them to one of these suppliers even in the domestic market. It is motivations such as these that have driven professional service firms in such industries as advertising, accounting, consulting, and legal services to become global. The transformation of the advertising industry has been particularly dramatic. The world's top ten advertising firms captured only 22 percent of global revenues in 1991. By 2001, this figure had increased to 73 percent!

Globalization of competitors. If your competitors start to globalize and you do not, you become vulnerable to a two-pronged attack. First, they can develop a first-mover advantage in capturing market growth, pursuing global scale efficiencies, profiting from knowledge arbitrage, and/or providing a coordinated source of supply to global customers. Second, they can use multimarket presence to cross-subsidize and wage a more intense attack in your own home markets. Underestimating the rate at which competition can accelerate the pace of globalization is dangerous. Look at SABMiller's inroads into the U.S. beer market, historically dominated by Anheuser-Busch.

The second dimension in our framework concerns the extent to which different lines of business require local adaptation to succeed in foreign markets. The greater the extent of required adaptation, the greater the degree to which new product or service features would need to be developed locally, as opposed to cloning proven and preexisting concepts and capabilities. As any new development involves risk, the greater the need for local adaptation, the greater the risks of failure—particularly when such development entails the already significant "liability of foreignness." Marriott Corporation exemplifies these principles. Compared to full-service lodging, the retirement community business is a very local business, and hence requires more local adaptation.

Combining both dimensions, as indicated earlier in Figure 2.1, full-service lodging emerged as a particularly attractive candidate for early globalization. In fact, as the spearhead for globalization moves, full-service lodging provided Marriott with a high-return, low-risk laboratory for developing knowledge and skills pertaining to foreign market entry and managing foreign subsidiaries. Leveraging the expanding global presence of its full-service brands (Ritz-Carlton, Marriott, and Renaissance), Marriott has positioned itself well to exploit the globalization potential of its other lines of business.

In sum, almost no line of business today is devoid of potential for exploitation on a global scale. However, any multiproduct firm which is starting to globalize must remember that a logically sequenced, as opposed to random, approach is likely to serve as a higher-return, lower-risk path toward full-scale globalization.

Choice of Strategic Markets

Consider the case of Wal-Mart, the world's largest retailer. Until 1991, Wal-Mart was a domestic company focused purely on the U.S. market. When Wal-Mart embarked on building a global presence, it could choose among a wide array of options as to the regional or country markets that it could enter. In a situation such as this, how does the company decide which markets it should enter first and what its sequence of global expansion should be? Of course, one option is to pursue opportunities in an ad hoc, random fashion. In a dynamic environment, we accept the relevance of an opportunistic stance. However, we have observed that, rather than merely muddling through the opportunities as they emerge, effective globalizers engage instead in *directed opportunism*, that is, opportunism guided by a systematic and logical framework. We present the logical framework below and, in the next chapter, use it to analyze the global expansion strategy pursued by Wal-Mart.

The sequence in which a globalizing company enters various markets should depend on two factors: the strategic importance of the market, and the firm's ability to exploit that market. Going after a strategic market without the ability to exploit it is generally a fast track to disaster.

The first factor—strategic importance of a market—encompasses current and future market size as well as the learning opportunities offered by that market. Notwithstanding the importance of GDP, the size of a country's market for any particular product or service often depends on multiple factors including total population, demographic characteristics, per capita income, geographic climate, population density, cultural norms and preferences, stage of economic development, and so forth. Consider, for example, mobile telephony. In mid-2007, the number of mobile phone subscribers was estimated to be around 500 million in China, around 240 million in the United States, and around 170 million in India. Notwithstanding these numbers, if we look at individual products and services, in 2007, the United States was expected to be the largest market for wireless e-mail services, China the largest market for text messaging services, and India the largest market for new mobile phones. As this example illustrates, in estimating the size of a country's current and future market potential, it is important to focus on the right level of "target market" aggregation.

In estimating the size of the market for your line of business in a particular country, it is also important to look at market opportunities through the lens of tomorrow rather than that of the past, and to be market-centric rather than product-centric. Consider, for example, a company such as John Deere. As the undisputed agricultural equipment leader in North America, John Deere's product portfolio consists predominantly of large machines. However, when John Deere looks at the market potential in a country such as India (where the size of the average farm and the buying power of the average farmer is much smaller than in the United States), it is important for John Deere to look at the potential market in India not in terms of the market for its current portfolio of products but in terms of the market for all types of agricultural equipment, including smaller size machines that the company could potentially design for and sell in India.

Let's look now at variations in learning opportunities offered by different markets. Such opportunities are likely to be high when the market is populated by sophisticated and demanding customers who would force the company to meet the world's toughest standards for quality, cost, cycle time, and a host of other attributes—thereby giving the company a head start in developing leading-edge innovations and in learning about the market needs of tomorrow. For example, France and Italy are leading-edge markets for the high-fashion clothing industry, a fact of significant importance to a company such as DuPont, which manufactures a variety of textile fibers. Learning opportunities also depend on the pace at which relevant technologies are evolving in the particular market. This technology evolution can emerge from one or more of several sources: leading-edge customers, innovative competitors, universities, local research centers, and firms in related industries.

The second factor—ability to exploit a market—depends on the height of entry barriers and the intensity of competition within the market. Entry barriers are likely to be lowest when there are no regulatory constraints on trade and investment and when new markets are geographically, culturally, and linguistically proximate to the domestic market. However, even when such entry barriers are low, the intensity of competition can hinder a company's potential for exploiting a market. For example, the large U.S. market in the apparel retailing industry has often proved to be a graveyard for foreign entrants such as Marks & Spencer, precisely because of the intensity of local competition. Figure 2.2 presents a conceptual framework that

Figure 2.2. A Framework for Choice of Markets

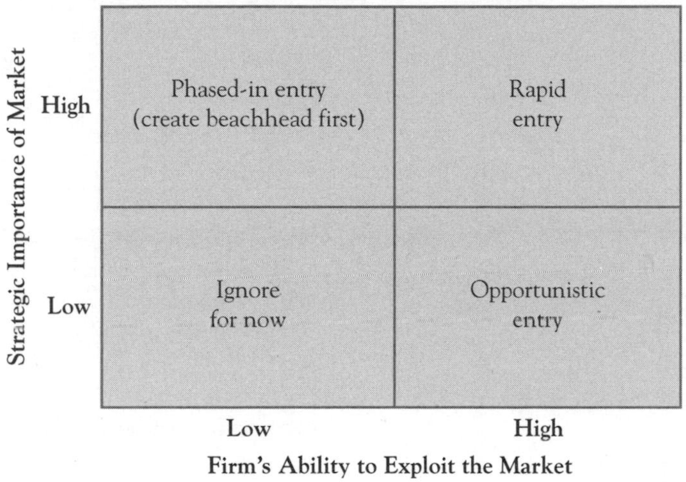

	Low (Firm's Ability)	High (Firm's Ability)
High (Strategic Importance)	Phased-in entry (create beachhead first)	Rapid entry
Low (Strategic Importance)	Ignore for now	Opportunistic entry

Strategic Importance of Market

Low   High

Firm's Ability to Exploit the Market

combines the two key dimensions—"strategic importance of market" and "ability to exploit"—to offer guidelines to firms that want to engage in directed opportunism in their choice of markets.

A firm's stance toward markets that have high strategic importance and high ability to exploit should be "must enter rapidly." By comparison, the firm can afford to be much more opportunistic and ad hoc in markets that have low strategic importance but are easier to exploit. In the case of markets that have high strategic importance but are also very difficult to exploit, we recommend an incremental, phased approach where the development of needed capabilities precedes market entry. One way in which a company can develop such capabilities is to first enter a beachhead market: this would be a market that, although closely resembling the targeted strategic market, provides a lower-risk opportunity to learn how to enter and succeed in the chosen strategic market. Typical examples of beachhead markets are Switzerland or Austria for Germany, Canada for the United States, and Hong Kong or Taiwan for China. Finally, the firm should steer clear of those markets that are neither strategic nor easy to exploit.

The next box shows how the global expansion of Ikea over the last two decades illustrates our framework for choosing target markets.

Timeline of Ikea Expansion

Year first store opened	Country	Year first store opened	Country
1958	Sweden (Almhult)	1987	United Kingdom (Manchester)
1963	Norway (Oslo)		
1969	Denmark (Copenhagen)	1989	Italy (Milan)
1973	Switzerland (Zurich)	1990	Hungary (Budapest)
1974	Germany (Munich)	1991	Poland (Platan)
1975	Australia (Artamon)	1991	Czech Republic (Prague)
1975	Hong Kong	1991	United Arab Emirates (Dubai)
1976	Canada (Vancouver)		
1977	Austria (Vienna)	1992	Slovakia (Bratislava)
1978	Netherlands (Rotterdam)	1994	Taiwan (Taipei)
		1996	Finland (Espoo)
1978	Singapore	1996	Malaysia (Kuala Lumpur)
1980	Spain (Gran Canaria)	1998	China (Shanghai)
1981	Iceland (Reykjavik)	2000	Russia (Moscow)
1981	France (Paris)	2001	Israel (Netanya)
1983	Saudi Arabia (Jeddah)	2001	Greece (Thessaloniki)
1984	Belgium (Brussels)	2004	Portugal (Lisbon)
1984	Kuwait	2005	Turkey (Istanbul)
1985	United States (Philadelphia)	2006	Japan (Tokyo)
		2007	Rumania (Bucharest)

	Strategic Importance of Market		
		Low Ability to Exploit	High Ability to Exploit
High		United States (Beachhead: Canada) China (Beachhead: Taiwan and Hong Kong)	Germany France Italy UK
Low			Norway Denmark Finland Holland

Strategic Importance of Market

Ability to Exploit

As a final observation, we would like to emphasize that these frameworks should be applied not at the level of the firm as a whole but at the level of the individual business units within the firm.

Mode of Entry

Once a company has selected the country or countries to enter and designated the product lines that will serve as the launch vehicles, it must determine the appropriate mode of entry. At this point, the company must look at two fundamental issues. The first is the extent to which it will rely on exports versus local production within the target market. Figure 2.3 depicts some of the choices available to a firm. It can rely on 100 percent export of finished goods, export of components but localized assembly, 100 percent local production, and so forth. The second issue is the extent of ownership control over activities that will be performed locally in the target market.

Figure 2.3. Alternative Modes of Entry

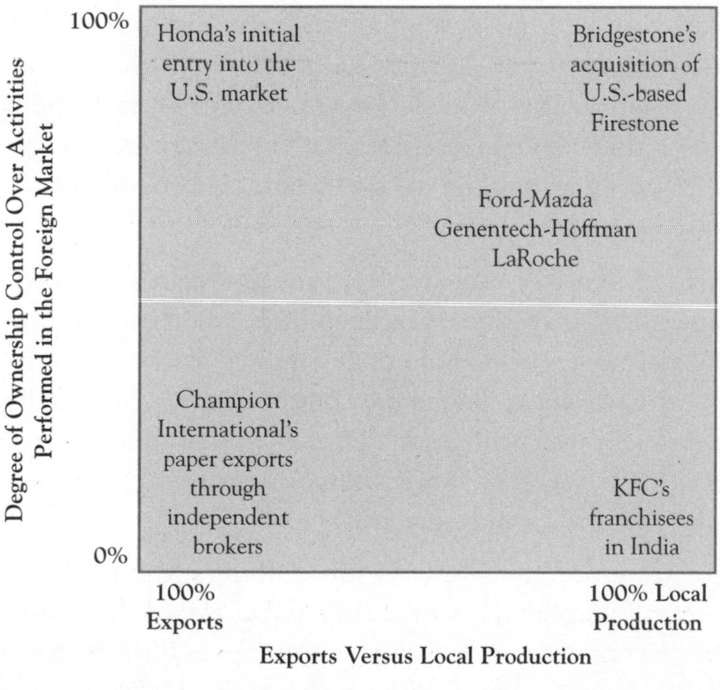

	100%	
Honda's initial entry into the U.S. market		Bridgestone's acquisition of U.S.-based Firestone
	Ford-Mazda Genentech-Hoffman LaRoche	
Champion International's paper exports through independent brokers		KFC's franchisees in India

Degree of Ownership Control Over Activities Performed in the Foreign Market — 100% to 0%

100% Exports — 100% Local Production

Exports Versus Local Production

Here, companies' options range from 0 percent ownership modes (licensing, franchising, and the like) or partial ownership modes (such as joint ventures or affiliates) to 100 percent ownership modes (fully owned greenfield operations or acquisitions).

Choosing the right mode of entry is critical because this choice, once made, is often difficult and costly to alter. Inappropriate decisions can impose unwanted, unnecessary, and undesirable constraints on the options for future development.

Turning to the first issue, greater reliance on local production would be appropriate under the following conditions:

- *Size of local market is larger than minimum efficient scale of production.* The larger the local market, the more completely local production will translate into scale economies for the firm while minimizing tariff and transportation costs. Bridgestone's entry into the U.S. market by acquiring the local production base of Firestone instead of exporting tires from Japan illustrates this point.

- *Excessive shipping and tariff costs discourage exporting to the target market.* In some cases, shipping and tariff costs are so high as to neutralize any cost advantages associated with producing in any country other than the target market. This is the primary reason that cement companies such as Cemex and Lafarge rely heavily on local production in the countries that they have entered.

- *Need for local customization of product design is high.* Product customization requires two capabilities: a deep understanding of local market needs accompanied by an ability to incorporate this understanding in the company's design and production decisions. Localization of production in the target market greatly enhances the firm's ability to respond to local market needs accurately and efficiently.

- *Local content requirements are strong.* If the size of the local market is large and government regulations require significant local content, the globalizing enterprise has little choice but to comply. This is one of the reasons why telecom equipment companies such as Nokia, Ericsson, Motorola, and Siemens rely on significant local production in order to serve the Chinese market. Along the same lines, constraints imposed on foreign auto companies to adhere to local content requirements have forced them to rely heavily on local production in markets such as the EU, China, and India.

As noted earlier, the second issue pertains to the extent of ownership and control over the locally performed activities. Given their differing costs and benefits, neither alliances nor complete ownership are universally desirable in all situations. Unlike the complete-ownership mode, alliance-based entry modes have several advantages: permitting the firm to share the costs and risks associated with market entry, allowing rapid access to local know-how, and giving managers the flexibility to respond more entrepreneurially and more quickly to dynamic global competition than is offered by the conquer-the-world-by-yourself approach. However, a major downside of alliances is their potential for various types of conflict stemming from differences in corporate goals and corporate cultures.

Taking into account both the pros and the cons, alliance-based entry modes often are more appropriate under the following conditions:

- *Physical, linguistic, and cultural distance between the host and the home country is high.* The more dissimilar and unfamiliar the target market, the greater the need for the firm to rely on a local partner to provide needed local know-how and networks. Conceivably, the firm could obtain the requisite local knowledge and competencies through an acquisition. However, if no suitable acquisition candidates are available or if the firm's ability to manage an acquired subsidiary in a highly dissimilar market is quite limited, then an alliance-based entry mode may be the best strategy to access local know-how and relationships. It is this set of reasons that explain Wal-Mart's decision to enter many Latin American and Asian markets through the joint venture route.

- *The subsidiary's operational integration with the rest of the global operations would be minimal.* By definition, tighter integration between a subsidiary and the rest of the global network increases the degree of mutual interdependence between them. In this context of high interdependence, it becomes crucial that the subsidiary and the network pursue shared goals and that the firm be able to reshape the subsidiary according to the changing needs of the rest of the network. Shared ownership of the local subsidiary puts major constraints on the firm's ability to achieve such congruence in goals and on its freedom to reshape the subsidiary operations when needed. Thus, shared ownership becomes a more acceptable option in those situations where it seems unlikely that the subsidiary's activities will affect the rest of the network.

- *The risk of asymmetric learning by the partner is (or can be kept) low.* In the typical joint venture, two partners pool different but complementary know-how into an alliance. Ongoing interaction between their core operations and the alliance gives each partner an opportunity to learn from the other and to appropriate the partner's complementary know-how. In effect, this dynamic implies that the alliance often is not just a cooperative relationship but also a learning race.[6] If Firm A has the ability to learn at a faster rate than Firm B, the outcome is likely to be asymmetric learning in favor of Firm A. Over time, Firm A may seek to dissolve the alliance in favor of going it alone in competition with a still-disadvantaged Firm B.

- *The company is short of capital.* Lack of capital underlay Xerox Corporation's decision in the 1950s to enter the European market through an alliance with the U.K.-based Rank Organization.[7]

- *Government regulations require local equity participation.* Historically, many countries with formidable market potential (such as China, India, and Brazil) have been successful in imposing the joint venture option on foreign entrants, even when all other considerations might have favored the choice of a complete-ownership mode. Recently, however, it is noteworthy that the creation of regional economic blocks (such as the EU, NAFTA, and Mercosur) and the ongoing adoption of liberal trade and investment policies by most nations worldwide is lessening the impact of government regulations on the mode of entry decision in an increasing number of industries.

A firm that decides to enter the foreign market through local production rather than through exports faces a secondary decision: whether to set up greenfield operations or to use an existing production base through a cross-border acquisition. A greenfield operation gives the company tremendous freedom to impose its own unique management policies, culture, and mode of operations on the new subsidiary. In contrast, a cross-border acquisition poses the much tougher challenge of cultural transformation and post-merger integration. However, setting up greenfield operations also has two potential liabilities: lower speed of entry, and more intense local competition caused by the addition of new production capacity along with one more competitor. Taking into account both the pros and the cons, Figure 2.4 provides a conceptual framework to determine when greenfield operations or cross-border acquisitions are likely to be the more appropriate entry modes.

Figure 2.4. Greenfield Versus Cross-Border Acquisition

Market Growth Rate		Low	High
High Growth		Greenfield operations or cross-border acquisitions	Greenfield operations (Example: Nucor's entry into Brazil)
Mature or Declining		Cross-border acquisitions (Example: International Paper's entry into Europe)	Greenfield operations or cross-border acquisitions

Uniqueness of Corporate Culture

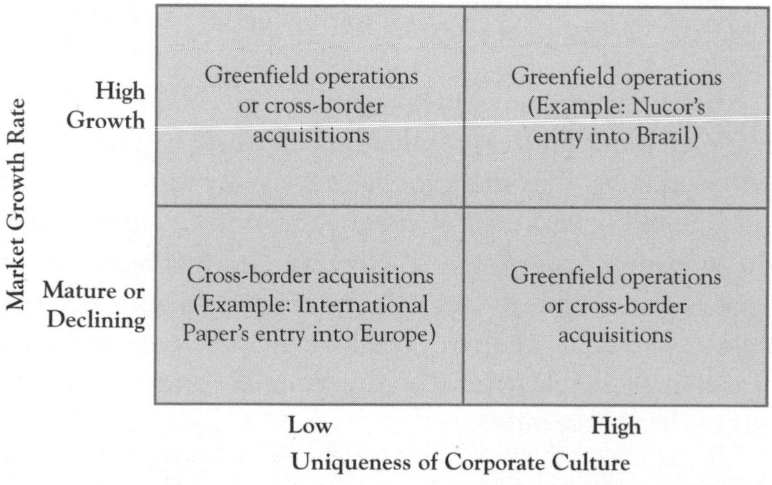

This framework has two dimensions. On the first dimension—the uniqueness of the globalizing company's culture—Nucor Corporation provides a good example of a company with a very strong and unique culture. Nucor differs significantly from other steel producers in its human resource policies, egalitarian work environment, performance-based incentives, teamwork, decentralization, and business processes.[8] The more committed a company is to preserving its unique culture, the more necessary it becomes to set up greenfield operations in foreign markets. Building and nurturing a unique culture from scratch (as would be feasible in the case of a greenfield operation) is almost always easier than transforming an entrenched culture (as would be necessary in the case of a cross-border acquisition).

Aside from corporate culture considerations, a firm must also consider the impact of entry mode on the resulting intensity of local competition. If the local market is in the emerging or high-growth phase (as in the market for mobile phones in India and China), new capacity additions would have little downside effect on the intensity of competition. In contrast, when the local market is mature (as in the tire industry in the United States), new capacity additions will only intensify an already high degree of local competition. For example, in the forest products industry, the Finland-based UPM-Kymmene has chosen the greenfield mode for its expansion into high-growth Asian markets. In contrast, it has relied on the acquisition mode for its expansion into the mature North American markets.

To sum up, a company with a highly unique culture should have a clear preference for the greenfield mode when entering a high-growth market. At the other extreme, a company with a less unique culture should have a clear preference for the acquisition mode when entering a mature market. However, in the mixed case of a company with a highly unique culture entering a mature market or one with a less unique culture entering a high-growth market, the choice of mode should depend on the particular circumstances and nature of the opportunity.

Transplanting the Corporate DNA

Having decided on the mode of entry for a particular product line into a particular target market, a company moves on to its next challenge: the implementation of actual entry. One of the most important things the globalizing company must figure out is how to transplant the core elements of its business model, its core practices, and its core beliefs—in short, its DNA—to the new subsidiary. The following examples illustrate the experience of two U.S. companies in their efforts to transplant their respective DNAs.

After acquiring two thousand employees from Yamaichi Securities, Merrill Lynch & Co. counted on its American-style investment adviser approach to establish a high-trust image in the securities brokerage industry in Japan. Historically, the brokerage industry in Japan had earned a poor reputation. "One well-known abuse . . . is 'churning'—in which sales people persuade naïve investors to buy and sell a lot of securities so the sales people can boost their commissions. Merrill Lynch promised that there would be no churning. Instead, its sales people were instructed to try to get an overall picture of customers' finances, ascertain their needs and then suggest investments. Something got lost in the translation, however. Japanese customers have complained that Merrill Lynch sales people are too nosy, asking questions about their investments instead of just telling them what stocks to buy."[9]

When the Walt Disney Company opened its Euro Disney theme park near Paris in the early 1990s, it faced considerable resistance from French applicants, employees, and labor leaders on the issue of grooming requirements. Following its core practices in the United States and their successful replication at Tokyo Disneyland in Japan, the company was strict in enforcing "a dress code, a ban on facial hair, a ban on colored stockings, standards for neat hair and fingernails, and a policy of appropriate undergarments."[10] These requirements were severely and publicly criticized by French labor leaders as well as the French media, which made recruitment and retention more difficult for the company, particularly in the beginning.

As these examples illustrate, obstacles to transplanting the corporate DNA can emerge from any of several sources: local employees, local customers, local regulations, and so forth. Given such obstacles, every company must be absolutely clear about exactly what its true core beliefs and practices are. Having achieved this clarity, the company would know where it should stay committed to its own beliefs and practices and where it should be willing to adapt. Then the company has to set to work constructing mechanisms to transfer core beliefs and practices to the new subsidiary. Finally, and most important, the company must be able to embed these beliefs and practices in the new subsidiary.

Clarifying and Defining Core Beliefs and Practices

Core beliefs and practices can be defined at any of several levels of abstraction—at the level of the central belief, as well as at the level of the symbols and practices that reflect the concrete manifestation of the central belief. It is generally wise for the globalizing company to remain committed to its central beliefs, but it is equally wise to remain flexible with respect to how these beliefs are concretely manifested within any particular local culture. As an example, take the case of the Chinese home appliance company, Haier Group. Zhang Ruimin, the CEO and architect of Haier Group, cares passionately about individual accountability. In the company's Chinese operations, he had even instituted the practice of printing a pair of yellow footprints on the factory floor; every day, a poor performer would be required to stand on the yellow footprints and to reflect on his or her mistakes.[11] Think now about what Haier should do as it expands into other countries and regions, such as the United States and Europe. It seems clear that the core idea of "individual accountability" can be viewed as universally relevant and thus transferable from China to other countries. It's also equally obvious that the concrete manifestation of this idea may have to be very different in different cultures and that the practice of "printed yellow footprints" may be totally unacceptable to American workers.

It is also important for the globalizing company to differentiate between core versus peripheral beliefs and practices. As an example, consider the establishment of the Mercedes-Benz plant to manufacture M-Class sport utility vehicles in Alabama during the mid-1990s. In the words of Andreas Renschler, leader of this project at the time, "We wanted the M-Class project to be more than just another plant building another car. We wanted it to be a 'learning field'—the creation of a new product and a new plant, with new administrative systems in a new country."[12] In this case, the company held steadfast to the view that the M-Class car must preserve the look and feel of a Mercedes-Benz, but many other practices (for example, the degree of plant automation, the formality versus casualness of attire) were viewed as flexible and subject to adaptation.

The definition of what constitutes a company's core beliefs and practices is and must always be the result of learning through experimentation. These definitions will be different across industries and, within any industry, across firms—and even for the same firm, different at different times. As a senior executive of a major global retailer observed, "Cut your chains and you become free. Cut your roots and you die. Differentiating between the two requires good judgment, something that you acquire only through experience and over time."

Transplanting Core Beliefs and Practices to the New Subsidiary

Transplanting core beliefs and practices to a new subsidiary, whether a greenfield operation or an acquisition, is always a transformational event, with the challenge much greater in the case of acquisitions. The transplanted beliefs and practices are likely to be at best only partly understood and, in the case of acquisitions, often seen as alien and questionable. Transferring core beliefs and practices to a new subsidiary usually requires physically transferring a select group of committed believers (the DNA carriers) to the new operation. The size of this group depends largely on the scale of the desired transformation effort. If the goal is essentially to replace an entire set of preexisting beliefs and practices (as with ABB's acquisitions in Eastern Europe), it may be necessary to send in a veritable army of DNA carriers. On the other hand, if the goal is to create a new business model (as in the case of Mercedes-Benz's Alabama plant), then fewer, carefully selected transplants would be needed.

Obloj and Thomas[13] have described vividly how the invasion process worked in the case of ABB Poland:

> The transformation began with an influx and invasion of external and internal ABB consultants that signaled clearly the introductory stage of organizational change. Their behavior was guided by their perception of the stereotypical behavior of an inefficient state-owned firm typically managed by a cadre of administrators who do not understand how to manage a firm in a market economy. They did not initially perform any sophisticated diagnosis or analysis of local conditions or develop a strategic vision for the transformation process. Rather, they forcefully implemented market enterprise discipline in the acquired former state-owned firms by a series of high-speed actions. They implemented massive training efforts aimed at exposing employees and managers of acquired firms to the principles of the market economy, modern management principles, and the ABB management system. This was adopted in all acquired firms following Percy Barnevik's dictum that the key to competitiveness is education and re-education.

The contrast between ABB's approach in Poland and Mercedes-Benz's slower, more open, more learning-oriented approach in Alabama is interesting:

> Of the six top executives in charge of the plant, three are native Germans. . . . Two are Americans. . . . There is one Canadian. . . . In late 1993, after the management team was hired, they were sequestered in Stuttgart, Germany, Daimler's base, for a year. They gathered each Wednesday at 10 A.M. in a temporary trailer office on a Mercedes

parking lot . . . often meeting past midnight. The executives clashed repeatedly. They disagreed over whether the plant should be highly automated—as Mercedes officials believed—or revolve around streamlined manual techniques—which the American executives supported. In the end, automation was kept to a minimum, compared with industry standards now.[14]

Embedding the Core Beliefs and Practices

The process of transplanting the corporate DNA, which begins with transferring a select group of DNA carriers to the new subsidiary, can be judged successful only when the new beliefs and practices have become internalized in the mindsets and routines of employees at the new subsidiary. Achieving such internalization requires visibly explicit and credible commitment by the parent company to its core beliefs and practices, a systematic process of continuous education within the new organization right down to middle managers and the local workforce, and concrete demonstration that the new beliefs and practices yield individual as well as corporate success.

The approach taken by the Ritz-Carlton chain at its hotel in Shanghai, China, illustrates how a company can initiate the successful embedding of its core beliefs and practices in a new subsidiary. Ritz-Carlton acquired the rights to manage this hotel, with a staff of about a thousand people, under its own name as of January 1998. The company believed that, consistent with its image and its corporate DNA, the entire operation required significant upgrading. The company brought in a sizable contingent of about forty expatriates from other Ritz-Carlton units in Asia and around the world to transform and manage the new property. What is particularly noteworthy, however, is the approach taken by Ritz-Carlton managers to embed the company's own standards of quality and service in the hearts, minds, and behavior of their local associates. Among its first actions in the very first week under its own control, the company decided to begin the renovation process with the employees' entrance and changing and wash rooms rather than from more typical starting points, such as the main lobby. The logic, as explained by a senior executive, was that, through this approach, every employee would personally see two radical changes in the very first week: one, that the new standards of quality and service would be dramatically higher, and two, that the employees were among the most valued stakeholders in the company. This approach served as a very successful start to embedding the company's basic beliefs in every associate's mind: "We Are Ladies and Gentlemen Serving Ladies and Gentlemen."

Winning the Local Battle

Winning the local battle requires the global enterprise to anticipate, shape, and respond to the needs and actions of three sets of players in the host country: its customers, its competitors, and the host country government.

Winning Host Country Customers

One of the ingredients in establishing local presence is an understanding of the uniqueness of the local market and of which aspects of the company's business model require little change, which require local adaptation, and which need to be reinvented. If the targeted segment in the foreign market is similar to the one served in the home market, the company's business design will need little adaptation. However, if the firm wants to expand the served customer base in a foreign market, then adapting the business model to the local customers' unique demands becomes mandatory. The following cases illustrate the varied experiences of U.S. companies in their pursuit of host country customers.

When FedEx entered the Chinese market, it had to decide, as an element of its entry strategy, who its target customers should be: local Chinese companies or multinational corporations. FedEx chose to target multinational companies, a customer segment identical to the one it has historically served. Given this decision, FedEx was able to export the U.S. business model into China, including employing its own aircraft, building a huge network of trucks and distribution centers, and adopting the aggressive marketing and advertising typical in the United States. In contrast, if FedEx had selected local Chinese companies as its targeted customer segment, winning host country customers would have required a much greater degree of local adaptation of the business model.

Nike suffered an initial setback in Europe when it mistakenly transplanted the U.S. marketing approach to the continent. In the United States, Nike became a huge success by projecting the image of an irreverent rebel who glorifies the lowly sneaker, worships athletes, and rebels against the establishment. Initially, Nike took the same approach in Europe. Two of the company's commercials in Europe were a team of Nike endorsers playing soccer against Satan and his demons and a French bad boy explaining how he had won a Nike contract by insulting his coach and spitting at a fan. Though these commercials might have done well in the United States, they backfired in the more tradition-bound European culture. Learning from this setback, Nike decided that it must "Europeanize" its approach and become more of a diplomat than a rebel. As Phil Knight, chairman of Nike, remarked: "The fine line is gone from being a rebel to being a bully. Nike is now making an effort to get along [in Europe]. Ten years ago, we would have never thought of doing that, because we were the antiestablishment."[15]

Winning the Battle Against Host Country Competitors

Whenever a company enters a new country, it can expect retaliation from local competitors as well as from other multinationals already operating in that market. Successfully establishing local presence requires anticipating and responding to these competitive threats. Established local competitors enjoy several advantages— knowledge of the local market, working relationships with local customers, understanding of local distribution channels, and so on. In contrast, the global firm suffers from the liability of newness. When a global firm enters their market, local competitors are likely to feel threatened and their retaliation in defense of their position will act as a barrier to entry. The new invader has four possible options to overcome these barriers.

Acquire a Dominant Local Competitor. This option will prove successful if there is significant potential for synergies between the global firm and acquisition target, the global firm has the capability to create and capture such synergies, and it does not give away the synergies through a huge up-front acquisition premium.

An example of successful entry through acquisition of a dominant local competitor is Accor, the French hospitality company, which entered the U.S. low-priced lodging market by acquiring Motel 6, the best-managed market leader in this category. In contrast, Sony Corporation paid a huge premium to acquire Columbia Pictures and to date has had great difficulty in justifying this premium, despite significant potential synergies between Sony's hardware competencies and Columbia's content expertise and assets.

Acquire a Weak Player. This option is attractive when the global firm has the ability to transplant its corporate DNA into the acquired firm quickly so as to transform the weak player into a much stronger or even a dominant player. The sheer act of acquiring a weak player signals to other local competitors that they will soon be under attack. It is therefore to be expected that local competitors will retaliate. If the global firm is unable to transform the acquired operations in a very short time, these operations are likely to become even weaker due to more intense attack from local competitors.

Consider Whirlpool's entry into Europe in 1989 by acquiring the problem-ridden appliance division of Philips. Unfortunately, Whirlpool could not quickly embed the capabilities needed to turn Philips's struggling appliance business around. In the meantime, Whirlpool's entry gave two European rivals—Sweden's Electrolux and Germany's Bosch-Siemens—a wake-up call. Not surprisingly, both these companies invested very heavily in plant modernization, process improvements, new product introductions, and restructuring—all with the intent of improving their competitiveness to repel the new invader. The net result was a disappointment for Whirlpool, which had hoped to consolidate the white goods industry in Europe. By 1998, Whirlpool had only 12 percent market share in Europe, half of its expected position, and was also underachieving in profitability. To quote Jeff Fettig, Whirlpool's head of European operations at the time: "We underestimated the competition."[16]

As a different type of example, consider South African Breweries' entry into the U.S. market. The company, now known as SABMiller, entered the United States in 2002 by acquiring Miller Brewing Company from Philip Morris, the tobacco and food giant. In the U.S. market, Miller had been the perennial number two to Anheuser-Busch. However, within three years after the acquisition, Miller was gaining market share from Anheuser-Busch and, despite a market share of well over 40 percent, the latter was forced to cut prices, apparently for the first time. Unlike Miller Brewing's previous owner, Philip Morris, South African Breweries brought to its new subsidiary much deeper knowledge of the beer business and a much more aggressive mindset honed in the rough-and-tumble of Africa, Eastern Europe, and China.[17]

Enter a Poorly Defended Niche. If acquisition candidates are either unavailable or too expensive, the global firm has no choice but to enter on its own. Under these circumstances, it should find a poorly defended niche for market entry and, assuming such a niche exists, use that niche as a platform for subsequent expansion into the mainstream segments of the local market. Often the mobility barriers to move from the niche market to the mainstream segments are much lower than the barriers to direct entry in the mainstream segments.

In the early 1970s, Japanese automobile manufacturers entered the U.S. market at the low end, a segment that was being ignored by U.S. car companies and hence a "loose brick" in their fortress. In time, the Japanese companies used their dominance of the lower-end segment to migrate to the middle and upper ends very effectively.

Financial Times' entry into the U.S. market in 1997 also illustrates the wisdom of avoiding a frontal attack. To quote Richard Lambert, editor of *Financial Times* at that time:

> When we started our expansion here [in the United States], some existing readers told us they were worried we might be seeking to replicate the *Wall Street Journal*. This was the last thing on our minds: 800-pound gorillas are usually best left well alone. Instead, our aim has been to develop a paper that would be uniquely positioned for the new global market place. Here is what you can expect from *Financial Times*: a much broader and more consistent coverage of international business, economic, and political news than is available in any other publication, a global perspective on the comment and analysis pages, [and] strong coverage of the world's biggest and most dynamic economy. We seek to put U.S. business, economic, and political news into an international context.[18]

Stage a Frontal Attack. The global firm can choose a head-on attack on the dominant and entrenched incumbents, provided its competitive advantage is sufficiently large so that it can be leveraged outside its domestic market. If this were not true, taking on an eight hundred-pound gorilla with all the liability of newness could prove suicidal. Lexus's frontal attack on Mercedes and BMW in the U.S. market succeeded mainly as a result of its overwhelming advantage in such areas as product quality and cost structure. For instance, Lexus enjoyed a 30 percent cost advantage. Given the high labor costs that Mercedes and BMW faced in Germany, where they manufactured their automobiles, they could not neutralize the Lexus cost advantage quickly.

Managing Relationships with the Host Government

Local government can often be a key external stakeholder, particularly in emerging markets. Two points are worth noting in this context. First, the global firm can ill afford to ignore nonmarket stakeholders, such as the local government. For instance, in the late

1990s, the Chinese government's ban on all door-to-door selling had a negative impact on companies (such as Mary Kay Cosmetics and Avon) who depend on a highly personalized direct marketing approach. Second, managing nonmarket stakeholders should be seen as a dynamic process. Simply reacting to existing government regulations is not enough. Firms must anticipate likely future changes in the regulatory framework and even explore the possibility of helping to shape the emerging regulatory framework. Persistence and constructive dialogue with the local government, instead of appeasement or confrontation, are often critical elements of winning the local battle.

Microsoft's strategy in China is a remarkable example of how a company can engage in a proactive and constructive engagement with the government. It is also a story of transformation from an initially naive and confrontational strategy to a synergistic and mutually beneficial one. Microsoft entered China in 1992 and, for nearly a decade, faced one disaster after another. The company's initial strategy was to sell software at the same prices in China that it charged in other markets. Given the vast demand for the company's products in China and the inability of most customers to pay the official price for them, the inevitable happened. Almost everyone was using Windows and Office, just that nobody was paying for them, as counterfeit copies were available for just a few dollars. Microsoft went on the offensive and sued violators for using illegal copies. Not only did the company lose in the local courts, it also developed an image in the Chinese press and with the Chinese government for being arrogant and heartless. In the mid-1990s, Microsoft's own country manager resigned and wrote a tell-all book criticizing the company for being naive and heavy-handed. For its part, the Chinese government (including the Chinese Academy of Sciences) became a major proponent of Microsoft's scourge—open-source Linux.

The transformation started in 1999 when Craig Mundie, Microsoft's public policy chief, visited China and started to advocate that the company needed to take a cooperative approach with the government and to look at China as not just a market but also as a base for leading-edge research. Microsoft set up a new Asia Research

Center in Beijing. This R&D center would eventually become a powerhouse in terms of academic publications, patents, and contributions of key components to the company's global software products. Microsoft also decided to engage with China more comprehensively. It set up research labs with some of China's top universities, created Microsoft Fellowships for some of China's best computer science PhD students, and collaborated with the Ministry of Education to set up one hundred model computer classrooms in rural areas. Microsoft also decided to battle piracy head-on by dropping its own prices radically for students and government offices.

The turnaround in Microsoft's relations with the Chinese government has been dramatic. In 2006, President Hu Jintao visited the Microsoft campus in Redmond, had dinner at Bill Gates's home, and was reported to have said: "You are a friend to the Chinese people, and I am a friend of Microsoft." Later that year, the Chinese government enacted a new law requiring that local PC manufacturers load legal software on the computers before selling them and prohibiting them from selling "naked" machines. Microsoft's 2007 revenues from China were expected to be $700 million, three times the figure for 2004. In mid-2007, *Fortune* magazine quoted Bill Gates as now being "certain that China will eventually be Microsoft's biggest market."[19]

Speed of Global Expansion

Having commenced the journey to globalization, a company has yet another major issue to address, namely, how fast should it expand globally? Starbucks' rapid expansion around the world epitomizes using globalization for aggressive growth. By moving quickly, a company can solidify its market position rapidly. However, rapid global expansion can also deplete managerial, organizational, and financial resources, thereby jeopardizing the company's ability to defend and profit from its newly created global presence. Consider, for example, the Chinese company TCL Corporation. In 2003 and 2004, TCL made some very bold moves by acquiring the consumer electronics businesses of the French companies Thomson and Alcatel. The acquisitions included some iconic brands such as RCA. As reported by *China Daily*, TCL's goal was to use these acquisitions as vehicles to become another Sony or Samsung.[20] By 2007, these ambitions appeared to be in ruins. TCL learned that acquiring a foreign company is one thing, turning it around and integrating it with existing operations quite another. After hefty restructuring charges, by mid-2007, the acquired units had either been shut down or were put on the auction block. Accelerated global expansion is more appropriate under certain conditions:

- *It is easy for competitors to replicate your recipe for success.* Particularly vulnerable are fast-food and retailing companies, such as KFC and Starbucks, where competitors can take a proven concept from one market and easily replicate it in another unoccupied market with relatively low investment. This phenomenon is also observable in other, very different industries, such as personal computers, software, and e-commerce. The rapid globalization of companies like Compaq, Dell, Microsoft, Google, and Yahoo! reflects their determination to prevent replication or pirating of their product concepts and business models in markets worldwide.

- *Scale economies are extremely important.* Very high scale economies afford the early and rapid globalizer considerable first-mover advantages and handicap slower globalizers for long periods of time. For this reason, expeditious globalizers in the tire industry, such as Goodyear, Michelin, and Bridgestone, now hold a sizable advantage over tardy globalizers, such as Pirelli and Continental.

- *Management's capacity to manage (or learn how to manage) global operations is high.* Consider, for example, the case of such experienced global players as Nokia, Coca-Cola, Citicorp, Procter & Gamble, or ABB. Should these companies successfully introduce a new product line in one country, it would be logical and relatively easy for them to roll out this product line rapidly to all potential markets worldwide. In addition to the company's ability to manage global operations, the rate of globalization also depends on its ability to leverage its experience from one market to another. The faster an organization can recycle its knowledge about market entry and market defense from one country to another, the lower the risk of depleting its managerial and organizational capacity.

Conclusion

Becoming global is never exclusively the result of a grand design. Nor is it simply a sequence of incremental, ad hoc, opportunistic, and random moves. The wisest approach would be one of directed opportunism, an approach that maintains opportunism and flexibility within a broad direction set by a systematic framework. The central idea underlying the framework developed and elaborated upon in this chapter has been that when a company embarks on the road to globalization, six major issues need to be sorted out: choice of products, choice of markets, mode of entry, transplanting the corporate DNA, winning the local battle, and speed of global expansion. The final box, based on this framework, identifies a set of questions that managers can use to assess their firm's global presence at any given point in time and design a course of action to expand this global presence in the future.

Building Global Presence: A Manager's Guide to Action

Using Marriott as an illustrative example, the following is a list of questions that a firm should ask in its attempt to assess its globalization efforts to date and direct actions needed to secure its global presence in the future. As mentioned earlier in the chapter, until the early 1990s, Marriott Corporation was essentially a domestic company. Since then, the company has established a major global presence by using full-service lodging as its initial launch vehicle.

The Globalization Imperatives

- What goals have motivated our globalization efforts to date?
- What benefits have accrued from globalization so far?
- Are we ahead of, at par with, or behind the extent of globalization demanded by our target customers?
- Are we ahead of, at par with, or behind the extent of globalization of our actual (or benchmark) competitors?
- Would more proactive globalization give us an edge over our competitors?
- What goals should drive our globalization strategy over the next three to five years? The next five to ten years?

Choice of Products

- Why did we pick full-service lodging as the first launch vehicle for globalization?
- To what extent was full-service lodging a good or not-so-good choice? What have we learned?
- What logic should guide us in the selection of the next launch vehicle?
- What should the next launch vehicle be? Why?

Choice of Strategic Markets

- How have we picked the target markets for globalization so far? What logic, if any, have we followed?
- Based on our experience, what have we learned about the factors that differentiate good from not-so-good markets?
- Taking into account emerging market opportunities, push from customers, and the actual or expected market presence of our competitors, what should our goals regarding market presence be three to five years from now for full-service lodging? For the next product line to be globalized?

Choice of Entry Mode

- What logic has guided our choices between own-management versus franchise approaches to entering target markets?
- Based on our experience to date, what have we learned about the characteristics that differentiate good from not-so-good

franchisees, negotiating the terms and conditions with
the franchisees, and ongoing oversight and management of
franchise operations?

- Over the next three to five years, what logic should guide us in
  the selection of entry mode?
- Over the next three to five years, should we have any preference
  between the various modes? If so, what and why?

Transplanting the Corporate DNA

- Are we clear about exactly what our core (as distinct from
  peripheral) beliefs and practices are? What have we learned in
  our experiments in the past on what constitutes core versus
  non-core?
- What mechanisms have we used so far to transfer these beliefs
  and practices to the new subsidiary? How efficient and effective
  are these mechanisms?
- What processes have we used to embed these beliefs and
  practices in the new subsidiary? What have we learned from
  our successful as well as unsuccessful attempts?

Winning the Local Battle

- Which customer segments have we targeted in our foreign
  market entries to date? What have we learned regarding
  tailored versus standardized formats? How can we use this
  knowledge in the future?
- What logic has guided our choices between a loose-bricks
  approach versus a frontal attack in entering target markets?
  What have we learned?

Speed of Expansion

- What factors have determined the speed of our global expansion
  to date? What have been the (internally or externally imposed)
  constraints on faster expansion? What have been the facilitators?
- Based on our experience to date, what have we learned about
  how to maintain a high rate of global expansion or to increase
  it even further?
- For the next three to five years, what should be the pace of our
  global expansion efforts?

3

Lessons from the Globalization of Wal-Mart

> We'll lower the cost of living for everyone, not just
> in America, [and] we'll give the world an opportunity
> to see what it's like to save and do better.
> —*Sam Walton, Founder, Wal-Mart*[1]

In 2007, Wal-Mart was the largest retailer in the world. Headquartered in Bentonville, Arkansas, the company achieved sales revenues of $345 billion for the year ending January 31, 2007. Across the United States, Puerto Rico, and twelve other countries, Wal-Mart operated a diverse variety of retail stores ranging in size from as small as eight thousand square feet to as large as two hundred thousand square feet. Within the United States, the company operated four types of retailing outlets: Discount Stores, which offered a wide assortment of general merchandise and a limited variety of food products; Supercenters, which offered a wide assortment of general merchandise and a full-line supermarket; Neighborhood Markets, which offered a full-line supermarket and a limited assortment of general merchandise; and Sam's Clubs, large warehouse clubs, which marketed merchandise displayed in bulk and required customers to purchase memberships.

Since its first move outside the United States in 1991, Wal-Mart had pursued globalization aggressively (see Table 3.1). Whereas in 1993 just 1 percent of all Wal-Mart's stores were located outside the United States, by 2007, that figure had grown to 41 percent.

Did Wal-Mart have to go global? If yes, then was the company's timing for the start of global expansion right? Did Wal-Mart choose

Table 3.1. The Globalization of Wal-Mart

		Year ending January 31			
		1991	(%)	2007	(%)
Sales ($ billions)	United States	33	100	268	78
	International	0	0	77	22
	Total	33	100	345	100
Number of stores	United States	1,721	100	4,022	59
	International	0	0	2,757	41
	Total	1,721	100	6,779	100

Source: Wal-Mart annual reports.

the right sequence of entry into the global markets? Was the company wise in designing its entry strategies for the various markets? Did the company make the right choices regarding how much of its corporate DNA to transfer to foreign markets versus how much to adapt to local realities? Why did the company win (or lose) the local battles that it did? Finally, has the company's global expansion been too fast, too slow, or just the right speed? We explore these questions below using the framework for building global presence developed in the last chapter.[2]

Globalization Imperatives

Wal-Mart made its first concrete moves toward foreign expansion in 1991 when it set up a fifty-fifty joint venture with Mexico's largest retailer, Cifra, to open wholesale clubs in that country. The first two units, branded Club Aurrera, were opened in the fourth quarter of 1991. In order to examine whether this was indeed the right timing, it is useful to look at the company's trend line in the five years leading up to 1991.

Wal-Mart's stock price was certainly doing well at the time. From $4.00 at the close of 1985, the stock rose to $15.12 at the close of 1990 and was on its way to ending at $29.50 by the close of 1991. However, the excellent capital market performance also posed a challenge. At a price-to-earnings multiple of nearly 40, investors had very high expectations regarding the company's ongoing growth. At the same time, given the trajectory of Wal-Mart's actual growth during 1986–1991 (see Table 3.2), it was becoming rapidly clear that staying domestic would make it virtually impossible to meet the lofty shareholder expectations. In the late 1980s, Wal-Mart was adding four to six new states within the United States each year to its geographic portfolio. With presence in thirty-five states by early 1991, the company would very likely be operating in all fifty states by 1995. Further, the growth rates in Wal-Mart's revenues and earnings per share were in steady decline, from 41 percent and 38 percent respectively for 1985–1986 to 26 percent and 20 percent respectively for 1990–1991.

Clearly, globalization is not the only strategic path for a company's growth. For Wal-Mart, domestic diversification into other types of retailing or even other industries has always been a potential option (although not necessarily an equally attractive one). Wal-Mart's history from 1991 to 2007 indicates that it has pursued both strategic options—global expansion in its core discount retailing business as well as business diversification into other types of retailing, such as supermarkets and, more recently, financial services. Pursuing both approaches considerably increases the prospects for continued growth. However, data for the twenty-five-year period 1981 to 2007 (see Table 3.3) indicate that, despite attempting to

Table 3.2. Wal-Mart's Growth During 1986–1991

	Year ending January 31				
	1987	*1988*	*1989*	*1990*	*1991*
Number of U.S. states with Wal-Mart stores	23	23	25	29	35
Growth in sales over previous year (%)	41	34	29	25	26
Growth in earnings per share over previous year (%)	38	38	35	28	20

Source: Wal-Mart annual reports.

Table 3.3. Wal-Mart's Intensifying Growth Challenge

Average Annual Growth Rate in:	1981–1986	1986–1991	1991–1996	1996–2001	2001–2006
Sales (%)	39.7	30.8	23.5	15.4	10.3
Earnings per Share (%)	47.6	32.9	15.7	18.6	13.7

Source: Wal-Mart annual reports.

grow along both dimensions, Wal-Mart has continued to face severe growth challenges. As it has grown bigger, the company's growth rate has declined steadily. During 2001–2006, revenues and earnings per share grew at an annual rate of only 10.3 percent and 13.7 percent respectively. Had Wal-Mart not pursued global expansion, it would have hit a plateau much sooner.

Deciding not to grow was not really an option for Wal-Mart. Lack of growth not only hurts the stock price, it also makes the company a less attractive employer for ambitious hard-charging people. Note also that one of the key factors in Wal-Mart's historical success has been its dedicated and committed workforce. Because of its stock purchase plan, the wealth of Wal-Mart employees was directly tied to the market value of the company's stock, strongly linking growth to its positive effect on stock price and to company morale.

In sum, Wal-Mart's decision to commence global expansion in 1991–1992 appears to have been right on the mark.

Choice of Markets: Roads Taken Versus Roads Not Taken

Which market was optimal as Wal-Mart's initial launching pad: Europe, Asia, or other countries in the western hemisphere? It could not afford to enter them all at once in 1991, because at that time Wal-Mart lacked the competencies and resources (financial, organizational, and managerial) to launch a simultaneous penetration all over the globe. Further, for any company, a logically sequenced approach to market entry (as opposed to a do-it-all-at-once scheme) enables it to apply the learning gained from its initial market entries to its subsequent moves.

Table 3.4 chronicles the trajectory of Wal-Mart's choice of markets for expansion outside the United States. The company's early entry into Puerto Rico and Canada can be regarded as largely opportunistic. Both markets are geographically, economically, and culturally proximate to the United States. Also, they are relatively small markets. The real strategic question pertains to expansion outside of these two markets. As Table 3.4 indicates, Wal-Mart's initial targets were the big markets in Latin America (specifically, Mexico, Brazil, and Argentina). After that, the company started expansion in Asia and Europe. We can analyze Wal-Mart's initial choice of markets as a three-step decision: a higher priority to emerging rather than developed markets; within emerging markets, a higher priority to Latin America over Asia; and, within Latin America, a higher priority to the larger rather than smaller markets.

As targets for initial expansion, both developed and emerging markets had pros and cons, especially in 1991. The developed markets of Western Europe and Japan were much larger than any of the developing markets. Also, in terms of per capita buying power, these markets were closer to the United States than the developing markets. However, the developed markets also presented a major challenge. As mature markets, they housed entrenched local competitors that were large, experienced, and professionally managed. Thus Wal-Mart could expect to meet tough competition from local players. Wal-Mart's decision to give higher priority to emerging markets appears to have been well thought out. Given the much higher growth rates of the emerging markets, delayed entry into these markets was likely to suffer from much greater opportunity costs than delayed entry into the developed markets. Also, given the nascent stage of their development, Wal-Mart was likely to have a stronger competitive advantage over existing rivals in the emerging rather than developed markets.

Within the set of emerging markets, Asian markets were the largest, followed by Latin America, then Eastern Europe, and then Africa. Wal-Mart's choice of Latin America rather than Asia as the

Table 3.4. The Evolutionary Path of Wal-Mart's Global Expansion (1991-2007)

Number of Stores on January 31

	1991	1992	1993	1994	1995	1996	1997	1998	1999	2000	2001	2002	2003	2004	2005	2006	2007
U.S.	1,721	1,928	2,134	2,435	2,554	2,667	2,740	2,805	2,884	2,985	3,118	3,244	3,400	3,551	3,702	3,856	4,022
Puerto Rico	—	—	2	5	7	11	11	14	15	15	15	17	52	53	54	54	54
Canada	—	—	—	—	123	131	136	144	153	166	174	196	213	235	262	278	289
Mexico	—	—	8	23	96	126	152	402	416	458	499	551	597	623	679	774	889
Brazil	—	—	—	—	—	5	5	8	14	14	20	22	22	25	149	295	299
Argentina	—	—	—	—	—	3	6	9	13	13	11	11	11	11	11	11	13
C. America	—	—	—	—	—	—	—	—	—	—	—	—	—	—	—	—	413
Hong Kong	—	—	—	—	3	—	—	—	—	—	—	—	—	—	—	—	—
Indonesia	—	—	—	—	—	—	2	—	—	—	—	—	—	—	—	—	—
China	—	—	—	—	—	—	2	3	5	6	11	19	26	34	43	56	73
South Korea	—	—	—	—	—	—	—	—	4	5	6	9	15	15	16	16	—
Japan	—	—	—	—	—	—	—	—	—	—	—	—	*	*	*	398	392
Germany	—	—	—	—	—	—	—	21	95	95	94	95	94	92	91	88	—
U.K.	—	—	—	—	—	—	—	—	—	232	241	250	258	267	282	315	335
Total	1,721	1,928	2,144	2,463	2,883	2,943	3,024	3,406	3,599	3,989	4,123	4,414	4,688	4,906	5,289	6,141	6,779

* Wal-Mart acquired a minority stake in the Japanese chain Seiyu in late 2002 and converted it to a majority stake in December 2005.

Source: Wal-Mart annual reports.

launching pad for global expansion appears to have been wise. As a novice to global expansion, it was important that Wal-Mart choose the launching pads on the basis of not just market size but also the risk of failure. Compared with Latin America, Asian markets were not only geographically much farther, they were also separated from the United States by multiple time zones, vast language and cultural differences, as well as differences in political systems. Thus Latin America emerged as the most attractive choice for initial global expansion. Given proximity to the United States, the risk of failure would be moderate and these markets would provide excellent learning opportunities for entry into the larger Asian markets.

Within Latin America, the three largest markets were Brazil, Mexico, and Argentina, in that order. Starting with Mexico, the closest market to the United States, Wal-Mart entered these three markets in quick succession. Note also that Wal-Mart delayed any additional forays into Latin America until 2007 when it acquired a controlling stake in CARHCO (Central American Retail Holding Co.) thus acquiring stores in Costa Rica, El Salvador, Guatemala, Honduras, and Nicaragua. Relative to Mexico, Brazil, and Argentina, these and other markets in Latin America are much smaller and thus would constitute opportunistic entries where the timing of the entry would not have a significant impact on the company's fortunes.

As Table 3.4 indicates, after Latin America, Wal-Mart turned its attention first to Asia and then Europe. In Asia, the company focused first on China, using Hong Kong as a beachhead to learn how to manage operations separated by vast geographic, time, and cultural differences. As Wal-Mart's quick withdrawal from Hong Kong after just one year illustrates, it apparently was a good learning experience. A similar quick entry into and exit from Indonesia in 1997, where the entry timing coincided with political turmoil and President Suharto's ouster, also served as another learning experience. Building on these experiences, Wal-Mart's real thrust in Asia came via entry into China in 1997. As the world's largest and fastest growing emerging market, the company's decision to give primacy to the Chinese market within Asia appears to have been wise. India would have been another option. However, since the Indian government did not permit foreign retailers to operate within its borders, this was not a feasible option. After China, Wal-Mart's next moves in Asia were in South Korea (1999) and Japan (2003), both developed markets. As we discuss later, the South Korean move would prove to be a mistake and the company would exit from there in 2006. As of 2007, Wal-Mart also appeared to be struggling in Japan. Looking back, it appears that Wal-Mart would have been better off giving higher priority to the emerging markets of Southeast Asia rather than going after South Korea and Japan. Such a move would have been consistent with the strategic logic that guided Wal-Mart to give higher priority to other important emerging markets, such as Mexico, Brazil, Argentina, and China.

Close on the heels of its 1997 entry into China, Wal-Mart also entered Europe. Its first move was into Germany in 1998 followed by the United Kingdom in 2000. Wal-Mart's German strategy would prove to be an unmitigated disaster. In 2006, the company sold its stores in Germany to Metro and exited with a $1 billion loss. As of 2007, Wal-Mart was yet to make any moves into the emerging economies of Eastern Europe. It appears that, in Europe, as in Asia other than China, Wal-Mart appears to have given higher priority to the developed rather than emerging markets. In broad terms, this may be regarded as a questionable strategy. The opportunity costs of delayed entry into emerging markets are much higher than in the case of developed markets. Also, in the case of developed markets, the foreign retailer runs a high risk of running into problems irrespective of whether it enters by acquiring a small or a large player. Retailing is a very multidomestic industry. Thus, as Wal-Mart learned in South Korea and Germany, what matters is local size and market share within the country—not global size or global market share. If the company enters by acquiring a small player, it's almost impossible to scale up against the entrenched leader. But if the company enters by buying the leader in a mature developed market, given the multidomestic character of the industry, it is very hard for the acquirer to recover the up-front acquisition premium.

Choice of Entry Modes

The following box presents details on how Wal-Mart entered each foreign market and the follow-up strategic moves that it made in each market. As can be seen, there is no single strategy that Wal-Mart followed across the board. Consistent with our arguments in Chapter Two, the company adapted its entry strategy to the context of the market that it was entering.

Time Line of Wal-Mart's Globalization Moves

Wal-Mart in Mexico

1991	50-50 joint venture with Cifra, Mexico's largest retailer.
1994	Entered agreement with Cifra that all new Cifra stores will be operated through the joint venture.
1997	Acquired a controlling stake in Cifra.
2000	Changed name to Wal-Mart de Mexico.
2007	889 retail units, $19 billion gross sales, No.1 retailer in Mexico, with 17.0 percent market share (as of January 2007).

Wal-Mart in Brazil

1994	60-40 joint venture with Lojas Americana, Brazil's largest retailer.
1995	Opened two Supercenters and two Sam's Clubs.
1997	Acquired the 40 percent minority interest in the joint venture.
2004	Acquired 118 Bompreco stores from Ahold.
2005	Acquired 140 Sonae stores from Modelo Continente.
2007	299 stores, 258 of which through acquisitions; $5 billion gross sales (as of January 2007).

Wal-Mart in Argentina

1995	Entered without a local partner (100 percent Wal-Mart ownership).

2007   Thirteen stores, $752 million gross sales (as of January 2007).

Wal-Mart in Canada

1994   100 percent acquisition of 122 Woolco stores from Woolworth; rapidly converted into Wal-Mart stores.

2007   289 stores, $12 billion gross sales (as of January 2007).

Wal-Mart in Japan

2002   Acquired a 6.1 percent stake in Seiyu, Japan's fifth largest supermarket chain operator, established in 1963.

2005   Acquired a majority stake of 53 percent in Seiyu, making Seiyu a Wal-Mart subsidiary.

2007   392 stores, $9.7 billion gross sales (as of January 2007), posted five straight years of losses; comparable store sales turned positive at 0.6 percent for the first time in 2006, but turned negative again in the first six months of 2007; lost $479.5 million in 2006.

Wal-Mart in China

1994   Partnership with Thailand-based conglomerate C.P. Pokphand Co. to open Value Clubs (mini-warehouse clubs) in Hong Kong.

1995   Partnership with C.P. Pokphand Co. dissolved.

1996   Opened one Wal-Mart Supercenter and one Sam's Club in China through joint ventures with Hong Kong Pearl River Investment Co. and Shenzhen International Co.

2006   Total: sixty-eight Supercenters, three Sam's Clubs, and two Neighborhood Markets in thirty-six cities in China. Gross sales reached $1.4 billion.

2007   Purchased a 35 percent interest in Bounteous Company Ltd. (BCL) which operates 101 Trust-Mart retail stores in 34 cities in China.

Wal-Mart in Indonesia

1996   Opened a Supercenter in Jakarta through a contractual agreement with Lippo Group of Indonesia whereby Wal-Mart provided expertise and management services for the store to be owned by Lippo Group.

1998   Left Indonesia after the Jakarta store was burned down during the 1998 riots.

Wal-Mart in Germany

1997   Acquired the Wertkauf hypermarket chain of twenty-one stores, a German company owned by the Mann family.

1999   Acquired seventy-four Interspar hypermarket chain stores from Spar Handels AG, a German company that owned multiple retail formats and wholesale operations throughout Germany.

2006   Exited from Germany; sold its eighty-five Supercenters to Metro AG, incurring a pretax loss of approximately $1 billion.

Wal-Mart in Korea

1999   Acquired a majority interest in four units operated by Korea Makro.

2006   Exited from South Korea; sold its sixteen stores for $882 million to Shinsegae Co., South Korea's leading retailer with seventy-nine E-Mart hypermarkets, incurring a pretax gain of $103 million.

Wal-Mart in the United Kingdom

1999   Acquired Britain's third-largest food retailer, the supermarket chain Asda Group PLC (229 stores), for $10.8 billion.

2000   The first Asda Wal-Mart Supercentre opened.

2001   The last Asda store was converted over to Wal-Mart retail system; began sourcing jointly with Wal-Mart.

2006   337 stores total generated gross sales of approximately $31.7 billion representing approximately 36.8 percent of Wal-Mart's total international sales.

Discount retailing in everyday consumer goods is a very multidomestic business. Even in Canada, a market geographically and in almost every other way extremely close to the United States, Wal-Mart has always sourced over 80 percent of the products from local suppliers. Globally, cross-border procurement for its stores in various countries including the United States amounts to only about 10 percent of the total. Given this multidomestic industry structure, entering a new market via exports is not a feasible option. Wal-Mart must enter by setting up local operations—local procurement, local supply chain logistics, and local stores. At the same time, the company does have to decide whether it will set up greenfield operations or buy into the existing operations of a partner. It also must decide whether the entry mode should be to go alone (100 percent ownership) or rely on shared ownership with a partner.

As Box 3.1 indicates, in most emerging markets (Mexico, Brazil, Indonesia, and China), Wal-Mart's initial entry has been via greenfield operations set up through a joint venture with a local partner. The only exception was Argentina where Wal-Mart entered by setting up 100 percent owned operations. In contrast, in most developed markets (Canada, Germany, United Kingdom, and South Korea), Wal-Mart's initial strategy has been to enter via acquiring 100 percent ownership over a local player. The only exceptions were Hong Kong and Japan. In Hong Kong, Wal-Mart entered through a joint venture with a partner from Thailand and, in Japan, the company entered by taking first a minority 6.1 percent and then a majority 53 percent stake in a local retailer.

Did Wal-Mart follow sound strategic logic in its entry mode decisions? For the most part, the answer would appear to be yes. Emerging markets offer considerable potential for the addition of new retail stores, thereby eliminating the risk that greenfield entry will result in overcapacity in the market. Further, given the nascent stage of modern retailing in emerging markets, these economies offer limited opportunities to acquire existing stores that would not need to be torn down and rebuilt from scratch. Thus greenfield entry emerges as the most likely strategy for emerging markets. In contrast, developed markets are diametrically opposite on both counts. Greenfield entry is likely to be neither necessary (because modern chains would already be in existence) nor desirable (because it would lead to overcapacity). Thus entry via partial or complete acquisition of existing operations emerges as the most likely strategy for developed markets.

Focusing now on the question of entering via a strategic alliance versus complete ownership, the two most important drivers in discount retailing are: (1) the extent to which the local market is "foreign" to the globalizing enterprise thereby necessitating the need to rely at least initially on a local partner, and (2) whether or not local equity partnership is mandated by host country regulations. Wal-Mart entered Mexico, Brazil, Indonesia, Hong Kong, China, and Japan via local equity partners. With the possible exception of Hong Kong, all of these entry modes appear to have been logical. Mexico and Brazil were two of Wal-Mart's earliest forays outside the United States; also, both markets are economically and culturally quite different from that of the United States, thus necessitating the need to rely on and learn from a local partner, at least in the initial years. Along similar lines, Indonesia, Hong Kong, China, and Japan represented the challenges of vast cultural differences as well as large geographic and time zone distances between the United States and Asia. Thus initial entry via strategic alliance partners appears wise for all of these markets. Wal-Mart's "mistake" in Hong Kong lay not in the fact that it relied on a partner but in the fact that the partner was a company from Thailand rather than from Hong Kong; thus, in a context of "the blind leading the blind," both partners committed many errors leading to a very quick exit from Hong Kong. Finally, in Indonesia and China, Wal-Mart also faced regulatory mandates to rely on local equity partners.

In contrast to the above entries via partnerships, Wal-Mart entered Canada, Argentina, Germany, the United Kingdom, and South Korea via 100 percent ownership from the very beginning. Government regulations were largely a nonissue in all of these markets. However, it appears highly likely that Wal-Mart mistakenly downplayed the cultural differences between the United States on the one hand and the German and the South Korean markets on the other. Wal-Mart was never able to get the needed traction in either of these two markets and would exit from both in 2006. As we discuss in the next section, the reasons for Wal-Mart's failures in Germany and South Korea go beyond the company's lack of understanding of these markets. However, it appears likely that the decision to go alone rather than without a partner may have played a role in the company's challenges there.

Transplanting the Corporate DNA and Winning the Local Battles

As discussed above, discount retailing is a highly multidomestic industry. In this industry, markets differ greatly in terms of customer buying power, product mix preferences, buying patterns and buying behavior, population density, the availability and cost of real estate, cultural norms, and a host of other factors. Thus a multinational retailer such as Wal-Mart must excel not just at transplanting its corporate DNA (that is, its core capabilities) but also at giving a high degree of flexibility to its local managers in leveraging these capabilities to create highly responsive local operations. Further, unlike some other industries, such as semiconductors, where the high-cost activities (R&D and manufacturing) can be globally centralized, in the case of discount retailing, most key operations (such as sourcing, logistics, and store operations) must be performed locally. Thus, unlike semiconductors, in the case of discount retailing, global operations play a limited role in supporting local operations. This feature of the discount retailing industry makes market share and scale at the *local level* far more important than that at the *global level* in determining the local competitiveness of any competitor.

As a company that expanded rapidly and successfully within the very large U.S. market, Wal-Mart appears to excel at the task of transplanting the corporate DNA. By way of illustration, look at how Wal-Mart managed the transformation of Woolco Canada after acquiring the company in 1994.[3] Prior to the acquisition, a combination of high costs and low productivity had driven Woolco into the red. Wal-Mart turned the situation around by reconfiguring Woolco along the lines of its successful U.S. model, a strategy facilitated by the similarity between the U.S. and Canadian markets. This transformation occurred in four central arenas: the workforce, the stores, the customers, and the business model.

- *Workforce*. More than any other element, Woolco employees were in need of a cultural transformation. Once the purchase was finalized, Wal-Mart sent its transition team to Canada to familiarize Woolco's fifteen thousand employees with (indeed, to indoctrinate them in) the Wal-Mart way of doing business, especially the concept of total dedication to the customer. The transition team succeeded in clarifying and defining Wal-Mart's core beliefs and practices to its new "associates."

- *Stores*. At the time of the sale, many of Woolco's 122 stores were in very poor shape. Wal-Mart undertook the hefty task of bringing every single outlet up to its own standards in record time. Renovation of each physical plant was completed within three to four months on average. It took an additional three to four months to restock each store.

- *Customers*. Although the Woolco acquisition was Wal-Mart's first entry into Canada, the company had a head start in building a consumer franchise since many Canadians living near the U.S. border were already familiar with the Wal-Mart image. Wal-Mart leveraged this high brand recognition into customer acceptance and loyalty by introducing its "everyday low prices" approach to a market accustomed to high-low retail pricing.

- *Business model*. A broad merchandise mix, excellent customer service, a high in-stock position, and a policy of rewarding employees for diminished pilferage were among the U.S. core practices that were successfully transplanted and embedded into Wal-Mart's Canadian operation.

The transfer of Wal-Mart's corporate DNA to Canada produced dramatic results. Between 1994 (the time of acquisition) and 1997, sales per square foot almost tripled from C$100 to C$292. During

the same period, expenses as a percentage of sales in Canada declined by 3.3 percent. Wal-Mart's Canadian operation turned prof-
itable in 1996, only two years after the acquisition. By 1997, it had
outpaced Zellers and Sears to become the leading discount retailer
in Canada.

Based on the company's record until 2007, it would appear that
Wal-Mart has not been equally successful at the complementary
challenge of giving local managers the needed autonomy to adapt
to local market and cultural realities. These challenges have been
particularly difficult in markets that are culturally more distant from
the company's home base in the United States. Consider the following observations by *Fortune* magazine in a July 27, 2007, article
titled "Why Wal-Mart Can't Find Happiness in Japan."

> Wal-Mart is battling to survive in Japan. . . . [Employees] are fre-
> quently quoted in Japanese media complaining about Wal-Mart's ef-
> fort to instill an American operating model in Japan. The company
> says it is being flexible, but the carping persists: Wal-Mart is moving
> too aggressively to cut out distribution middlemen; it is making life
> difficult for managers by mandating that stores remain open for
> 24 hours; it is introducing products from China and elsewhere that
> don't meet Japanese tastes or standards of quality. "Seiyu became a
> completely different store after it came under Wal-Mart manage-
> ment," the magazine *Nikkei Business* quoted one store manager as say-
> ing. "National-brand food product prices have definitely come down,
> but high quality merchandise has disappeared, and customers have
> left.". . . "They need to completely change their strategy, but it's too
> late," says Tadayuki Suzuki, who worked at Seiyu for 20 years, is a for-
> mer Merrill Lynch retail analyst, and now runs the retail consultancy
> Clio Research. "They are doing it totally wrong.". . . . According to
> outsiders and retail analysts, Wal-Mart's decision-making regarding
> Japan is centralized in Bentonville.[4]

Wal-Mart's record also suggests that the company may have
downplayed the importance of local scale. Consider its experience
in Germany. Wal-Mart entered Germany in 1997 by acquiring two

relatively small players in a concentrated market dominated by local players such as Metro and Aldi. Ten years later, in 2006, its market share was still 2 percent. In a highly multidomestic industry such as discount retailing, a scale disadvantage of such magnitude is almost always fatal. Wal-Mart's experience in South Korea, another market from which the company exited in 2006, was roughly similar.

Table 3.5 contains data on market size, market structure, and Wal-Mart's position as of early 2007 in each of the non-U.S. markets. According to these data, Wal-Mart's local market share, when compared with the combined market share of its two largest local competitors, is particularly low in Brazil, Argentina, China, and Japan. Given the still highly fragmented structure of the retailing industry in China, low market share is perhaps not a major handicap at this stage. However, three of these (Brazil, China, and Japan) are really large markets. Thus, in order for Wal-Mart to ensure the viability of its long-term position in each of these markets, it would need to develop effective strategies to scale up the local market share in each country.

Speed of Global Expansion

Did Wal-Mart globalize too slowly, too quickly, or at just the right pace? The answer to this question depends on the benchmark against which Wal-Mart's speed of global expansion may be assessed. There are at least four possible benchmarks: other large firms in general (such as General Electric and Procter & Gamble), other large retailers (such as Carrefour and Metro), the company's internal capabilities (as judged by successes and failures in globalization), and the objective potential (as judged by the size of the retail market outside the United States). We consider each of these in turn.

Wal-Mart expanded its non-U.S. revenues from zero in 1991 to $77 billion, or 22 percent of total revenues by 2007. In comparison, GE's non-U.S. revenues increased from about $21 billion (40 percent of total revenues) in 1991 to $74 billion (45 percent of total revenues) by 2006.[5] In the case of Procter & Gamble, non-U.S. revenues

Table 3.5. Market Characteristics and Wal-Mart Store Size and Sales by Country

| | Wal-Mart sales for Year Ending January 1, 2007 ($ billions) | Country's Retail Market in 2006 | | Market Share of Modern Retail | | Average size of Wal-Mart Store (sq. ft.)[b] | Wal-Mart Sales per sq. ft. ($) |
		Total Market Size ($ billions)	Modern Retail as % of total[a]	Wal-Mart (%)	Two largest competitors (%)		
United States	267.9					154,000	433
Puerto Rico	1.2	13.6	59	15.1	17.5	73,000	310
Canada	12.3	205.7	55	10.8	33.0	115,000	370
Mexico	19.5	252.3	45	17.0	7.5	39,000	558
Brazil	4.8	284.1	31	5.5	15.0	49,000	328
Argentina	0.8	53.8	35	4.0	22.1	198,000	292
Costa Rica	0.7	3.3	75	26.6	13.7	16,000	305
El Salvador	0.5	8.6	33	17.6	13.0	13,000	592
Guatemala	0.6	16.4	31	12.2	1.4	13,000	592
Honduras	0.2	4.1	23	19.8	7.7	8,000	588
Nicaragua	0.1	2.8	22	11.7	5.5	9,000	196
China	1.4	781.3	63	0.3	2.2	176,000	111
Japan	9.7	1187.7	66	1.2	12.9	35,000	598
United Kingdom	31.7	474.7	76	8.8	26.9	45,000	2131

[a] The remainder are small "mom and pop" stores or "black" market.
[b] Rounded to the nearest thousand.

Source: Wal-Mart Stores, Inc. Citigroup Research Report, March 2007.

increased from about $10 billion (40 percent of total revenues) in 1990 to over $40 billion (over 60 percent of total revenues) in 2006.[6] Taking into account that Wal-Mart's retail business is much more multidomestic than many of GE's and Procter & Gamble's businesses, and that it is much more challenging to globalize a multidomestic business, these numbers suggest that, by the standards of large companies, the pace of Wal-Mart's globalization has been fairly aggressive.

The pace of Wal-Mart's global expansion also looks quite impressive in comparison with that of other large retailers such as the France-headquartered Carrefour and the Germany-headquartered Metro Group. Both Carrefour and Metro started to globalize many years earlier than Wal-Mart did. By 2006, of its total revenues of 78 billion euros (or $107 billion), Carrefour derived 47 percent from outside France but only 10 percent from outside Europe.[7] In the case of Metro Group, of the total revenues of 60 billion euros (or $82 billion) in 2006, the company derived 58 percent from outside Germany but only 3 percent from outside Europe.[8]

What about the pace of Wal-Mart's global expansion when judged against the company's own capabilities? Given Wal-Mart's acknowledged failures in Germany and South Korea and its ongoing difficulties in Japan, it appears reasonable to conclude that the company is still midway on the globalization learning curve. It appears likely that an even faster pace of global expansion would have significantly increased the probability of costly mistakes. It also appears reasonable to conclude that, until recently, Wal-Mart has given higher priority to expanding its geographic footprint across countries instead of increasing depth of penetration and market share within a smaller number of mega-markets. In a highly multidomestic industry such as discount retailing, depth of presence in a few mega-markets is a potentially much smarter strategy than shallow but broad presence in a larger number of markets. Thus it may have been better for Wal-Mart to go slower in expanding its footprint across countries but faster in increasing its market share within a few mega-markets. As of 2007, it appears that this is finally the strategy that Wal-Mart is now pursuing.

Table 3.6 compares the profitability of Wal-Mart's international versus U.S. operations for fiscal year 2007. The company's international operating margins are 5.6 percent, only slightly lower than the U.S. operating margins of 6.9 percent. However, there is a huge difference in asset turnover ratios. Asset turnover for international operations is only 1.4, one-fourth the U.S. figure of 6.5. There are two likely reasons for this huge difference in asset turnover: one, Wal-Mart's international asset base is much newer than that in the United States and includes a large proportion of recent acquisitions; two, because of Wal-Mart's relatively low market shares in most foreign markets, the company's investments in local supply chain operations are supporting a relatively low sales volume. An increased emphasis on depth of presence in mega-markets should help the company on both counts.

Table 3.6. Wal-Mart's Financial Performance: United States Versus International

		Fiscal Year Ending January 31		
		2005	2006	2007
Sales ($ billions)	United States	228.9	249.7	267.9
	International	52.5	59.2	77.1
Operating Income ($ billions)	United States	15.4	16.7	18.5
	International	3.2	3.5	4.3
Assets ($ billions)	United States	35.2	38.5	41.0
	International	38.0	49.0	56.0
Operating Margins (%)	United States	6.7	6.7	6.9
	International	6.1	5.9	5.6
Asset Turnover (Sales/Assets)	United States	6.5	6.5	6.5
	International	1.4	1.2	1.4
Operating Return on Assets[a] (%)	United States	43.8	43.4	45.1
	International	8.4	7.1	7.7

[a] Operating income for the year/year-end asset base.

Source: Wal-Mart annual report, 2007.

The final benchmark for assessing the speed of Wal-Mart's global expansion is the size of the discount retailing market outside the United States. Since the size of any country's retail market closely tracks its GDP, it is a reasonable estimate that, paralleling the ratio of U.S.-to-non-U.S. GDP, the retail market outside the United States is over 75 percent of the world's total. In contrast, as of 2007, Wal-Mart derived only 22 percent of its global revenues from outside the United States. Without any doubt, Wal-Mart has barely scratched the surface of the market opportunities in discount retailing that lie in front of it.

Summing Up the Lessons

In conclusion, the lessons from Wal-Mart's global expansion over the period 1991–2007 can be summed up as follows:

- Do not overlook the economic structure of your industry. It matters whether your company operates in a highly multi-domestic industry, such as discount retailing, or a more globally integrated industry, such as semiconductors or mobile phones.

- In developing the company's global expansion strategy, what matters is the size of the target markets that you are addressing and not the number of markets. Achieving a 10 percent market share in a mega-market such as China may be far more valuable than a 20 percent market share in each of twenty smaller markets.

- There is no universally optimal entry mode for all markets. In those markets where government mandates are not a factor, the appropriateness of going it alone versus a strategic alliance with a partner depends entirely on the extent to which the globalizing company lacks local knowledge and local relationships, the criticality of such knowledge and relationships, and the ability of the partner to fill in the gaps.

- In most industries, the globalizing enterprise must excel at two very different, often conflicting, and yet highly complementary

tasks: transplanting the corporate DNA that serves to differentiate the global enterprise from its local competitors in the
host country and giving sufficient autonomy to country managers so that they can adapt the company's products, processes,
and the business model to local imperatives.

- Global expansion requires a long-term outlook and commitment. As indicated by the financial performance of Wal-Mart's
  international versus domestic operations, even after fifteen
  years, the operating return on assets for the company's international operations is a small fraction of that for the U.S. operations. The lesson is not that Wal-Mart would have been
  better off without global expansion. Rather, the lesson is that
  succeeding at global expansion requires long-term commitment, persistence, a logical approach to the development of
  global strategy, and an openness to learning from experience.

4

Exploiting Global Presence

The question is not whether the global company
adds value. It is whether it adds more than it
simultaneously subtracts.

—*Tony Jackson*[1]

Marks & Spencer, the venerable British retailer, started its global
expansion in the early 1970s when it entered Canada by setting up
a joint venture with Peoples Department Stores, a Canadian retailer, and later acquiring a controlling stake in Peoples. In the mid-
1970s, the company opened stores in France and later expanded
into Belgium and Ireland. The global expansion continued in the
1980s with entry into the United States by acquiring Brooks Brothers, the upscale clothing retailer, and Kings Super Markets, a food
retailer. Through its established outlets in Japan, the Brooks Brothers acquisition also gave Marks & Spencer a presence in the Japanese market. Notwithstanding its dedication and efforts over nearly
twenty-five years, Marks & Spencer never really figured out how
to make these foreign operations yield the hoped-for returns. In
fact, over time, most of these ventures became weaker rather than
stronger. Apparently, what kept them going was the parent company's superior performance in the United Kingdom, its "home"
market. In the late 1990s, however, the company found itself in deep
trouble in the United Kingdom also. In 2001, as part of a radical
turn-around strategy, the board of directors decided that the company's global expansion was a drain and a distraction rather than
a source of strength and embarked on a strategy of de-globalization

that resulted in shutting down or divesting virtually all operations outside the United Kingdom.[2]

As Marks & Spencer's experience demonstrates, securing global presence is anything but synonymous with possessing global competitive advantage. Presence in strategically important markets is certainly a precondition for creating global competitive advantage. However, it says little about whether and how you will actually create such advantage. To use a sports analogy, once you have assembled a team (that is, created global presence), you must get the players geared up for battle, harmonize and coordinate their actions, plan your offensive and defensive strategies, and anticipate and respond to opponents' moves. Furthermore, winning one game doesn't ensure that you will win the next one. In short, transforming global presence into solid competitive advantage requires systematic analysis, purposeful thinking, and careful orchestration and is a never-ending process. Without a rigorously disciplined approach, global presence can easily degenerate into a liability that winds up distracting management and wasting resources. The end result can even be a loss of competitive advantage in the domestic market. A company's overall performance will generally worsen rather than improve if it does not effectively harness global presence.

Sources of Global Competitive Advantage

To convert global presence into global competitive advantage, the company must pursue six value creation opportunities, each of which encounters specific strategic and organizational obstacles:[3]

- Responding to local market differences
- Exploiting economies of global scale
- Exploiting economies of global scope
- Tapping the most optimal locations for activities and resources
- Maximizing knowledge transfer across locations
- Playing the global chess game

Responding to Local Market Differences

A direct implication of being present in multiple countries is that the company must respond to the inevitable heterogeneity it will encounter in these markets. Differences in language, culture, income levels, customer preferences, and distribution systems are only some of the factors to be considered. Even in the case of apparently standard products, at least some degree of local responsiveness is often necessary—or at least advisable. For example, in the case of cellular phones, it matters whether or not companies adapt their products to differences in language, magnitude of background noise on the street, affordability, and so forth. By responding to country-level heterogeneity through local adaptation of products, services, and processes, a company can reap benefits in three fundamental areas: market share, price realization, and competitive position.

Increased Market Share By definition, offering standard products and services across countries constricts the boundaries of the served market to only those customers whose needs are uniform across countries. Local adaptation of products and services has the opposite effect, expanding the boundaries to include those customers within a country who value different features and attributes. One of The McGraw-Hill Companies' products, *Business Week*, provides a good illustration of how local adaptation of products and services can enlarge the customer base. As *BW*'s editor-in-chief explained: "Each week, we produce three editions. For example, this week's North American cover story is 'The New Hucksterism.' The Asian edition cover is 'Acer, Taiwan's Global Powerhouse.' And the European-edition cover is 'Central Europe.' In addition, our writers create an additional 10 to 12 pages of stories customized for readers in Europe, Asia, and Latin America. They also turn out four pages of international-finance coverage, international editorials, and economic analysis, and a regional feature column called SPOT-LIGHT."[4] Similarly, anyone who travels abroad (or just about anywhere) knows that McDonald's has adapted the Big Mac to local tastes, ranging from lamb-based patties in India to teriyaki burgers in Tokyo and the McDeluxe, a salty and spicy hamburger, in France.

Improved Price Realization   Tailoring products and services to local preferences enhances the value delivered to local customers. As a corollary, a portion of this increased value should translate into higher price realization for the firm. Consider, for instance, the case of Yahoo! portals in various countries. The more tailored the portal is to local market needs (in terms of content, commerce, and community), the greater the number of users and the amount of time they spend with Yahoo! These advantages can be monetized by Yahoo! directly in the form of higher advertising rates and merchant commissions accruing to the company from its various commercial partners.

Neutralizing Local Competitors   One of the natural advantages enjoyed by most local competitors stems from their deep understanding of and single-minded responsiveness to the needs of the local market. For example, in the Japanese soft drinks market, Suntory Ltd. and Asahi Soft Drinks Co. have been among the first movers in offering new concepts, such as Asian teas and fermented-milk drinks. When a global player also customizes its products and services to local needs and preferences, this move is essentially a frontal attack on the local competitors in their market niche. In its efforts to neutralize Suntory's and Asahi's moves and attack them on their home turf, Coca-Cola has introduced several new products in Japan that are not offered by the company in other markets, including an Asian tea called Sokenbicha, an English tea called Kochakaden, and a coffee drink called Georgia.

Challenges. While seeking the benefits of local adaptation, however, companies must be prepared to face a number of challenges and obstacles.

In most cases, local adaptation of products and services is likely to increase the company's cost structure. Given the inexorable intensity of competition in most industries, companies can ill afford any competitive disadvantage on the cost dimension. *Thus managers have to find the right equilibrium in the trade-off between localization and cost structure.* For example, cost considerations initially led P&G to standardize diaper design across European markets, despite market research data indicating that Italian mothers, unlike those in other countries, preferred diapers covering the baby's navel. After some time, however, recognizing that this particular feature was critical to Italian mothers, the company incorporated this design feature for the Italian market, despite its adverse cost implications.[5]

In many instances, local adaptation, even when well intentioned, may prove to be misguided. For example, when the American restaurant chain TGI Friday's entered the South Korean market, it deliberately incorporated many local dishes, such as kimchi, in its menu. This responsiveness, however, backfired. Company analysis of the tepid market performance revealed that Korean customers anticipated a visit to TGIF as "a visit to America." They found local dishes on the menu inconsistent with their expectations. *Thus companies must take the pulse of their market continually to detect if and when local adaptation becomes misguided adaptation.*

As with many other aspects of global marketing, the necessary degree of local adaptation will usually shift over time. In many cases, the shifts may tend toward less need for local adaptation. A variety of factors, such as the influence of global media, greater international travel, and declining income disparities across countries, are paving the way toward increasing global standardization. Back to the example of *BusinessWeek*, we foresee a diminished need over time for geography-based customization. *Thus companies must recalibrate the need for local adaptation on an ongoing basis; overadaptation extracts a price just as surely as does underadaptation.*

Exploiting Economies of Global Scale

Building global presence automatically expands a company's scale of operations (larger revenues, larger asset base, and so on). However, larger scale will create competitive advantage if and only if the company systematically undertakes the tough actions needed to convert "scale" into "economies of scale." The potential benefits of economies of scale can appear in various ways—spreading fixed costs, reducing capital and operating costs, pooling purchasing power, and creating critical mass—as we describe next.

Spreading Fixed Costs over Larger Volume This benefit is most salient in areas such as R&D, operations, and advertising. For instance, Procter & Gamble can spread R&D costs over its global sales volume, thereby reducing its per-unit costs of development. Similarly, transaction processing companies such as First Data enjoy economies of scale in credit card processing where unit costs fall sharply with an increase in the size of the activity.

Reducing Capital and Operating Costs per Unit This type of benefit is often a consequence of the fact that doubling the capacity of a production facility typically increases the cost of building and operating the facility by a factor of less than two. The global consolidation of the tire industry is a direct result of the cost advantages resulting from global scale economies.

Pooling Global Purchasing Power over Suppliers Concentrating global purchasing power over any specific supplier generally leads to volume discounts and lower transaction costs. For example, as Marriott has raised its stakes in the global lodging business, its purchase of such goods as furnishings, linen, beverages, and so on has stepped up dramatically. Exercising its global purchasing power over a few vendors (as with PepsiCo for soft drinks) is part of Marriott's efforts to convert its global presence into global competitive advantage.

Creating Requisite Critical Mass in Selected Activities A larger scale gives the global player the opportunity to build centers of excellence for the development of specific technologies and products. To develop a center of excellence, a company generally needs to focus a critical mass of talent in one location. In view of the potential to leverage the output of such a center on a global scale, a global player will be more willing and able to make the necessary resource commitments required for such a center. For example, outside the United States, Microsoft has established a small number of highly focused research labs, each a center of excellence for well-defined and nonduplicative technology areas. The lab in Beijing specializes in speech technologies whereas the lab in Bangalore specializes in multilingual systems.[6]

Challenges. Few if any of these potential strategic benefits of scale materialize automatically. The following challenges await firms in their efforts to secure these benefits.

Scale economies can be realized only by concentrating scale-sensitive resources and activities in one or a few locations. Concentration is a double-edged sword, however. For example, with manufacturing activities, concentration means that firms must export centrally manufactured goods (components, subsystems, or the finished product) to various markets. For R&D activities, concentration means that firms must invest in linking the R&D centers with the needs of various markets and the capabilities and constraints of various production centers. *Thus, in making decisions about the choice of location for any activity, firms must weigh the potential benefits from concentration against increased transportation and tariff costs and/or possible misalignments between complementary value-chain activities.*

One unintended result of the geographic concentration of any activity is to isolate that activity from the targeted markets. Such isolation can be risky since it may cause delayed or inadequate response to market needs. *Thus another management challenge is to minimize the costs of isolation.*

Concentrating an activity in a designated location also makes the rest of the company dependent on that location. This "sole source" dependence implies that, unless that location has world-class competencies, you may wind up with global mess instead of global competitive advantage. As underscored by a European executive of Ford Motor Company reflecting on the company's concentration of activities as part of a global integration program: "Now if you misjudge the market, you are wrong in fifteen countries rather than only one." *Thus the pursuit of global scale economies raises the added challenge of building world-class competencies at those locations in which the activities will be concentrated.*

In situations where global presence stems from cross-border acquisitions, as with Tata Steel's acquisition of the Anglo-Dutch company Corus, realizing economies of scale will almost always require massive restructuring.[7] Firms must scale up at those locations at which activities are to be concentrated and scale down or even close shop at the other locations. This restructuring demands large financial investment, incurs huge one-time transition costs, and always results in organizational and psychological trauma. Furthermore, scale-downs or closures may damage the company's image and relations with local governments, local customers, and local communities. On top of all this, erroneous decisions in choosing locations are usually very difficult, expensive, and time-consuming to reverse. Nonetheless, firms cannot realize the advantageous economies of scale without making tough decisions. *Thus management must be willing to undertake a comprehensive and logical analysis and then have the courage to carry out timely and decisive action.*

Exploiting Economies of Global Scope

Global scope, as distinct from global scale, refers to the multiplicity of regions and countries in which a company markets its products and services. For example, consider the case of two hypothetical advertising agencies, Alpha and Beta, whose sales revenues are roughly comparable. Assume that Alpha offers its services in only five countries whereas Beta offers its services in twenty-five countries. In this instance, we would consider the global scope of Beta to be broader than that of Alpha. Global scope is rarely a strategic imperative when vendors are serving customers who operate in just one country or customers who are global but who engage in centralized sourcing from one location and do their own internal distribution.

In contrast, the economic value of global scope can be enormous when vendors are serving customers who, despite being global, need local delivery of identical or similar products and services across many markets. In fulfilling the needs of such multilocation global customers, companies have two potential avenues through which to turn global scope into global competitive advantage: providing coordinated services and leveraging their market power.

Providing Coordinated Services to Global Customers Consider three scenarios: the case of Procter & Gamble, as it rolls out a new shampoo in more than twenty countries within one year and needs to source advertising services in every one of the targeted markets; the case of McDonald's, which must source virtually identical ketchup and mustard pouches for its operations in every market; and the case of Shell Oil, which needs to source similar process control equipment for its many refineries around the world. In all of these examples, a global customer needs to purchase a bundle of identical or similar products and services across a number of countries. The global customer could source these products and services either from a host of local suppliers or from a single global supplier who is present in all of its markets. In comparison to local suppliers, a single global supplier can provide value for the global customer through greater consistency in the quality and features of products and services across countries, faster and smoother coordination across countries, and lower transaction costs.

Market Power Vis-à-Vis Competitors A global supplier has the opportunity to understand the unique strategic requirements and culture of its global customer. Since it takes time to build this type of customer-specific proprietary knowledge, particularly in the case of multilocation global customers, potential competitors are initially handicapped and can more easily be kept at bay. FedEx, a major supplier of logistics solutions and services to Dell, seems to enjoy this advantage. As a global logistics provider, FedEx has had the chance to deepen its understanding of its role in Dell's value chain in every one of its served markets. By definition, this under-standing is customer-specific and takes time to build. As long as FedEx continues to provide effective and efficient logistics services to Dell, this knowledge should serve as an important entry barrier for other local or global logistics suppliers.

Challenges. Notwithstanding the twin benefits outlined in this section, securing economies of global scope is not without its own specific challenges.

The case of a multilocation global vendor serving the needs of a multilocation global customer is conceptually analogous to one global network serving the needs of another global network. Every glob-al network, however effectively managed, typically has a plethora of power centers, accompanied by competing perspectives on the opti-mal course of action. Thus one of the management challenges for a global vendor is to understand the ongoing tug-of-war that shapes the needs and buying decisions of the customer network.

Even for global customer accounts, the actual delivery of goods and services must be executed at the local level. Yet local country managers cannot be given total freedom in their operations vis-à-vis global customer accounts. They must orient their actions around their global customers' need for consistency both in product and service features and in marketing terms and conditions. *Thus an-other challenge in capturing the economies of global scope lies in being re-sponsive to the tension between two conflicting needs: the need for central coordination of most elements of the marketing mix, and the need for local autonomy in the actual delivery of products and services.*[8]

Tapping the Most Optimal Locations for Activities and Resources

Even as global economies have become increasingly integrated and influenced by the global media so that cultures take on many of each other's aspects, most countries are and will continue to be largely heterogeneous for many years to come. As discussed earlier, inter-country heterogeneity has an impact on the need for local adaptation in a company's products and services. But differences across countries also reveal themselves in the form of differences in cost structures, skill levels, and resource endowments. If it is able to exploit these intercountry differences better than competitors, a firm has the potential to create significant proprietary advantage.

In performing the various activities along its value chain (for example, research and development, procurement, manufacturing, assembly, marketing, sales, distribution, and service), every firm has to make a number of crucial decisions, among them where the activity will take place. Several factors influence this decision. The next box elaborates on some of these factors and suggests that tapping the optimal locations for each activity can yield one or more of three strategic benefits: performance enhancement, cost reduction, and risk reduction.

Criteria for Location Decisions

Performance Enhancement

- *Criticality of customer proximity in the execution of the activity.* For example, for an aircraft manufacturer such as Boeing, the preflight checkup and maintenance activity must be performed at the various airport locations around the world.

- *Availability of needed talent.* For example, Microsoft has chosen Cambridge, England, as the location for one of its major corporate research centers. This decision was driven predominantly by the availability of outstanding graduates from Oxford and Cambridge Universities, and by the desire to build stronger alliances with the leading-edge software research labs of these universities.

- *Impact on the company's speed at improving critical competencies.* Locating an activity in a country or region that is the home base of particularly demanding customers or leading-edge competitors exposes the company's operations to the highest standards of excellence at close range, thereby increasing the speed at which the competencies underlying this activity are upgraded.

- *Impact on the quality of internal coordination.* To the extent that the successful performance of two or more activities depends on intense coordination on an ongoing basis, the choice of locations for these activities must take into account the ease with which frictionless coordination across locations can be achieved. In such situations, location decisions would also be guided by factors such as the quality of travel and communication links between locations as well as the extent to which the locations are separated by time and language.

- *Ability to work around the clock.* Distribution of certain activities (such as development projects) to three different time zones can dramatically accelerate the pace at which the activities can be completed.

Cost Reduction

- *Impact of location on the cost of activity execution.* Relative to other alternatives, any particular location will generally reduce some cost elements (say, labor costs) but increase some other cost elements (for example, infrastructure-related costs, such as power, transportation, and so on). In cost terms, an optimal location would be one that yields the lowest cost structure on a net basis.

- *Government incentives and tax structure.* In many instances, local governments give sizable direct or indirect incentives to specifically targeted companies as a means to boost capital investment and technology inflows into that location. Some examples of this phenomenon would be the incentives provided by the state of Alabama to Mercedes-Benz and the government of Italy to Texas Instruments. For any value-chain activity, such incentives (or disincentives in the form of higher taxes and tariffs) can also have a significant impact on the cost optimality of various locations.

Risk Reduction

- *Currency risks.* Given the unpredictable nature of exchange rate movements, companies can protect themselves against currency risk exposure by performing the particular activity in a small number of very carefully chosen countries. For obvious reasons, guarding against currency risks through locational decisions would be most critical in the case of those activities that account for a significant fraction of the firm's total cost structure.

- *Political risks.* Notwithstanding the presence of other advantages, a location can become unattractive if the political uncertainties associated with that location are particularly high.

Performance Enhancement Renault's decision to choose Romania rather than its native France to design and launch Logan (a low-priced car for emerging markets), and Microsoft's decision to establish research laboratories in England, China, and India are good examples of location decisions that were guided predominantly by the goal of building and sustaining world-class excellence in the selected activities.

Cost Reduction Two illustrative examples of location decisions founded predominantly on cost reduction considerations are Nike's decision to source the manufacture of athletic shoes from Asian countries, such as China, Vietnam, and Indonesia, and IBM's decision to transfer vast chunks of its global services operations to India.[9]

Risk Reduction Given the wild swings in exchange rates between the U.S. dollar and the Japanese yen (compared to each other as well as in terms of other major currencies), an important basis for cost competition between Caterpillar and Komatsu has been their relative ingenuity at managing currency risks. For these competitors, one of the ways to manage currency risks has been to spread the high-cost elements of their manufacturing operations across a few carefully chosen locations around the world.

Challenges. We examine now the challenges associated with using geographic differences to create global competitive advantage.

The way in which activities are performed depends not only on the characteristics of the factor inputs but also on the management skills with which these inputs are converted into value-added outputs. The choice of a seemingly optimal location cannot guarantee that the quality and cost of factor inputs will be optimal. *It is up to managers to ensure that the comparative advantage of a location is captured and internalized rather than squandered because of weaknesses in productivity and the quality of internal operations.* Notwithstanding its travails in the U.S. market, Ford Motor Company's experience in Mexico illustrates how a company's efforts can amplify the magnitude of proprietary advantage derived from locating some of its manufacturing operations in a lower-cost location. Ford has benefited not just from lower labor costs in Mexico but also from superior management of its Mexican operations, leading to productivity levels that have been higher than in the United States. People often assume that in countries such as Mexico, lower wage rates come side-by-side with lower productivity. Although this may be true statistically at the level of the country as a whole, it does not have to be so for a specific firm such as Ford. Unemployment levels in Mexico are higher than in the United States. Thus in its Mexican operations, Ford can be more selective about whom it hires. Also, given lower turnover of employees, the company can invest more in training and development. Thus the net result can easily be not just lower wage rates but also higher productivity than in the United States. It goes without saying that without conscious efforts of this type, the reverse can just as easily occur.

Furthermore, the optimality of any location hinges on the cost and quality of factor inputs at this location relative to all other locations. This fact is important because countries not only evolve over time but do so at different rates and in different directions. Thus, for any particular activity, today's choice location may no longer be optimal three years down the road. A relentless pursuit of optimal locations requires the global company to remain somewhat footloose. Nike's example is illustrative. Nike continuously assesses the relative attractiveness of various manufacturing locations and has demonstrated a willingness and ability to shift locations over time. *Thus managers should not let today's location decisions diminish the firm's flexibility in shifting locations, as needed.*

Optimal locations will generally be different for different resources and activities. Thus yet another challenge in fully capturing the strategic benefits of optimal locations is to excel at coordination across dispersed locations. This is illustrated by the case of Texas Instruments' high-speed telecommunications chip, TCM9055. This sophisticated chip was conceived in collaboration with engineers from Sweden, designed in France using software tools developed in Houston, produced in Japan and Dallas, and tested in Taiwan.[10]

Maximizing Knowledge Transfer Across Locations

Foreign subsidiaries can be viewed from several perspectives. For instance, one way to view Nokia's subsidiary in China would be in terms of its market position within China's mobile telecommunications industry. An alternate view would be to see Nokia China as a bundle of tangible assets, such as buildings, equipment, capital, and so on. Yet another view would be to see Nokia China as a reservoir of knowledge in areas such as wireless technology, the creation of world-class manufacturing operations in a developing country, market penetration, revenue and cost management, and dealing with local governments. Building on this last perspective, we can view every global company not only as a portfolio of subsidiaries with tangible assets but also as a portfolio of knowledge centers.

Given the heterogeneity of countries, every subsidiary has to create some degree of unique knowledge so as to exploit the resource and market opportunities of the local environment. Of course, not all locally created knowledge is relevant outside the local environment (for example, advertising execution in the Japanese language lacks pertinence outside Japan). However, other types of locally created knowledge may be relevant across multiple countries and, if leveraged effectively, can yield various strategic benefits to the global enterprise, ranging from faster product and process innovation to lower cost of innovation and reduced risk of competitive preemption.

Faster Product and Process Innovation   All innovation requires the incorporation of new ideas, whether they are developed internally on a *de novo* basis or acquired and absorbed from others. A global company's skill at transferring knowledge across subsidiaries gives these subsidiaries the added benefit of innovations created by their peers. And by minimizing, if not altogether eliminating, counterproductive reinvention of the wheel, product and process innovations get accelerated across the entire global network. For example, Yahoo! introduced a new service—Yahoo! Photos—in its U.S. portal in March 2000. Within just three months after the U.S. launch, the company had made this service available on its portals in eighteen other markets. P&G's highly successful launch of Liquid Tide in the late 1980s provides a different yet equally interesting example. This product incorporated technologies pioneered in Cincinnati (a new ingredient to help suspend dirt in washwater), Japan (cleaning agents), and Brussels (ingredients that fight the mineral salts present in hard water).[11]

Lower Cost of Innovation   A second by-product of not reinventing the wheel is considerable savings in the costs of innovation. For example, the efficient "stockist-based" distribution system developed by Richardson Vicks's Indian operations, now a part of Procter & Gamble India, found ready applicability in the company's Indonesian and Chinese operations. Such cross-border replication of an innovation from one country to another can eliminate or significantly reduce the costs associated with from-the-ground-up experimentation in that country.

Reduced Risk of Competitive Preemption   A global company that demands constant innovations from its subsidiaries but does not leverage these innovations effectively across subsidiaries risks becoming a fount of new ideas for competitors. Procter & Gamble is one company that is keenly aware of these risks. Several of P&G's subsidiaries are dedicated to improving the fit, the performance, and the looks of the disposable diaper. Over the last decade, P&G's ability to systematically identify the successful innovations and expedite a global rollout of these innovations has thwarted competitors' efforts to steal its new ideas and replicate them in other markets. Effective and efficient transfer of knowledge across its subsidiaries has helped P&G safeguard its innovations and enabled it to significantly reduce the risk of competitive preemption.[12]

Challenges. Most companies tap only a fraction of the full potential for enormous economic value inherent in the transfer and leveraging of knowledge across borders. The rest of this section presents some of the primary reasons why. (Chapter Six details these and other pathologies in greater detail.)

Knowledge transfer from one subsidiary to another cannot occur unless the source and the target units (or an intermediary such as regional or corporate headquarters) recognize both the existence of unique know-how in the source unit and the potential value of this know-how in the target unit. Because significant geographic, linguistic, and cultural distances often separate subsidiaries, the potential for knowledge transfer can easily remain lost in a sea of ignorance. *Thus companies face the management challenge of creating mechanisms that would systematically and routinely uncover the opportunities for knowledge transfer.*

A subsidiary with uniquely valuable know-how is likely to enjoy a knowledge monopoly within the global enterprise. Also, power struggles are both normal and ubiquitous in any organization. Taken together, these two facts imply that at least some subsidiaries will succumb to the "knowledge is power" syndrome, viewing uniquely valuable know-how as the currency through which they acquire and retain political power within the corporation. The symptoms of this pathology are most obvious in the case of manufacturing facilities where relative superiority on an internal basis often serves as survival insurance in a footloose corporation. *Thus another management challenge in making knowledge transfers happen is to ensure that subsidiaries are eager rather than reluctant to share what they know.*

Like the "knowledge is power" syndrome, the "not invented here" (NIH) syndrome is a chronic malady in many organizations. Two of the engines of the NIH syndrome are ego-defense mechanisms that induce some managers to block information suggesting the greater competence of others, and power struggles within organizations that lead some managers to pretend that the know-how of peer units is neither unique nor valuable. *Thus global enterprises committed to knowledge transfer must also address the management challenge of making subsidiaries eager rather than reluctant to learn from peer units.*

Only a subset of an organization's knowledge exists in the form of codified knowledge—a chemical formula, an engineering blueprint, or an operations manual. Such codified knowledge readily lends itself to transfer and distribution across subsidiaries through electronic or other mechanisms for document exchange. However, much valuable know-how often exists in the form of tacit knowledge, knowledge that is embedded in the minds, behavior patterns, and skills of individuals or teams—for example, a vision of a particular technology's future or a particular competency at managing global customer accounts. With effort and investment, it might be possible to articulate and codify some fraction of the tacit knowledge. Nonetheless, its embedded and elusive nature often makes tacit knowledge impossible to codify and thus difficult to transfer. *Thus another challenge for the global enterprise is to design and erect effective and efficient bridges for the transfer of knowledge (especially, noncodifiable tacit knowledge) across subsidiaries.*

Playing the Global Chess Game

In the global competition between Dell, HP, and Lenovo, Coke and Pepsi, or Cisco and Nortel, each side can adopt one of two different approaches. The first option would be to view this as a war where your subsidiaries slug it out with your opponents on a country-by-country basis. The other option would be to view the global war as analogous to a chess game; as in chess, you would continually identify specific target markets for attack, and, when you do launch the attack, you would do so through coordinated action of all your available resources. The latter is nearly always the smarter of the two approaches.

In playing the global chess game, one goal should be to weaken the competitor in its current strongholds. When launching such an attack, it is crucial to ensure a coordinated leveraging of worldwide resources (cash flow, scale economies, technological breakthroughs, and so forth). Otherwise, an attack on the competitor's strongholds could well prove to be very costly, risk-laden, even suicidal. Only through skillful coordination can a company minimize both the cost and the risk of an assault on potentially high payoff markets. It will be interesting to watch how the ongoing competition between Dell, HP, and Lenovo in the global personal computer business will unfold. Since the acquisition of IBM's PC business by Lenovo, these three companies have been the largest competitors in the industry. It appears that a major element of Dell's global strategy has been to intensify its attack on Lenovo in China, the latter's home base.[13] Keeping Lenovo on the defense in China may be an important substrategy whereby Dell can reduce the intensity of Lenovo's offensive moves in other major markets, such as the United States, Europe, and India.

A second goal should be to preempt the competitor from building a strong presence in future strategic markets. Procter & Gamble's early and aggressive entry into China shows how this course of action offers a major opportunity for the company to expand its future resource base more rapidly than competitors will.

A central challenge in playing the global chess game and capturing the consequent benefits is to ensure strategic coordination across countries. It may make sense to sacrifice profits in one market in order to reap even greater benefits in another. In the absence of suitable organizational mechanisms, local managers are unlikely to be willing to sacrifice their own profits for the greater good.

The magnitude of the economic value underlying each of the six value-creation opportunities discussed here varies across industries, and even across different segments within the same industry. For instance, take a company such as Unilever, which competes in cosmetics, detergents, and foods. The relative importance of a specific value-creation opportunity varies greatly from cosmetics to detergents to foods. For example, global scale economies are the most salient in cosmetics but the least salient in foods. Even within the same business, such as foods, the sources of global value differ dramatically across individual product lines. For example, cooking oil can be transported across countries, but ice cream cannot. Thus, whereas scale economies and location optimization are important in the cooking oil business, technology transfer is the most important source of value in the ice cream business. *Given these differences, analysis of how to exploit global presence must be undertaken not merely at the overall corporate level, but more important, also at the level of each individual business.*

Focusing on the individual business as the unit of analysis, the next box summarizes the key issues that must be addressed to clarify the scope of each value-creation opportunity and to uncover the underlying challenges.

Issues to Consider in Exploiting Global Presence

1. Adapting to Local Market Differences

   a. Have we accurately drawn a distinction between those attributes where the customer truly values adaptation and those other attributes where the customer is either neutral or averse to adaptation?

   b. For those attributes where adaptation adds value, how much is the customer willing to pay for this value?

   c. Do we manage our product design and manufacturing activities in such a manner that we can offer the needed intercountry variety at the lowest possible cost?

    d. Do we have sensing mechanisms (such as market research and experimental marketing) that would give us early warning signals about increases or decreases in customers' preferences for local adaptation?

2. Exploiting Economies of Global Scale

    a. In designing our products, have we exhausted all possibilities to employ such concepts as modularization and standardization of subsystems and components?

    b. Have we accurately drawn a distinction between those activities that are scale-sensitive and those that are not?

    c. Have we fully assessed the benefits from economies of scale against any resulting increases in other costs—transportation, tariffs, and so forth?

    d. Have we established effective and efficient coordination mechanisms so that we do not squander the benefits from scale economies?

    e. Have we built world-class competencies in the locations where we have chosen to concentrate the scale-sensitive activities?

3. Exploiting Economies of Global Scope

    a. Is our internal coordination of marketing activities across locations at least on a par with (and preferably ahead of) the extent to which our customers have integrated their own purchasing activities?

    b. How well do we understand the various pulls and pushes shaping the needs and buying decisions of our customers' global networks?

4. Tapping the Optimal Locations for Activities and Resources

    a. Have we ensured that our location-based advantages are neither squandered by our own staff nor neutralized by competitors because of any weaknesses in the quality and productivity of our internal operations at these locations?

   b. Do we have the organizational and resource flexibility to shift locations over time as some other locations begin to become preferable to our current locations?

   c. How frictionless is the degree of our coordination across the various locations?

5. Maximizing Knowledge Transfer Across Locations

   a. How good are we at routinely and systematically uncovering the opportunities for knowledge transfer?

   b. How enthusiastic are our subsidiaries about sharing knowledge with peer units?

   c. How eager are our subsidiaries to learn from any and all sources including peer subsidiaries?

   d. How good are we at codifying the product and process innovations generated by our subsidiaries? Have we built efficient communication mechanisms for the sharing of codified know-how across locations? How good are we at keeping codified knowledge proprietary to our company?

   e. Have we built effective mechanisms (people transfer, face-to-face interchange, and so forth) for the transfer of tacit knowledge across locations?

6. Playing the Global Chess Game

   a. Do we attack our competitors in a targeted or a random manner?

   b. When we launch an attack on a competitor's current or potential stronghold, do we have the organizational ability to bring together, if needed, our worldwide resources in support of such attack?

Creating Global Competitive Advantage: Action Implications

Exploiting any opportunity requires action. All action occurs at the level of activities in the firm's value chain. Therefore, capturing the six sources of value requires the firm to optimize on a global basis the organization and management of each value-chain activity— R&D, manufacturing, selling, customer service, and so forth. A look at Hewlett-Packard's PC business illustrates why disaggregated analysis is needed at the level of individual value-chain activities. Somewhat simplified, a list of the value-chain activities in this business would include the following:

- Technology development
- Product development
- Purchasing
- Manufacturing
- Selling
- Distribution
- After-sales service
- Human resource management
- Cash management

For each of these activities in the value chain, H-P must figure out how that specific activity can be managed in a way that unleashes its maximum value. Technology development, for example, might require centralization in a very small number of locations. In contrast, selling might demand a high degree of operational decentralization in a context of a globally coordinated sales strategy. In other words, for any given business, exploiting global presence requires taking actions to create an optimal R&D network, an optimal purchasing network, an optimal manufacturing network, and so forth.

Figure 4.1. Drivers of Global Value: The Star Framework

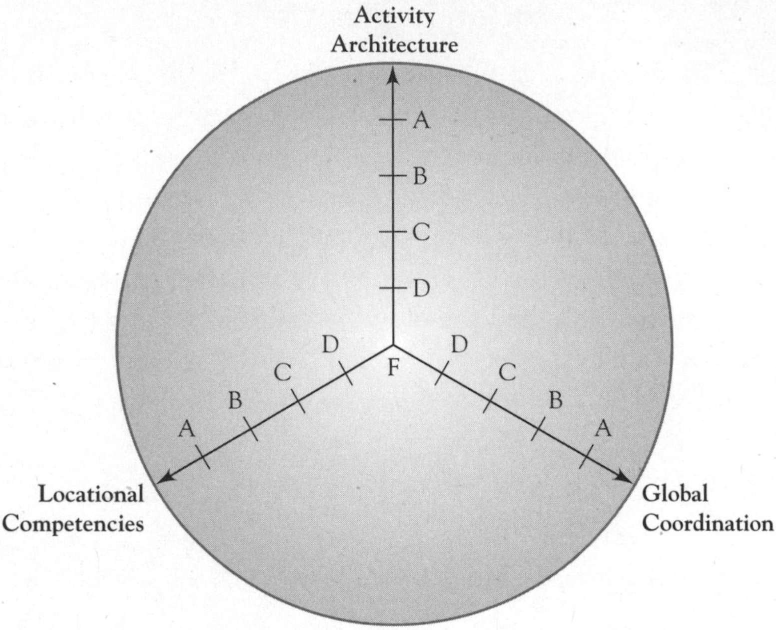

As depicted in the Star Framework (see Figure 4.1), creating and managing an optimal network for each value-chain activity requires optimizing three elements of the network: network architecture, competencies at the nodes of the network, and coordination among the nodes.

Designing an Optimal Architecture

For any activity, network architecture refers to the number of locations in which that activity is performed, the actual identity of the locations, and the specific charter of each location. Although an infinite number of choices exist for the design of activity architecture, three of the most common options are

- Concentration in one location (for example, the development of one-click check-out technology at Amazon.com)

- Differentiated centers of excellence (for example, specialized R&D centers in Microsoft)
- Dispersion to regional or local units (for example, the development of alliances with sellers and advertisers at Yahoo!)

It is worth noting that although activity architecture will shape organizational structure decisions, it is not the same thing as organizational structure. Take, for example, Honda's decision to build a design center in Italy. This is an activity architecture decision. In contrast, organizational structure deals with questions such as who should report to whom (for example, who should have direct control over the Italian design center: the country manager for Honda Italy, the president of Honda Europe, or the corporate design chief). Because they require commitment of investment on the ground, activity architecture choices are less reversible than those pertaining to organization structure. Consequently, getting the activity architecture right is far more important than getting the organizational structure right.

The issues that must be addressed in designing an optimal activity architecture are as follows: Does the number of locations where this activity will be performed ensure critical mass at each location and full exploitation of economies of scale? For each activity, does the choice of locations optimize both the quality with which this activity will be performed and its cost competitiveness, while minimizing the political, economic, and currency risks associated with it? Is the charter of each location defined in a way that eliminates unneeded duplication across locations?

It is essential to reassess the optimality of activity architecture on a periodic basis. Some of the important factors that can render today's optimal architecture less than desirable tomorrow are shifts in factor cost differences across countries, changes in tariff regimes, trends in demand patterns across countries, variations in product design, and adoption of new manufacturing technologies. In the late 1990s, ABB's declaration that it would shift thousands of jobs from Western Europe to the emerging economies over the next several years illustrates the need for such ongoing reassessment. The company believed rightly that this shift in manufacturing architecture would increase efficiency, take greater advantage of lower labor costs in the emerging economies, and heighten the company's responsiveness to customers in its largest growth markets.

Building World-Class Competencies

Once you have chosen the locations at which a particular activity will be performed, the next step is to build the requisite competencies at those locations. Otherwise, you could easily lose all the gains from creating a seemingly optimal architecture. As a hypothetical example, suppose you lead an American equipment manufacturer that has significant European presence and two production centers, one in Germany and the other in France, each supplying about 50 percent of your European market needs. With labor costs a significant portion, say 21 percent, of your total cost structure, you are weighing the option of consolidating your European production resources into one new facility in Spain. You anticipate about a 12 percent net reduction in the total cost structure: a 5 percent savings due to consolidating the two factories, and a 7 percent savings due to the one-third reduction in labor costs that would result from lower manufacturing wages in Spain. Is this change in the architecture of your European manufacturing operations the right move?

Despite the attraction of the projected reduction, you should not make this change unless you are confident that you can build the following competencies at the new Spanish location: the labor productivity in your Spanish plant will be greater than 67 percent of the average labor productivity in your existing German and French plants, the indirect effect of labor on other costs (for example, raw material usage and machine utilization) will be either neutral or positive, and the quality and performance of your products will remain world-class.

Objectively speaking, many countries with relatively lower wage rates also suffer from lower levels of productivity. Notwithstanding this generalization, companies should resist becoming prisoners of the aggregate statistics. As we noted earlier about Ford Motor Company's experience in Mexico, it is often possible for a company to locate production in a country with low labor costs and still achieve world-class productivity and quality levels. Both Motorola and Siemens have done this in China. This combination of low labor costs and world-class operations is particularly feasible under the following conditions:

- The developing economy, despite its relative poverty, has a large pool of highly educated workers (for example, India, China, and the Philippines).

- High unemployment levels in the economy furnish the multinational firm with a very talented and motivated pool of employees.

- The company is setting up greenfield operations, where it is possible to establish world-class processes from day one, a task that often is far easier than shaking up the status quo in a well-entrenched organization.

As you would expect, the greater a business's dependence on a particular location, the greater the need to have world-class competencies in the relevant activities there. The importance of any particular location is likely to be very high when it is the sole location or one of only a few locations where the particular activity is concentrated (as is often true in the case of upstream activities, such as R&D and manufacturing). But even in the case of downstream activities, such as sales, which often are dispersed across many locations, the need for world-class market-sensing and selling competencies is critical, especially in the major markets. For example, any weakness in Ikea's market-sensing competencies in a moderately sized market such as Spain would be far less costly for the company than in mega-markets such as the United States or China. Ikea's initial setbacks in the U.S. market can be attributed in part to major blind spots in its market-sensing capabilities.[14]

Ensuring Frictionless Coordination

In addition to creating an optimal architecture and ensuring requisite competencies at the different locations, the final component in creating an optimal global network is to develop and maintain smooth, indeed seamless, coordination across the various locations. The worldwide business team needs to foster this coordination along several dimensions: operational coordination between units performing similar activities (for example, two R&D labs or two production centers) as well as those performing complementary activities (for example, manufacturing vis-à-vis procurement and manufacturing vis-à-vis marketing). It also needs to promote the transfer of knowledge and skills across locations. *The pursuit of seamless coordination along these dimensions requires two types of concrete actions: (1) creating motivation, indeed eagerness, among those managers whose cooperation is essential, and (2) setting up mechanisms that will put the desired cooperation into practice.*

Some of the high-leverage organizational mechanisms to create eagerness for cooperation among managers working in different subsidiaries are as follows:

- *Using an incentive system that links at least part of the subsidiary managers' rewards to the business's regional or global performance.* For instance, Procter & Gamble gives explicit weight to both country-level, region-level, and global performance in computing annual incentives for its country-based business unit managers (for example, the general manager of the beauty business in Japan).[15]

- *Instituting a benchmarking system that routinely compares the performance of relevant subsidiaries along key indicators and makes these comparisons visible to the subsidiaries and their corporate superiors.* A system of this kind puts the desired spotlight and pressure on the weak performers, making them eager to learn from peers. For example, the typical business area headquarters within ABB distributes internally detailed monthly information on critical parameters, such as failure rates, throughput times, inventory turns, and days' receivables for each factory belonging to the business area. ABB management believes that these reports put even more intense pressure on the managers than external marketplace competition.[16]

- *Giving high visibility to individuals who achieve excellent business results through collaboration with peers in other subsidiaries.* For instance, Procter & Gamble regularly publicizes as "success models" those managers who demonstrate a zest for and ability to succeed at cross-border coordination.[17]

Focusing now on the creation of organizational mechanisms that make cooperation feasible, some of the high-leverage mechanisms are as follows:

- *Formal rules and procedures that enhance communication.* Examples would include the use of a standard format for reports, use of common terminology and language, and the routine distribution of the reports to the relevant managers. The Mexico-headquartered company CEMEX's standardized monthly reports from every plant in the world serve as an outstanding example of a formal communication system that works.[18]

- *The creation of global or regional business teams, functional councils, and similar standing committees that routinely bring key staff members from various subsidiaries into face-to-face or virtual communication with each other.* Global project teams at a consulting firm such as McKinsey and global account management teams at an advertising services firm such as Ogilvy & Mather are examples of effective coordination forums.

- *Corporate investment in cultivating interpersonal familiarity and trust among the key managers of various subsidiaries.* Examples of mechanisms that promote interpersonal familiarity and trust are: bringing managers from different subsidiaries together in executive development programs, rotating managers across locations, and building language skills among these managers so that these "get to know each other" encounters have high leverage. The McGraw-Hill Companies' Leadership Strategies for Growth Program, which periodically brings together groups of high-potential executives from various subsidiaries, is an outstanding example.

The next box summarizes the criteria by which a firm can systematically assess the optimal management of the three drivers—network architecture, nodal competencies, and network coordination—in the process of converting global presence into global competitive advantage.

Criteria for Assessment of the Firm's Global Network

Basis for Global Advantage	Typical Criteria for Assessment
Optimal Architecture (for each value-chain activity)	• What is the size of asset and employment base? • Have we captured economies of scale and scope in manufacturing, subcontracting, and raw material purchases? Are there any diseconomies of scale? • Do we have the needed sales and distribution strength in all key markets? Are our distribution systems too concentrated or too dispersed? • Do we have the needed critical mass in each key technology area? Is there unneeded duplication across technology centers? • Do locational choices automatically create push for excellence in the particular activity (as with miniaturization in Japan)? • Do we have critical talent available? • What will be the total impact on overall cost structure?

- What will be the impact of government inducements and tax considerations?
- What are the currency and political risks?

World-Class Competencies (by function, each facility)

- Do we define quality from our customers' point of view?
- Do we define quality narrowly (product durability only) or broadly (quality of products, services, and overall management)?
- Do we use measurable indicators of quality or operate on gut feel?
- Do we constantly compare ourselves with external benchmarks?
- How do we compare vis-à-vis competitors on key attributes of quality- and time-based competition?
- In delivering quality and speed, are we improving at a slower or faster rate than the competition?

Frictionless Coordination (between similar activities, between complementary priorities and activities)

- How direct and frictionless are the communication channels for customers' concerns to be heard not just by marketing, but also by production and R&D personnel?
- How direct and frictionless are the communication channels between units performing complementary activities? Between units performing similar activities?
- Do reward systems encourage or discourage needed coordination?
- Has the company created a frictionless internal market for ideas that reward both the producers and the buyers of a great idea? Is the head office active or sleepy in carrying out its "knowledge broker" responsibilities?

The Star Framework in Action

Every global business should use the Star Framework to assess the optimality of each activity in its value chain. Further, companies should undertake this evaluation separately for two different time frames—today and three to five years from now. The Star Framework is a diagnostic tool that can highlight the major problem areas and alert companies to the need to address these areas.

The global battle between ScanStar and GamMech[19] in a specific segment of the heavy machinery industry illustrates how a company can systematically improve its position along one or more dimensions of the Star Framework in order to launch an attack on a competitor or to strengthen a weak position. Both companies are headquartered in Europe, albeit in different countries. GamMech was founded a few decades ago and, in 1994, was the market leader at 36 percent market share. ScanStar was founded more recently by a former licensee of GamMech; with a 22 percent market share in 1994, it was the number two player in the industry.

Figure 4.2 depicts a comparative assessment of the two companies' production bases in 1994. At that time, ScanStar suffered a nearly 15 percent cost disadvantage vis-à-vis its arch rival, which, as indicated in Figure 4.2, resulted from relative weaknesses in its activity architecture and locational competencies. In 1994, both GamMech and ScanStar had production activities concentrated in single locations and exported to sales companies and distributors based in most major markets around the world. However, ScanStar's location placed it at a significant disadvantage in that wage rates there were, on average, 10 percent higher than those of GamMech. In terms of its locational competencies, ScanStar suffered from a competitive disadvantage as well. Given its shorter history, it had less cumulative experience relative to GamMech. ScanStar's cost structure was also affected negatively by its lower market share, which reduced its potential to capture economies of scale.

Figure 4.2. The Global Battle Between ScanStar and GamMech: Analysis of Production Activities (1994)

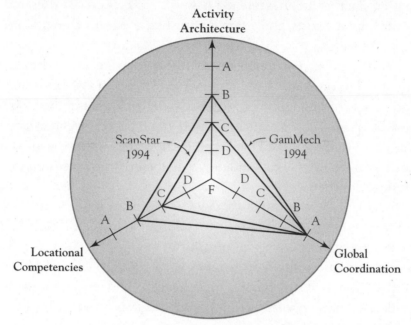

In 1994, ScanStar's founder retired and a new CEO was recruited from outside to bring fresh ideas and a more aggressive mindset to the company. The new management team concluded that continuing to play the historical game would only result in ScanStar continuing to be second-best in its industry. A thorough reexamination of the competitive situation via the Star Framework resulted in a turnaround plan that sought to remedy the two disadvantages. By 1998, ScanStar had established six new regional assembly centers in the heart of major markets around the world. The original home-base location was now a much smaller factory that manufactured only the core components—that is, components that were technology- and capital-intensive rather than labor-intensive and where ScanStar possessed a competitive advantage. The new regional assembly centers were located in lower-labor-cost markets and set up to obtain other (so-called noncore) components locally or from global suppliers under centralized sourcing agreements. This new production architecture led to lower production costs, sharply lower shipping costs, and a smaller finished goods inventory in the supply pipeline.

Furthermore, the new assembly centers were located much closer to final customers and were managed by a mix of expatriates and newly recruited local professionals. A by-product of these new market-specific competencies (largely nonexistent at GamMech) was that ScanStar gained much more knowledge about the unique needs of different markets and now was able to develop customized products for them.

As Figure 4.3 indicates, by 1998, it was ScanStar that had the competitive edge. During the period from 1994 to 1998, it had closed the market share gap, transforming a 22 percent versus 36 percent situation into a 30 percent versus 30 percent dead heat. With a lower cost structure than GamMech's and more customized products, it now appeared set to capture the global leadership of this industry.

Figures 4.2 and 4.3 are only synopses of the ongoing multifaceted battle between ScanStar and GamMech. A more complete analysis would require a separate evaluation of each major subactivity within manufacturing as well as of other value-chain activities, such as R&D, sales and distribution, after-sales service, and so forth.

Conclusion

Managers should never assume that global presence by itself is the same as global competitive advantage. Having presence in multiple markets implies that the firm now has available to it six distinct opportunities for the creation of global competitive advantage: adapting to local markets, capturing economies of global scale, capturing economies of global scope, optimizing the choice of locations for activities and resources, leveraging knowledge across subsidiaries, and

Figure 4.3. The Global Battle Between ScanStar and GamMech: Analysis of Production Activities (1998)

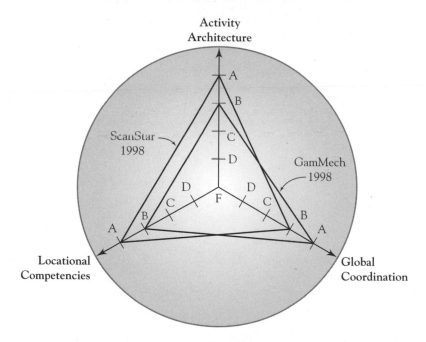

playing the global chess game. Realizing these opportunities requires the firm to adopt a two-step approach for analysis and action. The firm should first evaluate the optimality of the global network for each activity in the value chain along the following three dimensions: activity architecture, locational competencies, and global coordination. Based on this evaluation, the firm should then design and execute actions to eliminate or at least to reduce the suboptimalities.

5

Cultivating a Global Mindset

I define globalization as sourcing capital from where
it is cheapest, sourcing talent from where it is best
available, producing where it is most cost effective
and selling where the markets are without being
constrained by national boundaries.
> —N. R. Narayana Murthy, Chairman,
> Infosys Technologies[1]

There are no German or American companies.
There are only successful or unsuccessful companies.
> —Thomas Middlehoff, Chairman (1998–2002),
> Bertelsmann AG[2]

Individuals differ in how they sense and interpret the world around them. So do organizations. And these differences matter. They matter because it is how we perceive our environment as well as ourselves that determines which of the multitude of opportunities and problems we go after and how we do so.[3] Consider, for example, this seemingly simple question: "What is Marriott's market share in the lodging business?" The answer, or answers, would depend on your perception of the company's relevant opportunity space: the North American hotel market, the global hotel market, or the global lodging market including not only hotels but also other forms of lodging, such as apartments, college dormitories, and even prisons.

As part of our ongoing research on the global corporation, we posed the following question to the CEO of one of the world's largest pharmaceutical corporations: "What are the three things that might keep you awake at night?" His response: "First, people development. Second, setting business priorities to make sure that the short term doesn't drive out the long term. And, third, setting the tone for creating a global mindset." Although their words may differ, other CEOs and senior executives echo this viewpoint.

Any company that wants to emerge as the global leader in its industry has to lead in three tasks: discovering new market opportunities, establishing presence in key markets, and converting such presence into global competitive advantage. How does one do that in *today's* environment? Rooted in the premise that managers pursue only those market and resource opportunities that they discern, we would contend that a deeply embedded global mindset is a prerequisite for global industry dominance. As Sam Palmisano, CEO of IBM Corporation, observed:

> Today, for the first time in human history, everything is connected. There are a billion people and hundreds of millions of businesses on the World Wide Web. And, the Web has emerged as much more than a connectivity medium. It has become a global platform of work. . . . Think back to how we at IBM historically developed leaders all over the world. That model worked well if you put most of your global mission in the 'home country'—in our case the U.S.— and installed strong local leaders heading up local country organizations. In other words, management was still largely defined by national boundaries. But that approach does not necessarily prepare people to lead global missions headquartered in any part of the world. Already, we have moved our global procurement mission to China, global services delivery to India, and many of the services that support our external and internal Web sites to places like Brazil and Ireland. These people are not leading teams focused on China or India or Brazil or Ireland. They are leading integrated global operations. I am spending a lot of time on this leadership challenge at IBM. So are many of my fellow CEOs who are leading global companies.[4]

Straightforward as these words sound, developing a global mindset is far from easy. In a survey of fifteen hundred executives from twelve large multinational companies, the International Consortium for Executive Development Research asked executives to rank their performance along various dimensions deemed vital to sustaining competitiveness. "The respondents rated their ability to cultivate a global mindset in their organization dead last—thirty-fourth out of thirty-four dimensions."[5]

In this chapter, we address the following issues: why mindset matters, what a global mindset is, the value of a global mindset, and finally, what companies can do to cultivate a global mindset.

Why Mindset Matters

The concept of mindset, also referred to as *cognitive schema*, *mental map*, or *paradigm*, can be traced back to the research of cognitive psychologists who have addressed the question of how people make sense of the world with which they interact.[6] The central finding of this stream of research is that we, as human beings, are limited in our ability to absorb and process information. However, our information environment is not only abundantly rich in content but also complex, often ambiguous, and ever-changing. Thus we are constantly challenged by the problem of how to avoid becoming paralyzed by the complexity and ambiguity surrounding us. We address this challenge through a process of filtration. Without much if any conscious thought, we are selective in what we absorb and biased in how we interpret that which we absorb.[7]

For each of us, at any one time, these cognitive schemas are a product of our own peculiar and at least partially unique histories. Every mindset represents a theory of what the world is like. And like every theory, a mindset exists in the form of a "knowledge structure," that is, it consists of components as well as linkages among the components.[8] Suppose, for instance, that you are the European marketing manager for Hewlett-Packard's Home Products Division and are responsible for devising the company's strategy for the European home PC market. How would we uncover your mental map of the European PC market? The logical way would be to ask such questions as: What are your beliefs about the PC market in each country? And, what are your beliefs about the similarities, differences, and interlinkages among the PC markets across various countries?

Not unlike theories, mindsets evolve through an iterative process. The current mindset guides the collection and interpretation of new information. To the extent that this new information is consistent with the current mindset, it reinforces that mindset. From time to time, however, some elements of the new information appear to be truly novel and inconsistent with the existing paradigm. In this event, we either reject the new information or forge a change in our mindset. The likelihood that our mindsets will undergo a change depends largely on how explicitly self-conscious we are of our current mindsets: the more hidden and subconscious the cognitive schema, the greater the likelihood of rigidity.[9]

Furthermore, mindsets serve as doubled-edged swords. On one hand, they allow us to avoid becoming paralyzed by the richness and complexity of the information environment around us; on the other hand, they can blind us to alternate views of reality. In short, we operate in a paradox, viewing the world through cognitive schemas, yet being at the mercy of schema-driven information processing "can be at once enabling and crippling."[10]

The view that mindsets can differ and that they can have a powerful impact on corporate strategies is illustrated well by the case of Kenneth Olsen, founder and then-CEO of Digital Equipment (DEC). In the mid-1970s, DEC was the world's second-largest computer company and the market leader in the minicomputer segment. In 1977, Olsen observed that "there is no reason for any individuals to have a computer in their home."[11] This was the same year in which Steve Jobs and Steve Wozniak incorporated Apple Computer and launched the PC revolution. Olsen's mindset and his power over the company he had founded caused DEC to become a late entrant in the PC market, a delay that never allowed the company to recover its footing. By the mid-1990s, DEC ceased to exist as an independent company. It was acquired by Compaq, a personal computer manufacturer, and the rest is history.

The following question-and-answer excerpt from one of Coca-Cola's annual reports is another illustration of the power of mindsets to drive strategies:

Q: What's our most underdeveloped market?

A: The human body. People can do without most things for an entire day. But every day, every one of the 5.7 billion people on this planet must consume roughly sixty-four ounces of fluid to live. We currently account for less than two of those ounces.[12]

It is important to remember that mindset is not synonymous with behavior. Behavior is an outcome—a product of both what you consider worth doing (a derivative of your mindset) and what you are capable of doing (your competencies). Although having a less powerful theory of your industry is likely to constrain your efforts and imagination (probably channeling them in suboptimal directions), having a more powerful theory is no guarantee that you will emerge as the dominant and most successful player in your industry. For that to happen, you also need to assemble the competencies required to convert your vision into reality.

Although the concept of mindset applies to individuals as well as organizations, it is useful to draw a distinction between the two. When we talk about an individual's mindset, we are referring to how one human brain observes and interprets the signals it receives. But, given that organizations do not have an equivalent brain, what does it mean when we talk about an organization's mindset?

The question of whether or not it makes sense to conceptualize an organization (as distinct from an individual) as having the capability to think has long been debated.[13] The emerging and widely held view is that "when a group of individuals is brought together, each with their own knowledge structure about a particular information environment, some kind of emergent collective knowledge structure is likely to exist. This group-level representation of an information environment would act just like an individual's knowledge structure. It too functions as a mental template that when imposed on an information environment gives it form and meaning, and in doing so serves as a cognitive foundation for action."[14] Common experience—confirmed by scientific research—tells us that, although organizations cannot be said to have a brain as such, they do behave as if there exists a collective cognitive paradigm, a paradigm that transcends that of any single individual—including the CEO.

In making sense of the concept of organizational mindset, it is helpful to keep several points in mind. First, every organization is a collectivity of individuals. Each individual has a personal mindset that continuously shapes and is shaped by the mindsets of others in the collectivity. How this shaping and reshaping of mindsets occurs depends crucially on who interacts with whom, in what context, for what purpose, and so forth. Hence, how the firm is organized plays a decisive role in the emergence of a collective mindset. Furthermore, depending on both the type of decision and how the firm is organized to make various types of decisions, different individuals in the collectivity have varying degrees of influence on the decision-making process. Building on these dynamics, *we would define an organization's mindset as the aggregated mindset of individuals adjusted for the distribution of power and mutual influence among the group.* In this light, unless the CEO is exceptionally powerful or has played a major role in shaping the organization's history and culture (for example, Bill Gates at Microsoft), it would be incorrect to view the CEO's own personal mindset as synonymous with the organization's mindset.

From these observations, it follows that there are three primary ways in which organizational mindsets can undergo change:[15]

- *A change in the relative power of different individuals in the various decision-making processes.* In such an event, even without any change in the mix of individuals belonging to the collectivity, we would observe a change in how the firm as a whole appears to "think" and behave.

- *A change in the social processes through which individuals meet and interact with each other.* Such a change would alter the process through which individual mindsets bounce off and reshape each other.

- *A change in the mix of individuals composing the firm such that the mindsets of incoming individuals differ from those of outgoing ones.* As is well known, the need for a fresh mental template is one of the most common reasons for involuntary changes in CEO positions.

What Is a Global Mindset?

To use the terminology of cognitive psychology, every mindset represents a knowledge structure, and the two primary attributes of any knowledge structure are differentiation (the number of elements in the person or organization's knowledge base) and integration (the person or organization's ability to synthesize the various elements).

Differentiation in knowledge structures refers to the narrowness versus breadth of perspective that the individual or organization brings to the particular context. For instance, think of the proverbial functional expert with almost no exposure outside one functional area. In colloquial terms, we would say that this person has "tunnel vision"—a classic case of low differentiation in knowledge structure. In contrast, a manager with significant experience in multiple functional areas has a more highly differentiated knowledge structure and is unlikely to exhibit the tunnel vision syndrome.

Integration in knowledge structures refers to the extent to which the person or organization is able to rise above and integrate the various perspectives or knowledge elements. For those with low differentiation (that is, the person or organization with tunnel vision), integration is not an issue; multiple perspectives simply do not exist in the mental template so there is no need to integrate. However, integration becomes a critical attribute of mental templates in those contexts where differentiation is high.

Each of us, at one time or another, probably has met someone who appeared to swing from one position to another as a result of being swayed heavily by the opinions they encountered last. Using our terminology, such a person would be seen as exhibiting a combination of high differentiation coupled with low integration (High D–Low I). In contrast, an individual who seeks and values multiple opinions but then is able to develop and hold an integrative perspective is someone we would say has a combination of high differentiation and high integration (High D–High I).

At the organizational level, consider a new product development team that consists solely of technical experts. The mindset of such a team, operating in its own silo, would be Low D–High I. Compare this team to another whose composition includes experts from several functional areas, such as R&D, manufacturing, marketing, after-sales service, and accounting, but lacks strong leadership; the mindset of such a diffused and unfocused team would be High D–Low I. Finally, consider another team that in addition to being multifunctional has a strong leader who helps the team synthesize the diverse perspectives; the mindset of such a team would be High D–High I.

Borrowing from the language of differentiation and integration, we would define global mindset as a High D–High I mindset in the context of different cultures and markets. More concretely, as depicted in Figure 5.1, *we would define a global mindset as one that combines an openness to and awareness of diversity across cultures and markets with a propensity and ability to synthesize across this diversity.*[16] As Percy Barnevik, the architect of ABB and its first CEO, aptly observed: "Global managers have exceptionally open minds. They respect how different countries do things, and they have the imagination to appreciate why they do them that way. But, they are also incisive, they push the limits of the culture. Global managers don't passively accept it when someone says, 'You can't do that in Italy or

Spain because of the unions,' or 'You can't do that in Japan because of the Ministry of Finance.' They sort through the debris of cultural excuses and find opportunities to innovate."[17]

The simultaneous focus on developing a deep understanding of diversity and an ability to synthesize across diversity is illustrated well by Pacific Trade International, a U.S.-based household accessories company. Founded a little over ten years ago, the company is one of the fastest-growing manufacturers of household accessories, with a five-star customer base that includes some of the most prestigious retail chains in the United States. According to CEO David Wang, an immigrant from China, the company's strategy can be summarized succinctly as "combining Chinese costs with Japanese quality, European design, and American marketing. There are other

Figure 5.1. What Is a Global Mindset?

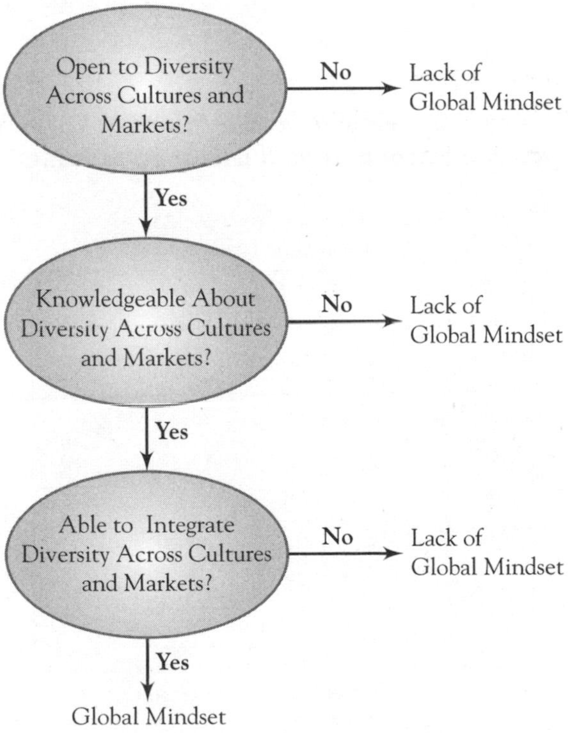

Chinese competitors in the market, but along with Chinese costs, what they bring is Chinese quality. On the other hand, our American competitors have excellent product quality but their costs are too high. We can and do beat both of them."

It is useful to compare and contrast a "global mindset" (High D–High I situation) with two alternative mindsets regarding the global economic environment (see Figure 5.2): a "parochial mindset" (Low D–High I situation), and a "diffused mindset" (High D–Low I situation).[18]

As an illustration of a parochial mindset, consider the situation at Ikea, the world's largest furniture retailer. Until as recently as slightly over a decade ago, Swedish nationals constituted virtually the entire top management team of the company. Fluency in the Swedish language was considered essential at the senior levels. And when the company entered foreign markets, for example, the United States, it replicated traditional Swedish concepts: no home delivery, a Swedish cafeteria, beds that required sheets conforming

Figure 5.2. How a Global Mindset Differs from a Parochial or a Diffused Mindset

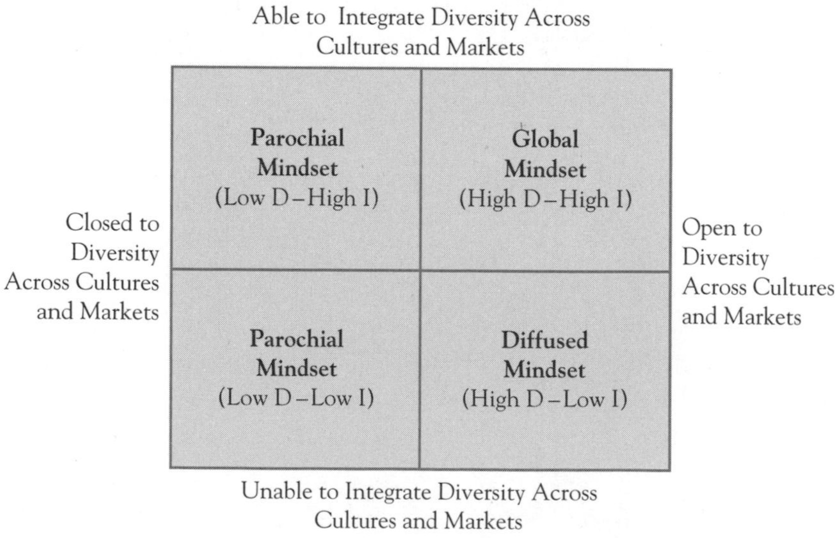

Able to Integrate Diversity Across Cultures and Markets

	Parochial Mindset (Low D–High I)	Global Mindset (High D–High I)	
Closed to Diversity Across Cultures and Markets	Parochial Mindset (Low D–Low I)	Diffused Mindset (High D–Low I)	Open to Diversity Across Cultures and Markets

Unable to Integrate Diversity Across Cultures and Markets

to Swedish rather than U.S. standards, and so forth. In short, Ikea saw the world through a Swedish filter. It was almost blind to alternative views of market reality, and not surprisingly, the outcome was a very disappointing performance and unambiguous feedback that this mindset would be a major barrier to success in the U.S. market. As Ikea reexamined its format for U.S. operations, it faced two challenges: first, to develop a better understanding of how the needs and buying behavior of American customers differ from those of the customers it had served in the past, and second, to synthesize this understanding with its beliefs and competencies pertaining to the furniture business. Without the former, the company would continue to suffer from a misalignment between its product and service offerings and market needs; without the latter, it would be unable to develop competitive advantage over incumbent players. For Ikea, the shift from a parochial to a more global mindset required an understanding of differences between Europe and the United States and, equally important, also a commitment to synthesize these differences and develop a more integrative perspective on the global retailing industry.

In contrast to a parochial mindset, we have observed a diffused mindset most often in the case of professional service firms (for example, in accounting, management consulting, and legal services). Often, such firms are structured as networks of local partner-owned organizations. In such contexts, the power of the CEO and even the senior management team is severely constrained. While certain individual executives at the top may have highly developed global mindsets, the firm as a whole behaves as if it has a diffused mindset. The appreciation for and understanding of local issues and local differences is great, but often the ability to see the bigger global picture is inadequate.

The following boxes present sets of diagnostic questions that individual managers or organizations can use to assess the extent to which they have a global mindset, along with the results of global mindset audits conducted by the authors with senior executives in three Global 500 corporations.

Do You as an Individual Have a Global Mindset?

A Set of Diagnostic Questions

1. In interacting with others, does national origin have an impact on whether or not you assign equal status to them?

2. Do you consider yourself as equally open to ideas from other countries and cultures as you are to ideas from your own country and culture of origin?

3. Does finding yourself in a new cultural setting cause excitement or fear and anxiety?

4. When visiting or living in another culture, are you sensitive to the cultural differences without becoming a prisoner of these differences?

5. When you interact with people from other cultures, what do you regard as more important: understanding them as individuals or viewing them as representatives of their national cultures?

6. Do you regard your values to be a hybrid of values acquired from multiple cultures as opposed to just one culture?

Does Your Organization Have a Global Mindset?

A Set of Diagnostic Questions

1. Is your company a leader (rather than a laggard) in your industry in discovering and pursuing emerging market opportunities in all corners of the world?

2. Do you regard each and every customer wherever they live in the world as being as important as a customer in your own domestic market?

3. Do you draw your employees from the worldwide talent pool?

4. Do employees of every nationality have the same opportunity to move up the career ladder all the way to the top?

5. In scanning the horizon for potential competitors, do you examine all economic regions of the world?

6. In selecting a location for any activity, do you seek to optimize the choice on a truly global basis?

7. Do you view the global arena not just as a playground (that is, a market to exploit) but also as a school (that is, a source of new ideas and technology)?

8. Do you perceive your company as having a universal identity and as a company with many homes or do you instead perceive your company as having a strong national identity?

Survey Results from Global Mindset Audits in Three Major Corporations

The following list shows the percentage of executives who, using a five-point scale ranging from "Strongly Disagree" to "Strongly Agree," responded with "Agree" or "Strongly Agree" to the mindset assessment questions.

Mindset Assessment Questions	Alpha	Beta	Gamma
1. My company is a leader in discovering and pursuing emerging market opportunities in all corners of the world.	70	47	5
2. My company regards each and every customer wherever they live in the world as being as important as a customer in our own domestic market.	46	27	5
3. My company draws employees from the worldwide talent pool.	67	27	5

Mindset Assessment Questions	Alpha	Beta	Gamma
4. Employees of every nationality have the same opportunity to move up the career ladder all the way to the top.	27	33	30
5. We examine all economic regions of the world when we scan the horizon for potential competitors.	55	40	36
6. In selecting a location for any activity, my company seeks to optimize the choice on a truly global basis.	58	47	30
7. We view the global arena not just as a playground (that is, a market to exploit) but also as a school (that is, a source of new ideas and technology).	46	57	48
8. My company has a universal identity with many homes (as contrasted with having a strong national identity).	36	33	5

Note: "Alpha" is a major electronics company (data from thirty-three senior executives), "Beta" is a major heavy equipment company (data from thirty senior executives), and "Gamma" is a major forest products company (data from twenty-one senior executives).

As the results shown in the box indicate, significant differences do exist in the extent to which different firms possess global mindsets. As we would expect by looking at the mindset of Gamma, this firm has been one of the slowest globalizers in its industry. The differences between Alpha and Beta are also instructive. Both firms, although headquartered in the United States, derive more than half their revenues from non-U.S. markets. Yet Alpha's global mindset is more highly developed than Beta's, which would suggest that Beta is likely to be less effective than Alpha at exploiting global presence. Interviews with executives in these two companies appear to support this expectation. The results box also illustrates that the concept of global mindset is a multidimensional construct. A firm's mindset regarding different cultures and markets can be and often is more (or less) global along different dimensions.

The Value of a Global Mindset

A look at Microsoft's entry into the Chinese market attests to the value, indeed the centrality, of a global mindset. It is obvious that China presents a huge market for software today and promises an even larger market tomorrow. However, the promise of the Chinese market is accompanied by perils. Software piracy has been rampant, at least historically. Public policy tends to be unpredictable and often favors local over foreign enterprises. The sophistication level of the market lags a few years behind the more economically developed countries, though this gap is closing. At the same time, the Chinese market leads all others in some important respects. For example, the estimated mid-2007 number of mobile subscribers in China is around five hundred million and the number of Internet users over two hundred million, both figures larger than for any other country in the world. Also, the use of Chinese characters requires, at the very least, a major adaptation of the software's user interface and possibly even the internal code. We would contend that when Microsoft formulates and reformulates its strategy for China, it would not be successful if its mindset regarding China were wanting along either of the two dimensions: if it were shallow in its understanding of what is happening in China, or if it were not sufficiently able to see events in China from a more integrative global perspective. China is not the only country where Microsoft faces dedicated pirates, nor is it the only one with a nationalistic public policy regime. Can Microsoft bring to bear lessons from other markets as it analyzes China? Alternatively, might lessons from China be relevant in other markets? What does Microsoft's experience in other countries say about the rate at which the sophistication of the Chinese market might evolve and about how quickly the company should bring leading-edge products and services to China? Might China be one of the best global centers for Microsoft's research into voice and character recognition technologies as well as technologies for mobile Internet devices? Given a global mindset, these are just some of the fundamental questions that would get raised in the process of developing the company's China strategy. In the absence of a global mindset, on the other hand, few if any of these questions would be identified or addressed.

As the discussion of Microsoft illustrates, what a global mindset does is enable the company to outpace its rivals in assessing various market opportunities, in establishing the necessary market presence to pursue the worthwhile opportunities, and in converting its presence across multiple markets into global competitive advantage. *The central value of a global mindset lies in enabling the company to combine speed with accurate response*. It is easy to be fast, simplistic, and wrong. It is also easy to become a prisoner of diversity, be intimidated by enormous differences across markets, and stay back—or, if the company does venture abroad, to end up reinventing things in every market. The benefit of a global mindset derives from the fact that, while the company has a grasp of and insight into the needs of the local market, it is also able to build cognitive bridges across these needs and between these needs and the company's own global experience and capabilities. It is instructive to compare the mindsets of the CEOs of two of America's largest retailers, Sears Roebuck and Wal-Mart, both of them looking at the same global reality. Their views on the globalization potential of the retailing industry, as illustrated in the following quotes, are as starkly different as were those of DEC's Kenneth Olsen and Apple Computer's Steve Jobs on the future of personal computers.

Arthur C. Martinez, CEO (1995–2000), Sears Roebuck & Co.:

I think the order of difficulty is geometric because you are dealing not only with the translation of your format, you're dealing with different business practices. You're dealing with different sourcing strategies. The degree of difficulty in a global strategy is very very great. . . . It's tough. You have to understand distribution patterns. You have to understand how goods are advertised, the role of promotions in driving your business. The whole dynamics are different. So, it's not simply a matter of picking up your store and dropping it in a new environment. The degree of complexity represents a major challenge. I know it looks tempting because of all those consumers over there, and because we have too many stores in America. But a lot of people are going to stub their toes.[19]

David D. Glass, President and CEO (1988–2000), Wal-Mart Stores:

We are confident that the Wal-Mart concept is "exportable."[20]. . . If Wal-Mart had been content to be just an Arkansas retailer in the early days, we probably would not be where we are today. State borders were not barriers, and people and ideas moved freely from one area to another. . . . We believe the successful retailers of the future will be those that bring the best of each nation to today's consumer. We call it "global learning." We are committed to being a successful global retailer and we believe the attributes that made us successful in the United States will also lead to success internationally.[21]

Indeed, the corporate behavior of Sears Roebuck and Wal-Mart has mirrored their CEOs' perspectives. Sears has chosen to remain confined inside North American borders; even within this region, it has reduced its equity commitments in Canada and Mexico. In contrast, Wal-Mart has charged ahead aggressively into a wide range of international markets spanning North and South America, Asia, and Europe.

There are several concrete ways in which a global mindset can yield beneficial outcomes. One of the key advantages it confers is speed.

An early mover advantage in identifying emerging opportunities. Consider, for example, the aggressiveness of GE Capital in Asia. In the late 1990s, one of the by-products of the Asian financial crisis was that market valuations of industrial as well as financial services companies in the region dropped dramatically and appeared to offer knock-down bargains. Yet, as reported in the business press at the time, "Few giant multinationals have swooped down to pick up the pieces. . . . Only a handful of deals have been consummated, and those mostly between existing partners. There is one company, however, that looks set to break the deadlock in a rather grand fashion . . . GE Capital. . . . 'They're everywhere,' groans the head of one competing bank."[22] Why did GE Capital see tremendous opportunities in a region when most other competitors saw only tremendous risks? We believe that the answer lies in the fact that, under Jack Welch, GE Capital was much more successful in developing a global mindset.

Similarly, think about airport authorities. Most airport authorities see themselves simply as local (indeed, one-location) organizations. Yet, given a global mindset, the strategic charter of even an airport authority can undergo radical change. This is illustrated by the case of NV Luchthaven Schiphol, the organization that manages Amsterdam's Schiphol airport, which has signed a thirty-year lease with the Port Authority of New York and New Jersey to operate the Arrivals Building at New York's John F. Kennedy Airport.[23]

Greater sophistication and more fine-grained analysis regarding the trade-off between local adaptation and global standardization. Procter & Gamble's Organization 2005 program, launched in 1998, was designed explicitly to help the company become more globally efficient as well as more locally responsive to consumer needs in various markets. The company reorganized itself into a number of global business units (GBUs) as well as a number of regional market development organizations (MDOs). Working in collaboration with the GBUs, the mission of the MDOs was to own the "first moment of truth"—the moment when consumers make their purchase decision. In turn, working in collaboration with the MDOs, the mission of the GBUs was to own the "second moment of truth"—the moment when consumers use the product. The career development of Ravi Chaturvedi, President-Northeast Asia MDO in 2007, illustrates how Procter & Gamble attempted to foster a global mindset among its managers. Chaturvedi, born in India, joined P&G India in 1983 soon after finishing his MBA. After rotating through various assignments in a number of Asian countries, he was promoted to become the General Manager of Thailand MDO in 1997. In 2000, he was transferred to the United States as Vice President of North America Hair Care. In 2003, he became Vice President, Greater China Health and Beauty Care. In 2004, he was appointed President-Northeast Asia MDO.[24]

Smoother coordination across complementary functional activities distributed across borders. Liberalization of trade and investment barriers, coupled with the technology revolution, has added and continues to add significant fuel to the engine driving firms to achieve global scale and scope. We view the ongoing spate of cross-border mergers (such as Mittal Steel and Arcelor, Alcatel and Lucent, Lenovo and IBM's PC division) as a logical outcome of these forces. However, building or buying into global presence is anything but synonymous with having global competitive advantage. A company's ability to capture cross-border synergies (for example, in the form of lower costs, faster product development, or faster market development) more effectively and more efficiently than competitors lies at the heart of what distinguishes global presence from global competitive advantage. Without doubt, information technology plays a major role in the quest for effective and high-velocity coordination and communication. Yet, as every executive knows from experience, effective coordination among people depends on more than technology. It depends also, and crucially, on such factors as how well the people know each other, understand each other, like each other, and—most important—trust each other. A global mindset has the potential to serve as the foundation for the development of the necessary interpersonal glue.

Faster rollout of new product concepts and technologies. It took Procter & Gamble twenty-eight years to get Pampers, one of its diaper brands, into twenty-seven countries. It took the company only seven years to get Pert and Rejoice shampoos into sixty countries. Even more recently, it took the company only two years to get Vidal Sassoon, another shampoo, into forty countries. How do we explain the increasing velocity with which P&G is able to roll out new products on a global scale? In part, the company's mindset clearly has become increasingly global over time.

More rapid and efficient sharing of best practices across subsidiaries. Take a company such as Marriott International, with several thousand properties spread across virtually all continents. Let's say that one of the properties in Asia has experimented and succeeded with a new service concept whereby a frequent-stay customer is greeted and assisted at the airport. How rapidly can the company first discover this innovation and then roll it out wisely to its other properties? The answer would depend heavily on the extent to which individual hotel general managers and their superiors have developed a global mindset.

Lower failure rate in expatriate assignments. Expatriate failure (that is, early return or below expected performance) is a very costly experience for any company: on average, expatriates cost three times as much as local nationals. Yet failure rates among expatriates tend to be alarmingly high, ranging anywhere from one-third to one-half of all expatriates.[25] In addition to the direct costs of failure, the company also must contend with the indirect costs that any failure imposes on the individuals in question, on their families, on other colleagues, as well as on the company's market position. Screening for and cultivating a global mindset among expatriates ready to embark on foreign assignments can have a huge impact in several pivotal areas; for example, the quality of the communication and social ties that they are likely to build with their hosts and on the depth of understanding they develop regarding the local culture and market, and thus, ultimately, on their effectiveness.

Cultivating a global mindset among local nationals based in their respective countries can also reduce the need for a company to rely on expatriates for global coordination. The resulting benefits, in terms of cost savings as well as cultural closeness to local customers, can be substantial. For example, during the 1990s, Standard Chartered, a London-based international bank then employing about twenty-five thousand people, parlayed its investment in cultivating a global mindset into a nearly 50 percent reduction in the number of expatriates—from about 800 to about 420 people.[26]

Does Every Company Need a Global Mindset?

By now, the value of a global mindset is obvious for any company that already operates in multiple countries or that is currently local but is about to embark on building a presence outside its domestic boundaries. But is a global mindset likely to have value for a company that is local and has no plans to venture outside domestic borders in the foreseeable future? This is often the situation of companies in industries where the most effective and efficient size of an operating unit is very small relative to the global size of the industry, as is true of many industries (often, but not always, in the service sector), such as nursing homes, hospitals, radio stations, TV stations, commercial cleaning services, and so forth.

Even assuming that the organization's decision to stay local is wise, having a global mindset—and looking at the local market as a fragment of the global market—can yield at least two benefits. One, a global mindset should make the organization much more proactive in benchmarking and learning from product and process innovations outside its domestic borders. This is illustrated well by the case of Nucor Steel, which, from its inception as a steel manufacturer in the late 1960s, has remained as a largely domestic steel producer. Yet right from the beginning, Nucor benchmarked itself against the most efficient steel manufacturers worldwide and was often the steel industry's first mover in sourcing the latest steel-making technology wherever it was available. It was the first American company to adopt the minimill technology, to commercialize thin-slab casting and make flat rolled steel in a minimill, and to commercially produce iron carbide; all of these technologies originated outside the United States, especially in Germany and Japan. Two, a global mindset should make the organization much more alert to the entry of nontraditional (that is, foreign) competitors in its local market. In today's globalized market, it is always possible (and increasingly likely) that, whether you are a local TV station, a local supermarket, or a local commercial cleaning service, a global consolidator will acquire one of your local competitors and change the rules of what you viewed as just a local game. This is precisely what has happened in the U.S. beer industry. Until 2002, the bulk of the market share in the U.S. beer industry was controlled by two *domestic* companies—Anheuser-Busch at around 50 percent of the market and Miller Brewing at around 20 percent. However, in July 2002, South African Breweries, an aggressive foreign player, changed the rules of the game by acquiring Miller Brewing. Within three years, Miller Brewing had been transformed from a placid competitor into one of the most aggressive fighters in the worldwide beer industry. In the colorful words of Norman Adami, the newly appointed South African CEO of Miller Brewing: "When you play with the big boys, you don't piss like a puppy."[27]

Does Every Employee Need a Global Mindset?

Let us assume that you are persuaded that, as an organization, your company needs to cultivate a global mindset. Does this mean that every employee needs to develop a global mindset, or is it sufficient for just a few people to focus on cultivating a global mindset?

The imperative of cultivating a global mindset is most obvious in the case of those individuals responsible for managing activities that span borders (for example, a global product manager, a Europe region marketing manager). It also is obvious for those individuals who interface routinely with customers, suppliers, or peers from other countries (for example, scientists on global product development teams, sales managers on global customer account management teams, and so forth). However, what about those individuals who not only have purely local responsibilities (for example, a production supervisor or a machine operator) but who also have little if any routine interaction with customers, suppliers, or peers in other countries? Can these employees—as well as the company—benefit from the cultivation of a global mindset? Our unambiguous answer is yes.

Consider, for example, the job of, say, paint shop supervisors in a global car company such as Toyota or Hyundai. The company is likely to have dozens of such individuals, and it is very unlikely that any of them will ever be sent on an expatriate assignment or engage in cross-border negotiations. Nonetheless, the company can build a global learning community of its own paint shop supervisors. They might, for instance, all receive and contribute to a global paint shop newsletter and might have easy connectivity to each other through electronic mail. Their children might enjoy being pen-pals. The net result would almost certainly be that, in a company with these types of practices, the need for a hierarchical push to create a learning organization deep within its operations would be dramatically reduced. In today's technology-networked environment, nothing—other than the lack of a global mindset—prevents even assembly line workers from developing their own global learning communities. In the absence of a global mindset, creating a global learning organization will almost certainly be a much tougher challenge.

This discussion is not meant to imply that the global mindset imperative is equally strong across the entire spectrum of employees. Although we contend that the returns to investment in cultivating a global mindset would always be positive, we do not expect them to be uniform. The value added by a global mindset, and the value subtracted by its absence, is likely to be strongest in the case of those individuals who are directly responsible for managing cross-border activities (for example, the president of GE Lighting), followed by those who must interact frequently with colleagues from other countries (for example, members of a cross-border research team at Alcatel-Lucent). Thus, if a company is in the early stages of becoming systematic about cultivating global mindsets, the highest returns would come from focusing on these more senior levels. Nonetheless, if the company's goal is to capture and sustain global market leadership in its industry, it absolutely has to regard the development of a global mindset as a goal that encompasses each and every unit and each and every employee.

Cultivating a Global Mindset

In thinking about how to cultivate a global mindset, it is critical to remember that the key word is cultivation, and that the quest for a global mindset is a ceaseless journey. Living as we do in a complex and dynamic world, there is no upper limit to the extent to which one could continue to explore the world's diversity as well as the linkages across this diversity. No matter how developed the global mindset of a Nokia, a Toyota, or a Cisco Systems may appear to be today, surely twenty years from now, these companies' current mindset would appear, in relative terms, quite naive.

Remember too, as we described earlier, that mindsets represent knowledge structures (that is, cognitive templates). As a result, the development of mindsets follows the same generic path as the development of all types of knowledge: a child learning to walk, a team of scientists pushing the limits of microprocessor technology, or an organization like eBay learning about the world's cultures and markets. As we know from research in a variety of areas, including evolution of species, human development, cognitive psychology, and even technological innovation, all development occurs through a sequence of evolutions and revolutions. In other words, the ongoing cultivation of a global mindset, whether at the individual or the organizational level, must be seen as taking place through a series of S-curves (see Figure 5.3).

Figure 5.3. Development of a Global Mindset

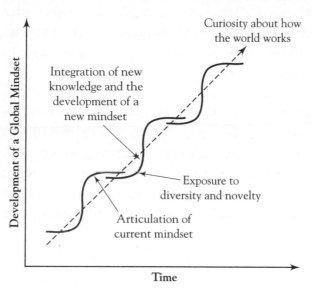

As a vivid illustration on a personal level, consider the experience of one of our interviewees—Jenny Stephens, a thirty-five-year-old American executive working for the French subsidiary of an American multinational in Paris. She had moved to Paris seven years earlier, having met and married a Frenchman in New York. She spoke fluent French, interacted with French relatives, friends, and colleagues on an ongoing basis, and was by most standards very well informed about France. Yet when we asked her if she felt she now understood France and the French culture, she replied, "I have been here for seven years. In an almost predictable manner, I have found that whenever I begin to get a sense that now I really do understand the French, something strange will happen that will throw me off completely. As I would reflect on the event and talk it over with my husband and friends, I would begin to develop a more complex view of the French. Then, things would seem to go fine for several months until the whole process would repeat itself in some other area."

As Jenny Stephens's experience points out, at any one time, we have a frame of reference, and we think we know how the world works. From time to time, however, something novel happens, an element of perplexity is introduced, and we are forced to go back to the drawing board. After some struggle, we emerge with a new frame of reference and begin to relearn and assimilate data within this new framework until the next discrepancy or challenge forces us to start the process all over again.

If we accept that the development of mindsets must take place through a series of S-curves, the interesting question then becomes: What can managers and companies do to accelerate the process of moving from one S-curve to another? Building on our own research as well as research in cognitive psychology and the development of knowledge, we would contend that the speed with which any individual or organization can cultivate its global mindset is driven by four factors:

- Curiosity about the world and a commitment to becoming smarter about how the world works
- An explicit and self-conscious articulation of current mindset
- Exposure to diversity and novelty
- A disciplined attempt to develop an integrated perspective that weaves together diverse strands of knowledge about cultures and markets

Cultivating Curiosity About the World

Curiosity and openness about how the world works reflects an attitude, an element of the individual's personality makeup. Like other elements of personality, this attitude is shaped heavily by early childhood experiences and becomes more resistant to change as the individual gets older. Thus, although a company does have some maneuvering room in further cultivating curiosity among its existing employees, its greatest degree of freedom lies at the point of selection and in managing the company's demographic makeup.

In situations where a company has the luxury of hiring a younger workforce (for example, Nokia, where the average age across the entire company is around thirty), it may be able to develop an inherent corporate advantage in the degree to which its employees will strive to develop a global mindset. In any case, every company has a good deal of discretion in including curiosity about diverse cultures and markets among the selection criteria at the point of hiring and again at the point of promotion. These considerations appeared to lie behind newly created DaimlerChrysler's appointment of Andreas Renschler as the head of executive management development in 1999, a role that gave him broad power to help shape the careers of the top three thousand managers globally. Renschler came to this job not with a background in human resource management but with a track record of having successfully managed the launch of Daimler-Benz's M-class sports utility vehicle out of a newly built U.S.-based car plant in Alabama, a challenge that required effectively melding a team of managers from diverse national and corporate backgrounds. According to Renschler, in his new role, he was looking for "people who are willing to change."[28]

Promotion decisions to senior executive levels that place high value on global experience and global mindsets, as illustrated by the appointment of India-born Indra Nooyi as the CEO of PepsiCo in 2006, also have a corollary effect in terms of sending strong signals regarding the increasing criticality of openness to and curiosity about diverse cultures and markets.

Articulating the Current Mindset

Mindsets evolve through a process of interaction between a person and the environment. Our current mindsets shape our interpretations of the world around us; in turn, these interpretations affect whether or not our mindsets change or remain unaltered. Unless this iterative process allows for new learning, it is easy to get trapped in one's own mental web. One powerful mechanism to reduce the likelihood of falling into this trap is to cultivate self-consciousness about one's mindset. This self-conscious articulation requires accepting the possibility that our view of the world is just one of many alternative interpretations of the reality. The thought process behind this articulation significantly enhances the likelihood of new learning.[29]

How might an individual manager or team of managers cultivate self-consciousness regarding their current mindsets? In our experience, two approaches work best: *direct mapping* and *indirect comparative mapping*. Direct mapping requires managers or teams to articulate their beliefs about the subject domain (for example, as Hewlett-Packard, what are our beliefs regarding the structure of the personal computer market in Europe?). In contrast, indirect comparative mapping works through an examination of how different people or companies appear to interpret the same reality (for example, as Hewlett-Packard, how does our view of the Indian personal computer industry compare with that of Dell, Lenovo, Intel, and Microsoft?). Since indirect comparative mapping rests on the premise that any particular mindset is just one of several possibilities, we would argue that it is the more effective of the two approaches for helping a manager, a team, or a company to uncover their often deeply buried cognitive maps.

As an example of how the indirect comparative mapping approach works, consider the experience of one company where we succeeded in persuading the CEO that, at least once every quarter, the agenda for the board meeting must include a strategic review of why a different competitor behaves the way it does. After a year of this relatively simple exercise, the quality of discussions in the board meetings had changed dramatically. It became clear that the company's own perspective on the market potential of different countries and on whether or not joint ventures were a sensible entry mode in this particular industry were not necessarily shared by some of the key players. As a by-product, board deliberations on action issues facing the company became more comprehensive and even led to the abandonment of what the CEO had earlier believed to be some of the seemingly "obvious" rules of this industry; in fact, this comparative mapping approach resulted in the CEO's becoming a proponent rather than an opponent of strategic alliances in this industry.

Cultivating Knowledge Regarding Diverse Cultures and Markets

Companies have recourse to two approaches for cultivating exposure to and increasing knowledge of diverse cultures and markets: they can facilitate such knowledge building at the level of individuals, and they can build diversity in the composition of the groups making up the company. These approaches complement each other: the former focuses on building cognitive diversity inside individuals' own mindsets, and the latter focuses on assembling a diverse knowledge base within the organizational collectivity. Both approaches are essential for every company. Cultivating a global mindset at the individual level is a slow process that can take years of learning through experience in multiple cultures; thus relying exclusively on the globalization of individual mindsets would be woefully inadequate vis-à-vis industry and competitive imperatives.

The following are some of the most effective mechanisms available to help companies cultivate literacy of and enthusiasm for diverse cultures and markets.

Formal education. Formal education (language skills and knowledge building regarding diverse cultures and markets) can take place in the form of self-study courses, university-based education, or in-company seminars and management development programs. For example, at its Global Management Development Institute, South Korea's Samsung Group routinely offers substantive courses in international business management as well as in country histories, cultures, and economies, and in foreign languages. In-company programs have an added advantage in that the learning occurs at multiple levels—not only in the classroom but through interactions with colleagues from other locations around the world, as well.

Participation in cross-border business teams and projects. Consider, for example, a leading U.S. bank which created a "Euro" team to coordinate the company's response to introduction of the new European currency in 1999. Should such a team be composed only of selected managers from the company's European units, or should the team also include a very small number of Americans from the company's U.S. operations? The latter approach, in our view, can be extremely effective in building in-depth knowledge regarding diverse cultures and markets—in addition to the obvious benefits of by-products such as development of interpersonal ties.

Utilization of diverse locations for team and project meetings. This approach has been used successfully by VeriFone, a global market leader in the automation and delivery of secure payment and payment-related transactions. As one of several mechanisms adopted to keep becoming more attuned to the global environment, the company's top management team had instituted a policy of meeting for five days every six weeks at a different location around the globe (see the box for a summary of the various mechanisms employed by VeriFone to cultivate a global mindset among its people and within the company as a whole). This generic approach can be implemented easily at any relevant level of the corporate hierarchy, from the board of directors to a multinational R&D team within one of the business units.

Cultivating a Global Mindset: The VeriFone Approach—Circa 1997

VeriFone was a market leader in the automation and delivery of secure payment and payment-related transactions. Headquartered in Silicon Valley, the company was founded in 1981. VeriFone's stated mission was to create and lead the transaction automation industry worldwide. In 1997, the company had three thousand employees based at more than thirty facilities in North America, South America, Asia, Australia, Europe, and Africa. The following are some highlights of how VeriFone cultivated a global mindset among its people and more broadly at the level of the entire company:

- Hatim Tyabji, VeriFone's CEO, disdained the idea of an all-powerful corporate headquarters and preferred to view the company as a network of locations. He likened the company to a blueberry pancake where all berries were created equal and all had the same size. Many corporate functions (for example, human resource management and management information systems) were managed in a decentralized fashion out of multiple global locations such as Dallas (Texas), Bangalore (India), Taipei (Taiwan), and Honolulu (Hawaii).

- Virtually all employees of the company were provided with laptops and were connected to each other electronically. Every company facility was also equipped with videoconferencing facilities. Upon signing on to their e-mail systems, employees automatically saw a list of holidays and local times at various VeriFone locations.

- The top management team, consisting of the CEO and his ten direct reports, met for five days every six weeks at a different location around the globe.

- The leadership was dedicated to instilling the company's core values among all employees. The CEO wrote the corporate philosophy manual himself. This manual was then issued in a number of languages, including English, Chinese, French, German, Japanese, Portuguese, and Spanish. When rolling out corporate programs, senior managers traveled personally to various locations to get local input and to provide guidelines regarding how the program could be tailored to the local context.

- Prior to its acquisition by Hewlett-Packard, VeriFone published the CEO's letter to shareholders (in its annual report) in multiple languages.

- The company conducted recruitment on a global basis and instituted a uniform performance assessment system and incentive structure around the globe.

- One of the company's recognized core competencies was its ability to leverage know-how from various locations in order to serve customers or pursue new opportunities. As an example, a large customer in Greece informed one of the company's sales reps that a competitor was raising concerns about VeriFone's expertise in debit cards. The sales rep sent out an e-mail request to colleagues within the company for information and references on debit installations. Within twenty-four hours, he had sixteen responses and multiple references, including the contact information of established customers with debit card installations. The next day, armed with this information and able to say that VeriFone had four hundred thousand installations worldwide, the rep closed a major deal with this customer. Stories such as these not only provided a concrete illustration of VeriFone's already well-developed global mindset but also served to reinforce the notion of what constitute desirable attitudes and behaviors within the company—thereby leading to a further deepening of the global mindset.[30]

Immersion experiences in foreign cultures. Immersion experiences can range from two- or three-month training assignments to more extensive cultural learning programs. Standard Chartered, a London-based global bank, has used the former approach, sending trainees recruited in London to Asian locations and those recruited in Asia to London. Samsung Group's Overseas Area Specialist Course is an example of an extensive program. Every year, each of over two hundred carefully screened trainees selected one strategically important country of interest, underwent three months of language and cross-cultural training, and then spent a one-year period devoted solely to understanding the chosen country. There was no specific job assignment and trainees were forbidden to make contact with the local Samsung office. While abroad, they were even encouraged to use modes of travel other than airlines, as these generally resulted in a deeper immersion in the local culture. At the end of the immersion period, trainees returned to headquarters in Seoul and reported on their experiences during a two-month debriefing period.[31] Recent interviews with a senior Samsung executive indicate that this program continues to be regarded as highly valuable.

Expatriate assignments. Multiyear expatriate assignments are by far the most intensive mechanism through which an individual can learn about another culture and market. However, this is also probably the most expensive mechanism for cultivating a global mindset—for the company and, given the increasing preponderance of dual-career marriages, often for the individual as well. Accordingly, companies need to pay greater attention to targeting expatriate assignments toward high-potential managers (as distinct from the common practice of selecting people that you don't want to see too much of) but also to ensuring that their stay abroad fosters cultural learning rather than cultural isolation. As Gurcharan Das, former head of Procter & Gamble India, has observed astutely:

> There are powerful . . . rewards for an international manager on transfer overseas who chooses to get involved in the local community. When such people approach the new country with an open mind, learn the local language, and make friends with colleagues and neighbors, they gain access to a wealth of a new culture. . . . Unfortunately, my experience in Mexico indicates that many expatriate managers live in "golden ghettos" of ease with little genuine contact with locals other than servants. . . . The lesson for global companies is to give each international manager a local "mentor" who will open doors to the community. Ultimately, however, it is the responsibility of individual managers to open their minds, plunge into their local communities, and try to make them their own.[32]

Cultivating geographic and cultural diversity among the senior management ranks. Notwithstanding the value of the various mechanisms discussed thus far, there do exist limits to the speed with which a company can cultivate a global mindset among its employees, the number of employees that it can efficiently target for this objective, and the rate of success in cultivating global mindsets. Accordingly, virtually all companies face the imperative of expanding the cognitive map of the organization by cultivating geographic and cultural diversity more directly among the senior management ranks. Such efforts can be targeted at many levels of the organization, from the composition of the board of directors and the office of the CEO to the composition of business unit management teams. For example, in 2007, the board of directors at IBM included Minoru Makihara, former chairman of Japan-headquartered Mitsubishi Corporation, Juergen Dormann, chairman of the board at Switzerland-headquartered ABB Ltd., and Lorenzo Zambrano, chairman and chief executive officer at Mexico-headquartered Cemex S.A.B. de C.V.[33] Similarly, in mid-2005, at Procter & Gamble, the group president for Global Fabric Care was a Greek, the corporate treasurer a Brit, and the president for Greater China an Italian.[34]

Location of business unit headquarters. By dispersing business unit headquarters to carefully selected locations around the world, companies can also further their cognitive diversity (that is, their knowledge about diverse cultures and markets). Among major corporations, ABB was perhaps the pioneer in dispersing the locations of business area headquarters away from the corporate center. Other examples would include Eaton Corporation, which shifted the worldwide headquarters of its light and medium truck transmission business to Amsterdam, The Netherlands, and that of its automotive controls business to Strasbourg, France.

Cultivating Ability to Integrate Diverse Knowledge Bases

Notwithstanding the fact that cognitive diversity is critical for navigating today's complex and dynamic environment, it can also be paralyzing. A management team composed of seven people representing four nationalities adds value only when the diverse perspectives can be melded into a coherent vision and a coherent set of decisions and actions. Otherwise, what you get is conflict, frustration, delay, and at best either a forced or a compromised decision. To emerge as a winner in the global battle in its market, becoming a more knowledgeable company must be accompanied by developing the ability to make and implement smart decisions faster than competitors. This, in turn, requires that the company be able to integrate the diverse knowledge bases so they become a usable resource.

Fortunately, many effective mechanisms are available to aid companies in developing an ability to integrate knowledge about diverse cultures and markets.

Defining and cultivating a set of core values throughout the corporation. By definition, core values are those values that cut across subsidiaries no matter where located. A set of deeply ingrained and widely shared core values (as in the case of companies such as Marriott, GE, Honda, and Google) can serve as an intellectual as well as a social integrating mechanism. Intellectually, belief in core values implicitly requires people to make sense of their local observations from the perspective of the company's global agenda. And on a social level, shared values give people with diverse cultural backgrounds and diverse knowledge bases a common platform on which to base a constructive rather than unproductive, conflict-ridden dialog.

Widespread distribution of ownership rights on a global basis. Ownership rights in the global parent provide a powerful mechanism to ensure that every employee, regardless of location or nationality, would be inclined to look at local opportunities, local challenges, and local resources from a global perspective. Companies such as Eli Lilly (which issues stock options to every employee worldwide through the company's GlobalShares program) significantly increase the likelihood that every employee becomes more cosmopolitan, more global in outlook.

Cultivation of an internal labor market driven by pure meritocracy. Companies such as IBM, McKinsey, Citigroup, and PepsiCo, which are committed to using merit rather than nationality as the prime driver of career mobility right up to the CEO level, create an environment in which all managers see themselves as global resources. Such an environment goes a long way toward removing impediments to viewing local knowledge as idiosyncratic and of only local value.

Job rotation across geographic regions, business divisions, and functions. Job rotations across countries have long served as an effective mechanism to promote openness to and knowledge about diverse cultures and markets. If well planned, they also help cultivate an ability to integrate across this diversity. Consider the approach adopted by Nokia. In the late 1990s, Sari Baldauf, formerly the head of Nokia's Asia-Pacific operations, was appointed to lead corporate R&D. Similarly, Olli-Pekka Kallasvuo, the former head of Nokia's U.S. operations, became the new corporate chief financial officer. From a management development perspective, one major outcome of these shuffles is to cultivate a thorough understanding of diversity (through regional responsibilities for Asia or North America) as well as an ability to integrate across this diversity (through global responsibilities for R&D or finance).

Cultivation of interpersonal and social ties among people based in different locations. Typically, the frequency and openness of interaction between two people is a function of the strength of interpersonal and social ties between them. Accordingly, the more successful a company is at cultivating interpersonal and social ties among people based in different subsidiaries, the more effective it should be at integrating their diverse perspectives and knowledge bases. For instance, Microsoft's Speech Technologies Group, charged with doing basic research in speech technologies, is spread across two locations—Beijing and Redmond. Scientists at each location serve as affiliate members of the team at the other location. Further, both groups of researchers meet each other often, virtually as well as in face-to-face contexts. Such direct interaction is critical to the development of trust, open communication, and thereby effective working relationships. It also helps build a global mindset whereby every researcher is open to ideas from other locations and, in conducting his or her own research, looks at the needs of Microsoft on a worldwide basis.[35]

Conclusion

The economic landscape of the world is changing rapidly and becoming increasingly global. For virtually every medium-sized to large company in developed as well as developing economies, market opportunities, critical resources, cutting-edge ideas, and competitors lurk not just around the corner in the home market but increasingly in distant and often little-understood regions of the world as well. How successful a company is at exploiting emerging opportunities and tackling accompanying challenges depends crucially on how intelligent it is at observing and interpreting the dynamic world in which it operates. Creating a global mindset is one of the central ingredients required for building such intelligence. The conceptual framework and mechanisms provided in this chapter can guide companies in moving systematically toward this goal.

6

Building a Global
Knowledge Machine

> Market success is only part of globalization. We must
> globalize every activity in the company. We've made
> some progress in sourcing products and components
> so critical to survive and win in a price-competitive
> deflationary world, but our challenge is to go beyond
> that—to capitalize on the vast intellectual capital
> available around the globe.
>
> —*John F. Welch Jr., CEO (1981–2001),*
> *General Electric Company*[1]

Whenever a company extends its presence across borders, it is confronted with diversity. Diversity, however, represents not just a challenge with which the firm must cope but also a critical resource that the firm can use to create value for customers as well as shareholders. The process of adapting products and processes to the vagaries of each location forces each subsidiary to engage in at least some local innovation. Every such local innovation represents the creation of new knowledge. Although some of the new knowledge may be too idiosyncratic to have much value outside the local environment, a good chunk of what starts out as locally created knowledge often has global relevance and value. For instance:

- Unilever has long fostered a culture of entrepreneurship among its subsidiaries. As one example, Hindustan Unilever, the subsidiary in India, took the initiative to develop Wheel— a new laundry detergent targeted at the bottom tier of the economic pyramid. To create, market, and distribute a product that would be effective yet within the price reach of targeted customers, Hindustan Unilever created a separate business unit and charged it with inventing a new business system. Wheel delivers significantly lower margins than other detergents on a per-unit basis; yet, given its very much higher asset turnover and a large market size, it has been an economic success. Unilever has since replicated this concept and business idea in other markets, most notably the case of Ala, a similar detergent brand in Brazil.[2]

- China is rapidly becoming one of the fastest-growing markets for Microsoft. However, given the vast linguistic differences between English and Chinese, both written and spoken, Microsoft's success in China depends very heavily on its effectiveness in customizing the user interface of its products, something more easily said than done. Not surprisingly, Microsoft has decided to locate one of its biggest research programs in language and speech technologies in China. The technological knowledge emerging from these China-based activities has been of critical value to Microsoft's operations not only in China but in all corners of the world.[3]

Despite widespread awareness of the economic value that can be unleashed by creating and mobilizing intellectual capital, for most companies, reality remains well below potential. As the CEO of a commercial services company lamented in an interview: "We provide pretty much the same services in every location. But my regional managers would rather die than learn from each other." Our research suggests that this anecdote is hardly an isolated case. As our survey research indicates (see Figure 6.1), not only is actual knowledge sharing well below corporate expectations, it also is notably below corporate executives' perceptions of today's reality.

Building on the observation that there exists a wide gap between the rhetoric and the reality of knowledge management, this

Figure 6.1. Potential Versus Reality of Knowledge Sharing: Survey Results from Three Large Global Corporations

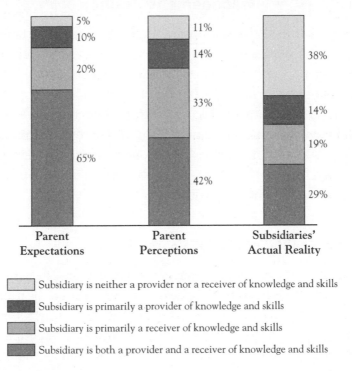

Parent Expectations   Parent Perceptions   Subsidiaries' Actual Reality

Subsidiary is neither a provider nor a receiver of knowledge and skills

Subsidiary is primarily a provider of knowledge and skills

Subsidiary is primarily a receiver of knowledge and skills

Subsidiary is both a provider and a receiver of knowledge and skills

Note: Total number of subsidiaries = 79.

chapter proposes that building an appropriate social ecology is a crucial requirement for effective knowledge management. We explicitly uncover the pathologies and pitfalls that prevent companies from realizing the full potential of knowledge management, and present a detailed analysis of how one company—Nucor Corporation, one of the world's most innovative and fastest-growing steel companies over three decades—has created an exemplary social ecology for accumulating and mobilizing knowledge. We use these insights to present a general framework for converting any company into an effective knowledge machine.[4]

Unpacking the Knowledge Management Agenda

Because all knowledge starts as information, many companies tend to regard knowledge management as synonymous with information management. Carried to an extreme, such a perspective can result in a profoundly mistaken belief that the installation of a sophisticated information technology infrastructure is the be-all and end-all of knowledge management. Departing from such thinking, our central thesis is that effective knowledge management depends not merely on information technology platforms but more broadly on the social ecology of the organization.

The Centrality of Social Ecology

We define *social ecology* as referring to the social system in which people are embedded. Social ecology drives the organization's formal and informal expectations from individuals; witness, for example, the impact of stock options on the motivation of people at any Silicon Valley start-up. It shapes the degree of freedom that individuals have to pursue actions without seeking prior approval; witness, for example, the 70-20-10 rule at Google that allows people to devote 10 percent of their time to purely exploratory projects that may have no immediate or direct connection to current core projects. Social ecology signals to the individual the desired norms of behavior; witness, for example, the power of "the credo" at Johnson & Johnson. It sends signals about which dimensions of performance are more or less highly valued by the organization; witness, for example, the impact of Harold Geneen's financial controls on the behavior of people during his tenure at ITT. It defines the types of people who will be welcomed by the organization and those who will be rejected; witness, for example, the salience that Nordstrom attaches to hiring and retaining only those people who truly enjoy serving customers. It defines for people the meaning of important concepts such as quality; witness, for example, the implications of Jack Welch's and then Jeff Immelt's passion for Six Sigma on the behavior of people at GE. Social ecology affects the way people interact with each other both inside and outside the organization; witness, for instance, the impact of P&G's "Connect and Develop" program on its scientists' openness to innovations originating from outside the company. In short, the social ecology of an organization is critical because it affects people's motivations and abilities and thereby shapes their behavior.

As illustrated in Figure 6.2, the determinants of social ecology are culture, structure, information systems, reward systems, processes, people, and leadership. The term ecology suggests that the social system should be viewed not as a random collection of disparate elements but as a package where the various elements interact with each other.

Figure 6.2. How Social Ecology Shapes People's Behavior

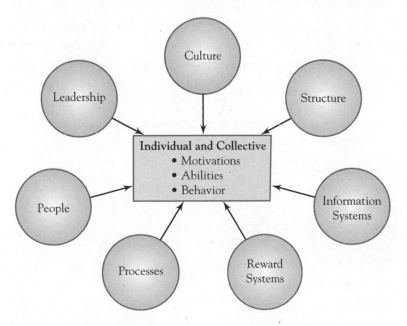

Information technology (IT) certainly plays a central role in knowledge management in any organization. Yet, in our view, information technology is only one part of the total picture and far from a panacea for the challenge of knowledge management. IT is perhaps the only viable mechanism to connect large numbers of people based far apart and located in different time zones. Yet, like any powerful tool, IT can be used effectively, misused in wasteful ways, and even abused. It also is important to note that we live in an era of open systems and the interest of technology providers lies in making the technology available to as wide a customer base as possible rather than to only a select few. Thus, for most companies, IT platforms provide at best a temporary advantage. Sustainable advantage depends on how smart the company is in using the technology. That depends fundamentally on the social ecology of the organization. As the survey data in Figure 6.3 indicate, senior executives appear to echo our perspective. As Gelacio Iniquez, former chief information officer of Mexico-headquartered CEMEX, a global leader in the cement industry, aptly observed: "I don't like information technology! The interpretation of IT is really poor. I have never focused on the technology part. I understand the technical issues but I don't want them to be the center of our conversation. . . . it's a waste of time. During my stay in CEMEX, the center

Figure 6.3. Drivers of Knowledge Management: Survey Results from Senior Executives Within Global Fortune 500 Companies

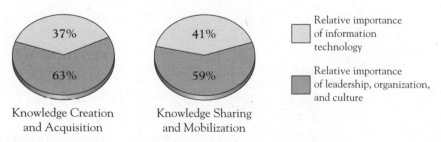

Note: Data are from one senior executive in each of forty-three companies.

of IT was human beings. We could leverage human beings and business processes with technology."[5]

Knowledge Accumulation and Knowledge Mobilization

The intellectual capital of any enterprise is a function of two primary factors: the stock of knowledge created or acquired by individual persons and units in the enterprise, and the extent to which such knowledge is shared and mobilized across the enterprise. A direct parallel exists between the concept of a company's intellectual capital and the concept of an economy's money supply. Economists measure money supply in the form of a multiplicative product of two factors: the stock of notes in circulation multiplied by the velocity of circulation. Similarly, we need to view an enterprise's intellectual capital as the product of individual- and unit-level stock of knowledge multiplied by the velocity at which such knowledge is shared and mobilized throughout the enterprise. This notion of a multiplicative relationship is rooted in the premise that an increase in either the stock of individual and unit knowledge or in the sharing of knowledge has an amplified impact on the magnitude of collective knowledge. Thus the knowledge management agenda of any firm must include boosting both the stock of knowledge among individuals and units and the sharing of knowledge across individuals and units.

As depicted in Figure 6.4, the knowledge accumulation task can be further disaggregated into three subtasks: *knowledge creation*, whereby individuals and units learn from their own internal experiments and experience; *knowledge acquisition*, whereby individuals and units acquire and internalize knowledge developed by entities outside the company, such as technology suppliers, competitors, and so forth; and *knowledge retention*, that is, minimizing the loss or leakage of internally created or externally acquired knowledge.

Also depicted in Figure 6.4 is the disaggregation of the knowledge mobilization task into a set of subtasks: *knowledge identification* (systematic uncovering of opportunities for knowledge sharing

Figure 6.4. Unpacking the Knowledge Management Agenda

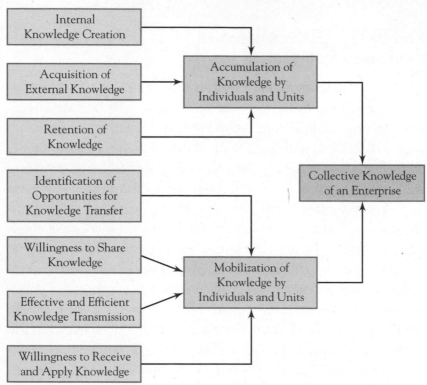

within the enterprise), *knowledge outflow* (creating willingness on the part of potential senders to share their knowledge), *knowledge transmission* (building effective and efficient channels for the actual transfer of knowledge), and *knowledge inflow* (creating willingness and ability on the part of potential receivers to accept and use knowledge from other units within the enterprise).

Pathologies and Pitfalls in Knowledge Management

The box summarizes the myriad pathologies and pitfalls that can (and often do) bedevil every element of the knowledge management process in many organizations.[6]

Common Pathologies and Challenges in Knowledge Accumulation and Knowledge Mobilization

Element of the Knowledge Management Process	Common Pathologies and Challenges
Knowledge Creation	• Complacence • Low decision-making discretion • Absence of an internal market for ideas (in most companies, lack of support from just one person, the immediate superior, kills the initiative)
Knowledge Acquisition	• Failure to be an early mover in knowledge acquisition • Inability to integrate and apply external knowledge
Knowledge Retention	• Employee turnover • Bleed-through of proprietary knowledge to competitors
Knowledge Identification (identification of knowledge-sharing opportunities)	• The "halo" effect (high performers have nothing to learn, and low performers have no good ideas of value to other units) • "Garbage in, garbage out" syndrome (a common result of asking all units to upload their "best" practices into shared databases)
Knowledge Outflow (willingness to share knowledge)	• "How does it help me?" syndrome • "Knowledge is power" syndrome • Incentives tied to internal relative performance
Knowledge Transmission (effective and efficient transmission channels)	• Mismatch between structure of knowledge and structure of transmission channels • Use of multiple links in the transmission chain
Knowledge Inflow (willingness to receive knowledge)	• "Not invented here" syndrome • Reluctance to acknowledge the superiority of peers

Barriers to Knowledge Creation

The creation of new knowledge is always a nonroutine activity, involving some risk and requiring some resources. When a company finds that it is falling behind in discovering new ideas, it is almost always due to one or more of three pathologies: lack of motivation to experiment (complacence); lack of freedom to experiment (low decision-making discretion); and premature killing of new ideas (absence of a market for new ideas).

Complacence. By definition, complacence implies a lack of dissatisfaction with the status quo and thus an absence of felt need to experiment with new ways of doing things. It is no wonder that many companies commit some of their biggest blunders during periods when their financial performance is exceptionally strong; some notable examples would be IBM and Digital Equipment in the early 1980s.

Low decision-making discretion. Another pathology that impedes knowledge creation is not giving people the discretion and slack resources needed to explore new pathways. Without discretion, there can be no experimentation. Consider, for instance, companies such as Ikea or Marriott. The need for consistency demands that the basic format and standard operating procedures be replicated in every location. Yet, if carried too far, such an approach would put the burden of innovation solely on corporate headquarters and rob the company of the creative potential of its global network.

Absence of a market for ideas. Typically, in any firm, requests for approval of and financial support for new initiatives must go through the normal hierarchical channels. The net result is that a denial by just one person, the immediate boss, almost always results in the demise of the new initiative. Contrast this scenario with that of the independent entrepreneur who can shop any idea to multiple venture capitalists. Not surprisingly, most radical innovations occur not within but outside established corporations.

Pitfalls in Knowledge Acquisition

Failures at successfully internalizing externally available knowledge result from one or both of two types of pitfalls: weaknesses in accessing external knowledge, and weaknesses in integrating and applying such knowledge once it has been accessed.

Failure to be an early mover in knowledge acquisition. Externally created knowledge is almost always available to multiple acquirers. That being the case, creating competitive advantage requires that the company be an early mover in identifying and acquiring the relevant knowledge. This is precisely the challenge faced by companies such as Cisco, Nortel, Nokia, among others, as they compete with each other to acquire innovative young ventures that are developing leading-edge technologies, products, and services for the emerging communications market. The relevant question for any of these companies is not whether it can acquire (or create) new technologies, but whether it can do so faster and better than its competitors.

Inability to integrate and apply external knowledge. By definition, all external knowledge is created in a different organizational setting and culture. Even if they are aware of and able to access the external knowledge, companies will not profit from it unless they are able to integrate and use such knowledge within their own organizational setting and culture. We observed this relatively common pitfall in a large pharmaceutical company that acquired a biotechnology firm. Unfortunately, the acquiring company lacked the organizational capability to successfully integrate the knowledge base from the biotech side with its own pharmaceuticals know-how. After many years of losses, the acquired biotechnology firm had to be divested.

Pitfalls in Knowledge Retention

Companies face two types of challenges in dealing with the retention of knowledge created internally or acquired from external sources.

Employee turnover. Useful and proprietary knowledge can be lost through the departure of people who possess such knowledge either voluntarily (due to dissatisfaction) or involuntarily (due to downsizing or layoffs during recession periods). Any company whose employee turnover is higher than the average for its industry runs the risk of significantly depleting the return on its investment in knowledge creation.

Bleed-through of proprietary knowledge. Another risk is the conversion of proprietary knowledge into a commodity, which can result from the leakage of such knowledge to competitors or alliance partners who could become future competitors. Otis Elevator rues to this day its post–World War II joint venture with Toshiba, now a major global competitor in the elevator industry. Toshiba got its start in the elevator industry by drawing heavily on staff and technology from the Otis joint venture.[7]

Pitfalls in Identifying Opportunities for Knowledge Sharing

As noted earlier, knowledge cannot be shared between or among units unless the source and target units or an intermediary recognize both the existence of leading-edge knowledge in the source unit and its potential value for the target unit. Two common pathologies prevent companies from uncovering a large proportion of knowledge-sharing opportunities.

The "halo" effect. This effect manifests itself in the form of a generalized belief that a unit with good financial performance has little to learn and a lot to teach, whereas a unit with poor financial performance has little to teach and a lot to learn. We have observed this syndrome most often in subsidiaries that have strong financial performance in major markets, such as the United States, Japan, or Germany. The halo effect, when coupled with arrogance and complacence, can make the situation for these subsidiaries rather perilous.

"Garbage in, garbage out" syndrome. In studying a major service sector company, we discovered that this company had established a knowledge management system for sharing of best practices. Units were encouraged to enter information about what they regarded as their own best practices into this internally public database. As it turned out, this database became less a forum to share knowledge

and more a forum to engage in one-upmanship; no unit wanted to appear as if it had nothing to offer. The result, in the words of a senior manager, was that the database became flooded with "a lot of garbage" rather than becoming a catalog of validated and truly best practices.

Pathologies That Block Knowledge Outflow

There are at least three pathologies that can seriously inhibit a source unit's willingness to share valuable know-how and information with peer units: the "how does it help me?" syndrome, the "knowledge is power" syndrome, and incentive systems that reward relative performance.

"How does it help me?" syndrome. This syndrome manifests itself when units view sharing knowledge with other units as a diversion of scarce time, energy, and resources away from managing their own business. For instance, in our study, a marketing subsidiary in a multinational company was clearly more successful at generating new orders than most other peer units within the company. Any efforts by managers within this leading-edge unit to share their best practices with peer units would certainly have benefited those other units, but, within the unit itself, such efforts were perceived as an incurred cost without any compensating benefits. What managers in this unit really wanted to do was to remain focused on increasing their own competence base and not get distracted by the abstract notion of helping peer units catch up.

"Knowledge is power" syndrome. Managers and units within every company operate in a state of both cooperation and competition vis-à-vis each other. This natural tension has several sources. First, corporate resources are always finite, and units must compete with each other to get their requisite share. Second, given the fact of pyramidal structures, managers are well aware that they compete with their colleagues for promotion to higher-level positions. Finally, at least some senior managers have a high need for power and value greater relative power for its own sake. The ubiquity of these

phenomena implies that preserving an asymmetric distribution of power in one's own favor is often viewed as advantageous by those managers who are able to do so.

This pathology is illustrated well by the case of Alpha, a Europe-headquartered global engineering company. At the time of our interviews, the company had three business areas (BAs). Each BA president had complete responsibility for his business globally—except North America. In North America, all operations reported to the president of Market Area (MA)-North America who reported directly to the CEO. The three BA presidents disagreed with this arrangement, advocating that the MA-North America position be abolished and they be given direct control over activities in this region. The net result was an extremely limited transfer of technological know-how from Europe to North America. As one BA president explained: "People know that it is the BAs who create the technology and control it. They also realize that, in the middle of the technology pipeline between BA headquarters and MA-North America, there exists a control valve. The hands on that control valve belong to us. We can open that valve or we can keep it shut. Sooner or later, people are going to realize where the power in this company lies. Of course, we want to share our know-how with North America, but we will really do so only after we have obtained complete control over them."

Incentives tied to relative performance. In our research, we came across one company in the retail industry that relied heavily on the performance of different locations relative to each other in determining the incentive bonus for unit general managers. Coincidentally, within this company, the heads of two neighboring areas were married to each other. Interviews revealed that these two general managers had chosen not to share some of their best ideas even with each other. If incentives tied to relative performance can have this level of inhibiting impact on knowledge sharing between two managers who are married to each other, imagine the barriers they can create in the sharing of knowledge between managers who are simply colleagues.

Barriers to Effective and Efficient Knowledge Transmission

Assuming that valuable knowledge exists within a unit and that managers in this unit are motivated to share this knowledge with peer units, the next hurdle in the knowledge-sharing process is to ensure that effective and efficient transmission channels exist. At least two pathologies can lead companies to create or rely on transmission channels that are highly inadequate for the task at hand: a mismatch between the structure of transmission channels and the structure of the knowledge to be transferred, and the use of multiple links in the transmission chain.

Mismatch between structure of knowledge and structure of transmission channels. As discussed earlier, knowledge exists in several forms: information, codified know-how, and tacit know-how. Instead of tailoring the channel to the type of knowledge being transmitted, many companies select the transmission channels on an ad hoc and almost random basis. In these cases, much knowledge transmission tends to be either highly inefficient or highly ineffective.

As an example, consider the case of a global product manager at one of the companies in our study. This company sells a relatively small number (less than two thousand annually) of very expensive machines, often as part of large greenfield projects. Thus, in any particular geographic market, for any particular type of machine, the number of units sold can vary significantly from one year to the next. This product manager wanted to collect market knowledge to develop production plans for the following year. Falling into the trap of relying on the most efficient (but not necessarily effective) communication mechanism, he sent a message to all sales subsidiaries asking for their forecasts for next year's sales. The response was deadly. Even after two reminders, less than 20 percent of sales subsidiaries had sent back any response. When we interviewed the presidents of the sales subsidiaries, they indicated that it was not possible to develop accurate forecasts a year in advance, so that sending back single point forecasts would be misleading. They could, of course, have developed a probability distribution of likely sales next year, but, as this would require communicating complex judgment-level knowledge, the sales unit presidents felt that the product manager should have arranged a face-to-face meeting (or, at least, a lengthy telephone discussion) rather than merely sending out an impersonal message. As one of the sales unit heads who did send back a reply indicated to us: "I hope that he (the product manager) does not actually believe in the forecast figures that I have sent to him. It's nothing but garbage. I sent it in because he was pestering me to respond."

Use of multiple links in the transmission chain. Between any source unit and any target unit that have useful knowledge to share, the number of intermediary links can vary enormously. As an example of how companies often create superfluous (and thereby counterproductive) links in the knowledge chain, consider the case of another company in our study. The norm in this company was that the sales units "own" the customers within their territories and that nobody else from the company was permitted to contact the customers directly. One of the unfortunate results was that global product managers learned about customers' evolving needs through the eyes and ears of the sales units rather than directly from the customers. In other companies, we observed the method of attempting transfer of best practices from one unit to another solely through a dialog among the unit general managers rather than through direct interaction between the operating personnel in the source unit (the knowledge holders) and their counterparts (the knowledge users) in the target units.

Pathologies That Block Knowledge Inflow

Other common pathologies diminish managers' willingness to seek and welcome incoming knowledge from other parts of the organization.

The "not invented here" (NIH) syndrome. The roots of the NIH syndrome, a chronic malady in many organizations, lie in ego-defense mechanisms that cause some managers, particularly those with successful track records, to erect a mental barrier to any novel idea coming from a source outside their own unit. In our research, we encountered this syndrome in one of the world's leading consumer products companies. At the time of our interviews, the very successful Japanese subsidiary of this company had gained a reputation for being totally closed to any idea originating elsewhere in Asia.

Reluctance to acknowledge the superiority of peers. Even in situations where managers may privately concede the superiority of a practice originating elsewhere in the organization, ubiquitous power struggles lead some managers to deny that the know-how of peer units is unique or valuable. Such power struggles often get magnified in companies where the CEO believes strongly in a high level of autonomy for and competition among SBUs. Overreliance on the SBU concept may be good for building knowledge islands, but it does little to build bridges across these islands.

The Social Ecology of a Knowledge Machine: The Case of Nucor

As of 2007, Nucor Corporation had been one of the most innovative and fastest-growing steel companies of the previous three to four decades. As an example of how a knowledge machine works, we see Nucor as a far more interesting company than, say, Accenture or McKinsey, because unlike professional service firms whose only output is knowledge, Nucor's end product is steel, a tangible and non-differentiable commodity. Yet for much of the three decades from 1970 onward, Nucor was a knowledge machine par excellence.[8]

Since the late 1960s (until the recent upturn in steel prices due to the rapidly growing demand from China and India), the U.S. steel industry has faced numerous problems, such as substitution by other materials, foreign competition, slowing of demand, and strained labor relations, and has reported one of the poorest profitability and growth records in the American economy. Yet, despite operating in a fundamentally troubled industry, during this time period Nucor enjoyed an annual compounded sales growth rate of 17 percent, all generated organically. Furthermore, the company's profit margins were consistently well above industry medians, and average annual return to shareholders exceeded 20 percent. (See the next box for a business profile of Nucor Corporation.) Nucor achieved this phenomenal and sustained success by excelling at a single task: creating and mobilizing knowledge in order to become and remain the most efficient producers of steel and steel-related products in the world. It did so by developing and constantly upgrading three competencies that were both strategic and proprietary: plant construction and start-up know-how, manufacturing process know-how, and the ability to adopt breakthrough technologies earlier and more effectively than competitors.

Nucor Corporation: A Business Profile

Products: Steel and Steel-Related Products

Summary Financial Statistics

Year	Sales ($ millions)	Earnings per Share ($)[a]
1970	51	0.005
1975	121	0.025
1980	482	0.14
1985	758	0.17
1990	1,482	0.22
1995	3,462	0.79
2000	4,757	0.95
2006[b]	14,751	5.73

[a] Adjusted for stock splits

[b] Worldwide steel prices increased dramatically from 2002 onwards, leading to significantly improved profitability at almost all steel producers. For example, U.S. Steel saw its earnings per share rise from $0.83 per share in 2002 to $11.88 per share in 2006.

Nucor's Performance During 1970–2000 Cannot Be Explained by External Factors

External Factors	Comments
Industry structure	The median profitability and growth rate of the steel industry was among the lowest of all sectors in the U.S. economy.
Access to minimill technology	Entry barriers into the minimill segment were significantly lower than those into the integrated steel mill segment. Further, the standard practice of minimill technology suppliers was to offer their technology on a nonexclusive basis to all customers, including technology first movers such as Nucor.
Access to raw materials	Nucor purchased scrap steel through third-party agents at market prices.
Access to locations	Nucor located its plants in farm areas. Such locations were anything but scarce.
Access to distribution channels	Nucor used nonexclusive third-party steel service centers (50 percent of sales) as well as direct selling (50 percent of sales) to powerful OEMs that faced almost no switching costs.
Brand name and market power	Steel was a commodity product where Nucor's market share was less than 10 percent, giving it almost no market power to charge premium prices.

Knowledge Accumulation at Nucor

Knowledge creation. Nucor's success at knowledge creation derived from three elements of its social ecology: superior human capital, extremely high-powered incentives, and significant empowerment, coupled with considerable tolerance for failure and a high degree of accountability.

At Nucor, accessing superior human capital began with the company's policy of locating plants in rural areas, which tended to have an abundance of hardworking and mechanically inclined people. Nucor was a leading employer in these locations and offered a top-of-the-line compensation package, enabling it to attract an unusually large pool of applicants for every job opening (for example, twelve hundred applicants for eight job openings at the plant in Darlington, South Carolina). As a consequence, the company was able to use stringent selection criteria to hire conscientious, dedicated, goal-oriented, self-reliant people. Furthermore, Nucor built on this foundation of superior human capital by investing in continuous on-the-job multifunction training.

Superior human capital ensures that people have the intrinsic ability to excel at tasks assigned to them. By itself, however, it does not ensure that people will be inclined to keep pushing the boundaries of knowledge rather than merely executing their current routines, albeit flawlessly. Nucor cultivated hunger for new knowledge through its extremely high-powered incentive system for every employee, from the production worker to the corporate CEO. (See the next box for a synopsis of Nucor's incentive systems.) As summarized in this box, there was no upper cap on the incentive payouts. Payouts for production employees averaged 80–150 percent of base wage, making them the best-paid workers in the steel industry.

Nucor's Incentive System

Nucor provided employees with a performance-related compensation system. All employees were covered under one of four basic compensation plans, each featuring incentives related to meeting specific goals and targets.

1. *Production Incentive Plan:* Employees involved directly in manufacturing were paid weekly bonuses on the basis of the production of their workgroups, which ranged from twenty-five to forty workers

each. Every workgroup included not only the production workers but also maintenance personnel and the production supervisor, all of whom received the same percentage of base wage as the bonus. In other words, the bonus was given not on the basis of an individual's output but on the basis of the group's output. Even if only one worker's tardiness or attendance problem caused the group to miss its weekly output target, every member of the group was denied the bonus for that week. No bonus was paid if the equipment was not operating. Further, the bonus was paid only for output that met quality standards and was based on a comparison between actual and "standard" output. For each workgroup, once the standard output was determined, the standard was not revised unless a significant change in the production process resulted from a source other than the workers in the bonus group. While there were no upper caps, in general, the production incentive bonus had averaged 80–150 percent of the base wage. Further, each production group's weekly output and the bonus received were visibly displayed at the front entrance to the factory.

The incentive plan was designed to induce highly disciplined behavior from every member of the workgroup. A group member who was late by five minutes or longer lost the bonus for the day. One who was late by thirty minutes or absent for any reason, including sickness (with the exception of four forgiveness days per year) lost the bonus for the entire week.

2. *Department Manager Incentive Plan:* Department managers were the immediate superiors of the production supervisors and, in turn, reported directly to the general manager of their plant. Nucor department managers earned an annual incentive bonus based not on the performance of their own departments but on that of the entire plant to which they belonged. The targeted performance criterion here was return on assets (ROA). Every plant operated as a stand-alone business unit and was expected to realize a 25 percent or better return on the assets employed within that plant. In recent years, these bonuses had averaged more than 80 percent of base salary.

3. *Non-Production and Non-Department Manager Incentive Plan:* This bonus was paid to all plant-level employees other than the general manager who were not on one of the first two plans. Its participants included accountants, engineers, secretaries, clerks, receptionists, or any of a broad number of employee classifications. The bonus was based primarily on each plant's return on assets and was paid out on a monthly basis. The ROA data as well as the bonus payout figures were posted visibly in the employee cafeteria. In recent years, this bonus had averaged around 25 percent of base salary.

4. *Senior Officers' Incentive Plan:* The designation "senior officer" included all corporate executives as well as plant general managers. Their base salaries were set at less than what executives received in comparable companies. A significant part of each senior officer's compensation was based on Nucor's return on stockholders' equity above a certain minimum level. On the upside, officers' total compensation could be several times base salary. On the downside, their compensation could be only base salary and therefore significantly below the average pay for this type of responsibility.

These incentives motivated Nucor's employees to push the boundaries of manufacturing process know-how in several ways. First, because incentives were a function of production output, employees could earn higher bonuses only by discovering or inventing new ways to boost productivity. Second, because the incentive payouts depended only on output that met quality standards, employees were motivated to develop process innovations that would help them "do things right the first time." Finally, because the magnitude of the bonus payouts was not limited and employees' discovery of new process innovations had no adverse impact on resetting the standards, people were stretched to keep pushing the frontiers of manufacturing process know-how.

Attracting and recruiting superior human capital and offering them high-powered incentives helps ensure that people are able and eager to innovate. However, creating an effectively functioning social ecology for knowledge creation also requires that they have the necessary freedom to experiment—and even fail—with new ideas. Nucor created such freedom by regularly pushing the limits to which its organizational structure could be made and kept flat. Its organization consisted of only four management layers, which, for a multibillion-dollar company, was radically flat. In addition, Nucor had only twenty-two people, including executives as well as clerical and other staff, located at the corporate head office. All other employees worked for and were responsible to one of the company's twenty-plus business units. The flatness of Nucor's structure implied that all of the business unit general managers reported directly to corporate headquarters without any intervening layer, such as group vice presidents. Similarly, the typical production supervisor was responsible for a team of twenty-five to forty people.

Whenever employees are encouraged to experiment, there is always the possibility of failure. A company that does not tolerate failure will severely inhibit experimentation. On the other hand, a company that only has failures will not survive. Thus a knowledge creation ecology requires high tolerance for failure within a context of very high accountability. The following observation by Ken Iverson, Nucor's architect, its CEO from 1965 until 1996 and its chairman until 1999, illustrates how Nucor cultivated a culture of experimentation within a context of accountability:

> We try to impress upon our employees that we are not King Solomon. We use an expression that I really like, and that is—good managers make bad decisions. We believe that if you take an average person and put him in a management position, he'll make 50% good decisions and 50% bad decisions. A good manager makes 60% good decisions. That means 40% of those decisions could have been better. We continually tell our employees that it is their responsibility to the company to let the managers know when they make those 40% decisions that could have been better. . . . The only other point I'd like to make about decision making is, don't keep making the same

bad decisions. . . . Every Nucor plant has its little storehouse of equipment that was bought, tried, and discarded. The knowledge we gather
from our so-called "failures" may lead us to spectacular success.[9]

Knowledge acquisition. Nucor was consistently the steel industry's
first mover in acquiring and adopting breakthrough technologies. It
was not only the first American company to adopt the minimill
technology but also the first company in the world to make flat
rolled steel in a minimill and to commercialize thin-slab casting.

Being a first mover in adopting breakthrough process technologies is always risky, and particularly so in an extremely capital-
intensive industry such as steel. Despite these risks, Nucor not only
pioneered technology adoption within its industry but also succeeded in commercializing these technologies earlier and faster
than competitors. The company's extraordinary success in technology acquisition over three decades can be traced back to various aspects of its abilities, mindset, and behavior. Specifically, Nucor had
its operating personnel deeply involved in the assessment of emerging technology options, and had a unique and proprietary ability to
remove the bugs in absorbing, implementing, and commercializing
the acquired technologies.

As described earlier, Nucor's social ecology drove every employee to search for better and more efficient ways to make steel and
steel-related products, so that, relative to competitors, Nucor's operating personnel had a deeper mastery of this industry's manufacturing processes. Nucor built on this foundation by employing a
unique approach to technology adoption decisions. Whereas other
steel companies sent senior executives and staff engineers to analyze emerging technologies being developed by equipment suppliers, Nucor's technology adoption decisions were made by teams
composed not only of managers and engineers but also of operators.
As a result, Nucor's technology assessment teams came to the
equipment suppliers with a significantly deeper knowledge of technology as well as operational issues. Further, given an effectively
functioning social ecology for knowledge creation, the teams also

had greater confidence in the company's ability to resolve unknown bugs that would inevitably appear during the process of implementing and commercializing the new technology. In short, when assessing new technology options, Nucor not only understood the associated risks and returns more clearly than other companies, it also had justifiably greater confidence in its ability to reduce the risks and increase the returns during the process of technology absorption.

Nucor's ability to excel at knowledge acquisition is illustrated well by the company's lead in the adoption of thin-slab casting technology. Until the mid-1980s, minimills could not produce high-end flat steel products serving the needs of automotive and appliance customers; the flat steel market was the monopoly of integrated steel producers. Nucor made history in 1987 by building the first minimill (in Crawfordsville, Indiana) that could make flat steel, an innovation that moved the company into the premium segment of the steel industry. In the Crawfordsville plant, Nucor gambled on the thin-slab casting technology developed by SMS Schloemann-Siemag, a German company that had demonstrated this technology in a small pilot plant but had not yet proved it commercially. According to our interviews with an SMS executive, technical staff from over a hundred steel companies had visited SMS to explore the technology. Yet, in a seemingly bet-the-company move, it was Nucor that first adopted the thin-slab casting technology. Nucor's investment in the Crawfordsville plant almost equaled stockholders' equity for that year and represented approximately five times the company's net earnings. Despite some initial hiccups, Nucor succeeded and, by 1997, had built two more minimills that use the thin-slab casting process. Despite the fact that Nucor obtained this technology from SMS by signing a nonexclusive contract with an additional technology flow-back clause, the first plant built by a competitor using this technology appeared in 1995, fully eight years after Nucor's pioneering effort.

Knowledge retention. Companies often lose sizable chunks of the knowledge they have created or acquired through the voluntary or involuntary departure of people possessing such knowledge. Nucor orchestrated an ecology to protect itself against such loss of knowledge by successfully implementing a policy of no layoffs during recessions and by cultivating very high loyalty and commitment among its personnel, thereby reducing voluntary turnover.

Nucor maintained a policy of not laying off or furloughing people during business downturns. Unlike other companies, when recession hit, Nucor reduced the workweek rather than the workforce. Given the company's rural locations and its role as the leading employer in these locations, employees regarded a reduced workweek and the correspondingly lower wages as a relatively attractive option.

Notwithstanding the no-layoffs policy, reductions in workweek did cause a reduction in wages and could potentially have weakened the fabric of loyalty and commitment between the employees and the company. To counter this threat, Nucor's workweek reductions were always accompanied by a "Share the Pain" program. Under this program, any reduction in workers' compensation due to workweek reduction was accompanied by a disproportionately greater reduction in managers' compensation and an even greater cut in the CEO's pay (by as much as 70 percent). In this way, Nucor's response to recessions ended up strengthening the mutual sense of trust and respect within the company. It further cemented this loyalty and commitment through policies such as college scholarships for employees' children, a profit-sharing plan, and a stock purchase plan. The net result of the high loyalty was that Nucor enjoyed the lowest turnover rate of any company in its industry. Moreover, Nucor's very low personnel turnover provided additional benefits in its efforts toward knowledge accumulation. First, the no-layoffs policy motivated employees to pursue process improvements vigorously without the fear of eliminating jobs—either their own or those of their colleagues. Second, the prospect of a long-term relationship between the employee and the company strengthened mutual incentives to invest in the building of human and organizational capital.

Knowledge Mobilization at Nucor

Knowledge identification. As described earlier, in every company, different units typically have different levels and areas of competence. Given this disparity across units, a company's success in creating value through knowledge sharing depends first on its ability to identify best practices. Nucor was fervently systematic in measuring the performance of every work group, every department, and every plant, and in making these performance data visible inside the company. With this routinized measurement and distribution of performance data, the units themselves, as well as corporate headquarters, could uncover the myriad opportunities to share best practices.

Creating willingness to share knowledge. Nucor's social ecology was fashioned to encourage eagerness on the part of every work unit to proactively share best practices with all the others. The genesis of this ecology lay in Nucor's reliance on group-based incentives at every level in the organization from shop-floor workers to plant general managers. More concretely, the bonuses of shop-floor workers depended not on their own performance but on the performance of their entire twenty-five- to forty-person workgroup, which was responsible for a particular stage of production. Similarly, within every plant, department managers earned an annual incentive bonus on the basis of the performance of the entire plant, rather than just their own department. For plant general managers as well, incentive bonuses depended on the performance of the whole company rather than on their individual plants. These group-based incentives, in the context of their large magnitude, implied that any individual's (or unit's) superior competence would have a minimal impact on the bonus amount if the performance of other individuals (or units) in the bonus group remained subpar. This provided a strong motivation to share one's own best practices with peer units in order to boost the performance of the entire bonus group.

Constructing effective and efficient transmission channels. A company's knowledge base encompasses a wide spectrum of different types of knowledge, from highly structured, codified, and thus mobile forms of knowledge (such as monthly financial data) at one end to highly unstructured, tacit, and embedded forms of knowledge (such as plant start-up know-how) at the other. Generally, information technology is a highly effective and efficient mechanism for the transfer of codified knowledge, and Nucor, like many organizations, exploited the power of information technology. Unlike many organizations, however, Nucor also excelled at the sharing of non-routine and unstructured forms of knowledge—a key driver for building and leveraging core competencies. The ability to transfer these forms of knowledge requires much richer transmission channels (such as face-to-face communication and transfer of people). Later we describe in some detail Nucor's approach to constructing these knowledge transmission channels within each plant as well as across plants.

Nucor's goal within each plant was to build a social community that promoted mutual trust and open communication, where each person knew everyone else personally and they all had ample opportunity to interact with one another. Achieving this goal began with the company's policy of keeping the number of employees in each plant between 250 and 300. This small number, coupled with employees' long tenure, fostered the development of very high interpersonal familiarity. In addition, each plant general manager routinely held annual dinner meetings for groups of twenty-five to a hundred at a time so that every employee could be invited. Like traditional New England town meetings, the format was free and open, but there were ground rules. All comments were to remain business-related and not be aimed at specific individuals. Management guaranteed that it would carefully consider and respond to every criticism and suggestion.

In the arena of interplant knowledge transfers as well, Nucor made use of a multiplicity of transmission channels. First, detailed performance data on each mill were regularly distributed to all plant managers. Second, all plant general managers met as a group with headquarters management three times a year (in February, May, and November) to review each facility's performance and to develop formal plans for the transfer of best practices. Third, not only plant general managers but also supervisors and machine operators periodically visited each other's mills. These visits enabled operations personnel, the true holders of process knowledge, to go beyond performance data and to understand firsthand the factors that make particular practices superior or inferior. Fourth, recognizing the special difficulties inherent in the transfer of complex know-how, Nucor engaged in the selective assignment of people from one plant to another, "detailing" them on the basis of their expertise.

In addition to sharing best practices across existing plants, Nucor strove to be systematic in recycling its process innovations from existing plants to new plant start-ups. The company's philosophy was to build or rebuild one or more mills a year. Rather than rely on outside contractors to build mills, Nucor put together a small group of engineers from their existing mills. This internal group was responsible for designing and managing the construction of new building or rebuilding projects. To top this off, the actual construction on these projects was done by workers hired from the local area, who were informed that they were likely to be recruited to subsequently operate the mills.

Nucor's unique approach to building or rebuilding mills yielded a handful of benefits. First, the existing process knowledge was recycled into new plant design and construction. Second, the construction workers knew that they were building the plant for themselves and had a natural incentive to build it well. Third, knowledge of the underlying process technology embedded in the plant design was carried over in the workers' minds from the construction phase to the operations phase. Fourth, the company was able to accumulate an additional core competence in plant start-up know-how.

Creating willingness to receive knowledge. Earlier, we discussed how the "not invented here" syndrome and the reluctance to acknowledge the superiority of others often inhibit units from seeking or welcoming knowledge from peer units. Nucor's social ecology countered such tendencies in two ways. One, both the magnitude and the steepness of the incentives signaled strongly to people that relying solely on one's own efforts at knowledge creation (and, thus, slower competence development) was likely to be very costly in terms of forgone compensation. Two, by making every unit's performance highly visible to others in the company, Nucor made the workplace somewhat of a fishbowl. Strong performers were showcased while weak performers were exposed and were likely to feel the intense heat of peer pressure.

Figure 6.5 depicts how Nucor's social ecology is the foundation of its position as the leading knowledge machine within the steel industry.

Guidelines for Building an Effective Knowledge Machine

In a world in which the half-life of new knowledge is becoming ever shorter, an effective knowledge machine must excel at two central tasks: creating and acquiring new knowledge, and sharing and mobilizing this knowledge throughout the global network. Unless new

Figure 6.5. Nucor's Knowledge Machine

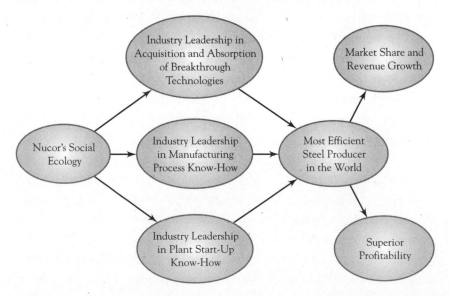

knowledge can be continuously generated, the enterprise will soon find itself playing tomorrow's game with yesterday's tools. And unless knowledge is pumped efficiently throughout the network, the enterprise will not only pay the price of reinventing the same wheel many times over, it will also risk becoming prey to competitors who are able to replicate and roll out the innovator's ideas more rapidly.

Building on our discussion of the pathologies that bedevil many companies and our in-depth analysis of Nucor Corporation, we would advance the following guidelines that companies can use to move toward becoming a more effective and efficient knowledge machine.

Maximizing Knowledge Accumulation

Stretch goals. The easier the target, the less the need for new approaches. Hence, the starting point for developing a culture of knowledge creation is to set targets that cannot be achieved without some innovation. As Jack Welch, CEO and architect of General Electric from 1981 to 2001, observed, "If you do know how to get there—it's not a stretch target. . . . The CEO of Yokogawa, our Japanese partner in the Medical Systems business, calls this concept 'bullet-train thinking,' i.e., if you want a ten-miles-per-hour increase in train speed, you tinker with horsepower—but if you want to double its speed, you have to break out of both conventional thinking and conventional performance expectations."[10]

Provide high-powered incentives. By definition, stretch goals increase a person's level of risk in performing a task. Unless the potential reward matches the higher level of risk, it would be irrational for smart people to stay with the company. Stretch goals without high-powered incentives are likely to end up as lofty exhortations lacking the real power to stir people to seek new approaches.

Cultivate empowerment and slack. Stretch goals and high-powered incentives stimulate a demand for new ideas. In contrast, empowerment and slack are supply-side tools that play a critical role in increasing the creative capacity of subunits. The 70-20-10 rule at Google is a good example of how empowerment and slack foster innovation. Under this rule, people at Google are expected to spend 70 percent of their time on core projects, 20 percent on projects that extend the core, and 10 percent on new projects that may even be unrelated to the core business.[11]

Equip every unit with a well-defined sandbox for play. By definition, creating a culture that values experimentation means encouraging a willingness to undertake risks. Although senior executives, in concert with the board of directors, must from time to time undertake bet-the-company types of moves, it would be suicidal to have a culture in which the power to make such moves is widely distributed in the firm. One mechanism that permits companies to sidestep this dilemma is to give people or units well-defined sandboxes—discretionary areas—for experimentation and play. If an experiment proves to be a fiasco, the risks are likely to be acceptable. Again, Google's 70-20-10 rule is one example of a well-defined sandbox. Here are some other potentially useful, although hypothetical, examples of a sandbox approach: a hospitality chain could specify that every hotel general manager has the freedom to experiment with 10 percent of the rooms on the property, or a specialty retailer could specify that every store manager has the freedom to design and create one new merchandise department. Within the limitations of the sandbox, employees can experiment with their own new, even radical, ideas.

Cultivate a market for ideas within the company. As the abundance of new product failures bears witness, not all new ideas that at first appear promising will prove to be promising in hindsight. Every company must have a screening mechanism to determine which of the multiplicity of ideas emerging from the various subunits deserve further support and which should be abandoned. When we read or hear about senior managers stifling good ideas emerging from the subunits, the problem usually is not that the company has screening mechanisms, but that the screening mechanisms are dumb rather than intelligent. Companies must accept the fact that no single individual, howsoever smart, has a monopoly on wisdom. Ac-

cordingly, they should create a culture whereby an idea that is rejected by the would-be innovator's immediate superior can still be
shopped around to other potential sources of support within the
company, without creating a perception of insubordination.

Maximizing Knowledge Mobilization

Ban knowledge hoarding and turn knowledge givers into heroes. Cultural
norms that treat knowledge hoarding as a violation of the company's
core values and treat knowledge givers as heroes serve as the best
foundation for building an ecology that maximizes knowledge sharing. Every company must decide, implicitly or explicitly, which resources are to be treated as if they were corporate resources ("loaned,
licensed, or leased" to the business units) and which resources are to
be treated as if they were owned by the business units. Consider, for
example, brand names such as Nokia, Honda, or IBM. In each of
these companies, business units use the corporate brand name as a
critical resource. It is clear, however, that the brand name does not
belong to any single business unit or subsidiary; in fact, through their
actions, subsidiaries are expected to strengthen the value of the
brand. To maximize knowledge sharing, companies must view knowledge similarly, that is, to treat knowledge as a corporate resource that
cannot be hoarded by any particular subsidiary or business unit. GE,
Procter & Gamble, and the consulting firm McKinsey & Company
are examples of companies with such policies.

Rely on group-based incentives. Group-based incentives, especially
if they are high-powered, reinforce knowledge-sharing as a cultural
norm. In companies such as Nucor, incentives take the form of cash
compensation. In other companies, such as Google, they take the
form of sizable stock options. The power of group-based incentives
stems from the fact that they direct attention to maximizing the performance of the whole system rather than just an individual unit. Of
course, a potential disadvantage of group-based incentives is that
they can lead to free-rider problems. However, this side effect can
be minimized by ensuring that incentives are large enough to be

meaningful, making individual behavior visible within the group, and giving the group power to expel the chronic underperformer.

Invest in codification of tacit knowledge. By definition, codified knowledge is much more mobile than tacit knowledge. A company's investment in codifying tacit knowledge can have very high payoffs. Consider the case of Marriott International. Over the three years 2007–2009, the company has indicated that it plans to add almost one hundred thousand rooms to its portfolio.[12] Assuming 1.3 employees per room, this means an addition of 130,000 new people, not counting replacement of any that may leave during this period. In order to sustain this level of growth effectively and efficiently, Marriott has been compelled to convert virtually everything it knows about the operation of a hotel into codified SOPs (standard operating procedures). Without codification, the outcome would be either highly inconsistent service or a much slower growth rate. Companies, of course, must recognize that there is a limit to how much knowledge can be codified. Even in a company such as Marriott, many critical types of knowledge (for example, how to integrate acquisitions) must remain at least partly tacit. Notwithstanding these limits, the returns from investments in codification can be very high in terms of both a wider sharing of knowledge within the enterprise and of spurring the development of new knowledge. Often, an explicit mapping of what we know today is the basis for discovering what we do not know.

Match transmission mechanisms to type of knowledge. The transfer of all knowledge occurs through one or more of the following transmission mechanisms: exchange of documents, conversations and coaching, and transfer of people and teams who carry the knowledge in their heads. To be both effective and efficient, transmission mechanisms must be tailored to the type of knowledge being transferred. By *effectiveness* of transmission channels, we refer to the extent to which the receiver receives what the sender has sent. And by *efficiency* of transmission channels, we refer to the cost and speed of the transmission channels. Document exchange (paper-based or electronic) is a highly effective and efficient mechanism for sharing codified knowledge. For transmitting tacit knowledge, however, this mechanism is often highly ineffective. In contrast, conversations and personnel transfers are relatively inefficient mechanisms for knowledge sharing; yet for the transmission of tacit knowledge, they may be the only effective mechanisms. Efficiency without effectiveness, as we know well, is useless.

Conclusion

The criticality of intellectual capital in creating competitive advantage is widely recognized today. However, in an era of relentless technological revolutions and ubiquitous benchmarking, intellectual capital by itself represents an ephemeral advantage. In the emerging economic landscape, competitive advantage must be recreated every day. To do this, companies must focus on creating and mobilizing new knowledge faster and more efficiently than competitors and not get caught up in the mechanics of measuring the worth of what they already know. As we have demonstrated, a company's ability to function as a knowledge machine depends not merely on the sophistication of its information technology infrastructure but more critically on the social ecology that drives the behavior of its people and teams. It is relatively easy for competitors to neutralize or even leapfrog a company's information technology architecture, but this infrastructure is only part of the equation. Creating a social ecology that is free from the many ubiquitous pathologies identified in this chapter is a much harder task. As the Nucor analysis points out, creating such an ecology is indeed feasible. However, doing so requires building a whole ecosystem of complementary and mutually reinforcing organizational mechanisms. The bad news is that this is a tough challenge to overcome. The good news is that, for the very same reasons, any success in building an appropriate social ecology will also be particularly hard for competitors to neutralize.

7

Dynamics of Global Business Teams

We are all angels with only one wing. We can only
fly while embracing each other.
                          —*Luciano de Crescenzo*[1]

In 2006, the merger of Arcelor and Mittal Steel created the world's first truly global steel company with operations on four continents and industrial presence in twenty-seven countries. ArcelorMittal, the post-merger enterprise, employed 320,000 people, produced 118 million tons of steel (more than two times the output of the second largest steel company), and had revenues of $88.6 billion in 2006. An immediate effect of the merger was to give the combined company greater resources, a larger market share, more production facilities, a wider footprint, more research and development centers, more distribution outlets; in short, a significantly larger scale and scope in all respects than either of the two predecessor companies.[2] As we've noted earlier, however, this kind of enlarged global presence does not automatically become global competitive advantage. A firm must be able to convert "scale" into "economies of global scale" and "scope" into "economies of global scope." Creating strategic advantage out of the merger would require a rationalization of research and development, procurement, manufacturing, and many aspects of marketing, sales, and distribution. It would also require the creation of organizational mechanisms to sell and deliver consistent quality and standard solutions to multinational customers. Last but not least, it would require ongoing and constant efforts to share best practices across the enlarged enterprise so that innovative ideas to improve quality or reduce costs at one facility could be rolled out and become a reality at other facilities. None of these opportunities to create value can be realized without establishing scores of cross-border teams consisting of members from different subsidiaries and functions. These teams would be akin to horizontal networks that would need to function smoothly and effectively with only a limited amount of hierarchical command and control.

For Groupe Schneider, a French multinational enterprise that specializes in electrical distribution, industrial control, and automation, managing global customer accounts (such as major automobile companies, petrochemical firms, and large pharmaceuticals) is an ongoing opportunity as well as a key challenge. When, for instance, Schneider automates a production line or installs a control and monitoring system for General Motors in China, Schneider's performance and service is expected to be just as efficient and effective in Beijing as in Detroit. Consistency across countries must be cultivated in every step of the value chain: project engineering, delivery, operator training, equipment maintenance, and after-sales service. Schneider has created focused cross-border and cross-functional account management teams to provide a coordinated and consistent response to global customers, such as General Motors, Renault, Volkswagen, and Merck. The same kind of management issues paralleling Groupe Schneider's dominate virtually all business-to-business marketing contexts (for example, IBM, Cisco Systems, McKinsey & Company, and even Procter & Gamble in its dealings with global retailers such as Wal-Mart).

ABB's competitive advantage is derived, in part, from its ability to transfer knowledge across countries. To quote Sune Karlsson, business area manager for ABB's Power Transformers unit in the 1990s: "Our most important strength is that we have 25 factories around the world, each with its own president, design manager, marketing manager, and production manager. These people are working on the same problems and opportunities day after day, year after year, and learning a tremendous amount. We want to create a process of continuous expertise transfer. If we can do that, it is a source of advantage none of our rivals can match."[3] ABB created dozens of cross-border teams to facilitate knowledge transfer within and across its many lines of business.

In each of the cases described so far—the integration of Arcelor and Mittal, Schneider's management of global customer accounts, and ABB's efforts to maximize knowledge transfer across countries—the underlying organizational thread is the global business team concept.

Multinational enterprises typically use one of three formal organizational structures: a global area structure, a global product structure, or a global matrix structure. We will not analyze the pros and cons of these structural alternatives here—formal organization is a topic that already has received considerable attention.[4] In addition, formal organization is merely the starting point in addressing the challenge of building and managing the global network. One could even argue that the formal organization is not the most critical variable. Companies often focus on issues of organizational structure not because they are the most critical but because they are the easiest to tackle. Changing the organizational structure—the boxes and arrows—is much easier than changing people's motivation, behavior, and mindset. However, it is the informal organization that makes the formal structure work. Having the right organizational structure but inappropriate informal processes and behavior is much more problematic than having an inappropriate organizational structure but the right informal processes and behavior.

No matter whether the formal organization is based on an area, a product, or a matrix structure, every company operating across borders requires a multidimensional perspective. Less formal and more flexible processes are needed to make the global network function effectively and efficiently. The concept of the global business team (GBT) is one of the most important of these process mechanisms. *By a GBT, we refer to a cross-border team of individuals of different nationalities, working in different cultures, possibly in different businesses and across different functions, who come together to coordinate some aspect of the multinational operations on a global basis.* These teams go by a variety of names: global management committees, world business boards, global product councils, global launch teams, global quality task forces, global supply chain teams, global purchasing forums, and global strategy teams, among others.

It is virtually impossible for any global enterprise to leverage its global presence (exploit economies of global scale and scope, maximize knowledge transfer, and so forth) without understanding and mastering the effective management of GBTs. Yet, in our survey of seventy GBTs, only 18 percent of the teams considered their performance "highly successful" and the remaining 82 percent fell short of intended outcomes. In fact, fully one-third of the teams in our sample rated their performance as largely unsuccessful.[5] In this chapter, we focus on the dynamics of creating and managing high-performing GBTs by addressing two issues: why GBTs often fail, and what steps can be taken to make GBTs more effective and efficient.

Why GBTs Fail

Some of the same problems that plague domestic teams also plague global teams: misalignment in the goals of individual team members, missing elements in the bundle of knowledge and skills necessary for the team to accomplish its task, and lack of clarity regarding team objectives. (The box presents details regarding these three problems.) However, given geographic distance, differences in languages, and cultural diversity, GBTs face some unique problems that relate to the difficulty of cultivating trust among team members and of overcoming communication barriers.

Generic Challenges Faced by Any Business Team

Business teams—whether domestic or global—often fail to accomplish their expected objectives because of misalignment in the goals of individual team members, lack of needed knowledge and skills, or lack of clarity regarding team objectives. Here is a quick review of these problems, which—although not unique to global teams—may well rise up to plague them, and may complicate efforts to deal with the problems discussed at greater length in the body of the chapter.

Misalignment in the goals of individual team members. The goals of individual members can often be at cross-purposes. This was the case when, following a cross-border acquisition, a U.S.-based industrial products firm set up a team consisting of plant managers from different countries belonging to both companies in an effort to consolidate the number of manufacturing facilities. Despite the clarity of its charter, the team had a great deal of trouble in rationalizing the plants on a global basis because individual plant managers were intent on protecting their territory and operations rather than working for the larger good. The team lacked a leader with clout to steer it toward tough decisions; thus its goals were misaligned, and the team was derailed.

As this example highlights, members often join teams with incompatible goals. An unresolved conflict between members' personal goals and corporate goals is almost always a sure path to failure.

Team lacks the needed bundle of knowledge and skills. Business problems generally assigned to a team are multifaceted and complex in nature. To tackle such problems successfully, every team must include among its members the requisite bundle of differentiated knowledge and skills. This fact is often overlooked.

For instance, take the case of Epsilon and Alpha (one European and the other American), two companies of equal size in a certain segment of the process machinery industry. In the 1990s, these two companies merged with the goal of becoming a globally dominant player. As one of the major post-merger tasks, the new company created a cross-border product development team charged with designing a common product line. The outcome was dismal failure. Not only did the team take twice as long as expected to accomplish its task, the basic platform for the new product was overengineered and too costly to manufacture. A post-audit revealed that the team had had no representation from any marketing subsidiary from any country. Rather, the team had gotten wrapped up in pursuing technological sophistication for its own sake and in accommodating the historical proclivities of the technology experts on the different sides of the Atlantic.

Lack of clarity regarding team objectives. This problem manifests when team objectives are defined too vaguely. For example, a major European multinational firm in the luxury goods sector formed a cross-border, cross-business team and defined the team's charter as "Make the principal customer more productive." The team struggled to understand the meaning of this mission and gave up on the project after two frustrating meetings.

If the team charter is unclear or incorrectly specified, team members can get caught in a web of fruitless and directionless debates as almost any plan of action or point of view can be rationalized or justified within a vague charter. And without a framework for conflict resolution, team members also have difficulty resolving substantive disagreements. In such a context, team deliberations can easily degenerate into endless debates with no resolution.

Even when the charter is reasonably clear, teams can fail if the broad charter is not translated into specific, measurable goals. In the absence of specific performance targets, teams struggle to define intermediate work plans and often flounder or lose momentum. In addition, they lose the opportunity to celebrate small victories along the way, which are critical in building confidence, momentum, and social cohesion among team members.

Inability to Cultivate Trust Among Team Members

By definition, trust implies "the willingness of a party to be vulnerable to the actions of another party based on the expectation that the other party will perform a particular action important to the trustor, irrespective of the ability to monitor or control that other party."[6] Trust is critical to the success of GBTs in that it encourages cooperation and minimizes unproductive conflict.[7] Owing to differences in national backgrounds, subsidiary affiliations, and functional orientations, each member of a GBT brings a unique cognitive lens to the group. If harnessed effectively, cognitive diversity can yield significant synergies, developing a collective wisdom that is superior to that of any single individual. However, without cohesiveness and a sense of trust, team members may shy away from revealing their true beliefs or, if they do share their viewpoints, they may not be heard. In one way or another, the absence of mutual trust is likely to turn a team's cognitive diversity into a liability rather than an asset.

If we look at the drivers of trust, it becomes obvious why GBTs tend to be particularly prone to start their work with problems of low trust among their members. Among the myriad factors that determine the level of trust among people, some of the most important are individual characteristics, quality of communication, and the broader institutional context. More specifically, research has discovered that, on average, people tend to trust each other more when they are more similar to each other, have more frequent communication with each other, and operate in a mutually embraced institutional and cultural context that imposes tough sanctions for behaving in an untrustworthy manner.[8] For obvious reasons, GBTs by their very nature suffer from severe limitations along all three dimensions. Not surprisingly, in our experience, when GBTs fail, it is usually the case that the team process was not managed with an eye toward cultivating trust.

Communication Barriers

One of the more obvious barriers to the effective functioning of GBTs arises from differences in geography, language, and culture.

Physical distance. With members living in different countries, separated by time zones and physical distance, and with often-conflicting schedules, arranging team meetings generally poses logistical challenges. Undoubtedly, technology (e-mail, teleconferencing, and videoconferencing) can enable team members to work together despite geographic distances. However, technology is a complement to and not a substitute for team meetings. Face-to-face meetings foster familiarity and build trust among team members, something that is not easily established through virtual meetings. Without the benefit of seeing body language and directly experiencing others' reactions, the emotional dimension—critical to team success—gets unduly downplayed. Moreover, certain types of team deliberations simply require face-to-face meetings. Brainstorming, for instance, requires unstructured, free-form interaction over an extended period of time, something not readily achieved in the context of a virtual meeting.

Language. Inability to understand what the other person is saying is always a barrier to communication, and is much more likely to occur in cross-cultural settings. One extreme would be a team in which every member speaks a different language and has very poor facility in a common language such as English. This team would undoubtedly require interpreters, who, regardless of their skills, are unlikely to capture the full richness of body language and other forms of nonverbal communication.

Even in the case of global teams where people speak the same language, differences in semantics, accent, tone, pitch, and dialect across different countries can become impediments. For example, whereas "table a motion" means to postpone discussion in the United States, in the United Kingdom it means to discuss the issue right away. If language barriers are not adequately dealt with, the likelihood of creating an atmosphere conducive to open and candid sharing of different viewpoints and perspectives is greatly diminished, as is the team's ability to achieve creative solutions.

Culture. The diversity of cultures frequently represented in GBTs means that their members are likely to bring different values, norms, assumptions, and patterns of behavior to the group. Consider, for example, cultural differences along the spectrum from "individualistic" to "collectivistic" norms for decision making.[9] The need for consensus deemed critical in collectivistic cultures is a relatively low priority in individualistic cultures. Take the case of a GBT in which some of the members come from highly individualistic cultures (such as the United States and Britain) and others from highly collectivistic cultures (such as Japan and Venezuela). Unless the differences in assumptions and beliefs inherent in such cultural diversity are explicitly addressed during team process, the cohesiveness of the members is likely to suffer—which, in turn, will impede the group's effectiveness.

The results of our survey of fifty-eight senior executives from five U.S. and four European multinational enterprises (see Table 7.1) confirm the importance of the global team challenges identified here. It should be emphasized that the unique problems of global teams—difficulty in establishing trust and communication barriers—tend to exacerbate the generic problems found in all teams, which were outlined in the preceding box.

Table 7.1.   The Challenge of Managing Global Business Teams

	Importance of the Task in Determining the Effectiveness of GBTs[a]	*Ease or Difficulty in Accomplishing the Task*[b]
Cultivating trust among team members	6.52	6.06
Overcoming communication barriers	6.35	5.56
Aligning the goals of individual team members	6.04	5.44
Ensuring that the team possesses the needed bundle of knowledge and skills	5.62	4.66
Obtaining clarity regarding the team objectives	6.05	4.61

Note: Data are from our survey of fifty-eight senior executives from five U.S. and four European multinational enterprises.

[a] Importance of the task in determining the success of GBTs was rated on a 1–7 scale, where 1 = "Not at all important" and 7 = "Very important."

[b] Ease or difficulty in accomplishing the task was rated on a 1–7 scale, where 1 = "Very easy" and 7 = "Very difficult."

Figure 7.1. A Framework for Designing and Managing High-Performing GBTs

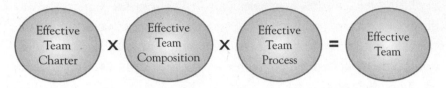

The performance of any team is a function of correct choices and decisions in three areas: team charter, team composition, and team process. Needless to say, the same three elements must be managed for a GBT, with a view to overcoming the unique challenges facing such teams. As Figure 7.1 indicates, a clear charter without an appropriate mix of team members would lead to failure. Similarly, when team composition is sound but team process is not, team effectiveness will suffer.

Defining Team Charter

As we have discussed in the preceding section, given diversity and distance, GBTs are prone to communication problems and trust issues. Hence, structuring and obtaining clarity regarding the team charter is particularly critical to the success of GBTs. In this context, three questions need to be addressed: Is the charter defined correctly? Is the charter framed correctly? And, is the charter clearly understood?

Is the Charter Defined Correctly?

The substantive validity of any GBT's charter depends, of course, on the specific situation. One of the first agenda items for any GBT (or, if the team is yet to be formed, for those championing it) must be to explicitly discuss and ensure that the team agenda is defined clearly and correctly. Many GBTs are doomed from the start because this step is skipped or the issues are not resolved. Likewise,

GBTs that succeed tend to be the ones where this step is given proper weight.

Consider the case of a European company that manufactures industrial components. This company set up a global customer account team to coordinate its marketing, sales, and service offerings to one of its largest customers. In setting up this team, the company was actually being proactive. Since this particular customer engaged in decentralized and uncoordinated sourcing, there was no immediate or obvious external pressure to establish a global account team.

At its first meeting, the team identified three possible alternative objectives: to encourage and help the customer move toward coordinated global sourcing at a faster pace, to offer the customer global volume discounts and thus lower prices, and to offer a more attractive bundle of products and services based on a better, more comprehensive understanding of the customer's global needs than the customer's individual buying locations might have. After considerable discussion, the team decided against the first two alternatives and embraced the third. The logic behind this choice was as follows. They decided that the first alternative was imprudent because, other things being the same, a coordinated supplier is better off dealing with an uncoordinated rather than a coordinated customer. However, were the customer to move toward coordinated global sourcing in the future, this team, having the advantage of its internal coordination, would be able to read the signals and quickly offer an appropriate response. The second alternative was rejected because the company's prices were already competitive, and the company's long-term strategy was to win on the basis of superior products and services rather than lower prices. The third alternative was seen as the most appropriate because it accomplished several key corporate objectives simultaneously: it eliminated internal price competition across plants, thus boosting gross margins; it made the company's product and service offerings to the customer more comprehensive; and it dramatically enhanced the company's ability to respond appropriately to any moves that the customer might make toward coordinated global sourcing.

Is the Charter Framed Correctly?

Ensuring that the charter is framed correctly is a more subtle challenge. By *framing* we mean the way an idea is expressed or a problem is formulated. Decision issues can usually be framed in multiple ways. In turn, different frames for the same problem can result in different outcomes.[10]

As the following example illustrates, it is generally best to frame the GBT's charter in terms of the company's position vis-à-vis the external marketplace (the external capital market, the external product market, and so forth), rather than giving it an internal focus—so as not to exacerbate any preexisting internal conflicts.

Take the case of a U.S.-headquartered consumer products company that assembled a global manufacturing team with the objective of rationalizing the company's production network. Given this objective, there were at least two alternative ways of framing this team's charter. Consider the following approach: "The team's charter is to cut costs by reducing the number of factories in our worldwide network from fifteen to nine and downsizing the workforce." Compare this to the following approach: "We want to be the clear industry leader in terms of creating customer and shareholder value. This goal requires that we be world-class in manufacturing—better than our best-in-class competitor in terms of cost, quality, and service. Given these targets, the team's charter is to propose the optimal network of factories for our business."

We contend that framing the charter using the second approach would yield more benefits than the first. An external and somewhat broader focus tends to encourage benchmarking and fosters greater creativity. Furthermore, in this case, it would provide a more compelling rationale for making the tough decisions inherent in any manufacturing rationalization and consequent workforce reduction.

Is the Charter Clearly Understood?

When teams have frequent face-to-face meetings, it is possible to iron out ambiguities in the team charter. If the team members meet less often, it becomes critical that the team charter be made clear so as to facilitate effective delegation of task execution. Because of physical distances, global teams tend to meet face-to-face on an infrequent basis. Given the resulting communication problems, it is imperative that the team members clearly understand the specifics of the charter—in particular, the scope of the project, the expected deliverables, and the time line.

The team must be sure about the raison d'être for the project. It must be clear from the start which topics are included within the charter, and which topics the team should not be working on. Furthermore, the expected output of the team must be fully understood as well. Is the team expected only to make recommendations on the best course of action? In such a case, what would be the process of hand-off to the implementation phase? Or is the team expected not only to make recommendations but also to implement the decisions? And, in terms of the time line, the team must know if it is intended to be an ongoing, permanent team. Such teams might be needed where the project scope extends to the implementation of decisions. Or is it a one-shot project team? Such teams might be appropriate when the project involves only recommendations, in which case the team must be clear about when it is expected to complete its assignment.

The successful experience of an industrial products firm illustrates this point. This company formed a team to examine the organizational design of its global businesses. Several meetings were arranged between the sponsor and the team members to ensure that the team charter was clearly understood. The project scope was defined to include the following:

- Analysis of the current organizational design across the company's five growth platform businesses. Part of the diagnostic phase was to focus on the question of whether a single organizational design made sense across the five businesses.
- External benchmarking of world-class global organizations and latest research on the best approaches to organizational design.

- Development of the business case and recommendations for an organizational design that would optimize global growth potential across the five businesses. Recommendations were to include approaches to capture potential synergies across the businesses in such areas as R&D, information technology, human resources, and supply chain.

The project was also intended to be a personal learning experience, designed to make the team members experts on the topic of organizational design and to expose them to the many facets of globalization within the company's businesses. Furthermore, the team members were explicitly told not to work on nongrowth business units or subsidiaries, or to reformulate the global strategies of the five businesses.

Finally, two deliverables were expected from the project team: a set of recommendations on the optimal worldwide organizational design for the five major growth platform businesses, and a presentation of the team's key findings, including a process or a methodology for tackling potential global organization issues.

The specificity of the objectives, project scope, and deliverables, along with the time spent at the start of the project getting the team members to internalize and accept the charter, helped them stay on course and make progress.

Configuring the Global Business Team

Differences among team members along such factors as age, education, organizational tenure, and personality imply that every team, global or nonglobal, has some degree of diversity within its composition. Global business teams, however, are characterized by particularly high levels of diversity for at least three reasons. First, they are composed of members from diverse cultural and national backgrounds. Second, team members generally represent different subsidiaries whose agendas may not be entirely congruent. In fact, given the ever-present possibility of consolidation or rationalization, peer subsidiaries often coexist in a state of both collaboration and competition vis-à-vis each other. Third, because team members often represent different functional units (marketing and manufacturing, for example), their worldviews and priorities may well be quite different.

Is the inevitably high level of diversity within a typical GBT a necessary evil that must be curbed or a source of strength that must be cultivated? We believe that the answer to this question depends very much on which dimension of diversity we focus on: "cognitive diversity" or "behavioral diversity."[11]

Ensuring Requisite Cognitive Diversity

We use the term *cognitive diversity* to refer to diversity in the substantive content of various team members' perceptions of the challenges and opportunities associated with the task, the options to be evaluated, and the optimal course of action. Cognitive diversity can originate from a variety of underlying factors, such as differences in nationality, subsidiary history and charter, and functional background. Differences in nationality can account for substantive differences on such issues as whether Chinese customers are positively or negatively disposed toward Japanese brands, what is the potential size of the market at the bottom of the pyramid in Mexico, and so forth. Differences in subsidiary histories and charters can account for substantive differences on such issues as whether Singapore, Hong Kong, Shanghai, or Tokyo should serve as the optimal location for the company's Asia region headquarters, whether or not it matters that Norway is not yet a member of the European Union, and so on. Similarly, variations in functional background can account for substantive differences on such issues as the relative importance of market-pull versus technology-push considerations in the company's new product development efforts.

Since no single team member can ever have a monopoly on wisdom, cognitive diversity is almost always a source of strength. Divergent perspectives foster creativity and a more comprehensive search for and assessment of options. There is, of course, an obvious requirement: the team must be able to integrate the diverse perspectives and actually come to a cohesive resolution. Otherwise, the GBT's outcome may well be little more than intellectual development of the team members. However, because there have been no decisions and no action, the business itself has not benefited from the GBT's collective wisdom.

How Nissan Motor's newly appointed CEO Carlos Ghosn managed this company's transformation after Renault acquired a 36.6 percent equity stake in Nissan in 1999 vividly illustrates the power of global business teams as well as the importance of ensuring that each team has a well-defined charter and composition. In the words of Ghosn:

> At a certain point in negotiations between the two companies, there was a discussion about how they would work together. Renault's negotiators assumed that the best way forward would be to set up a series of joint ventures, and they wanted to discuss all legal issues surrounding a joint venture: who contributes what and how much, how the output is shared, and so forth. The Nissan team pushed back; they wanted to explore management and business issues, not legal technicalities. As a result, negotiations were stalled. Renault CEO Louis Schweitzer asked me if I could think of a way to resolve that impasse. I recommended abandoning the joint venture approach. If you want people to work together, the last thing you want is a legal structure that gets in the way. My solution was to introduce informal cross-country teams (CCTs). Some teams focused on specific aspects of automobile manufacturing and delivery—there was a team focusing on product planning, for instance, and another on manufacturing and logistics. Others focused on a region—Europe, for instance, and Mexico and Central America. All told, we created 11 such cross-country teams. . . . The experience of the Mexico regional CCT is a good example. At the time of the alliance in early 1999, Nissan was suffering from overcapacity in the Mexican market because of sluggish domestic demand and flagging sales of the aging

Sentra model to the United States. Renault, on the other hand, was thinking of reentering the Mexican market, which it had abandoned in 1986. Putting managers from both companies together meant that they immediately recognized the synergy opportunity. In just five months, they put together a detailed plan for producing Renault cars in Nissan's plants. Just over a year later, in December 2000, the first Renault models rolled off the assembly lines.[12]

Minimizing the Negative Effects of Behavioral Diversity

We use the term *behavioral diversity* to refer to diversity in language as well as culture-driven norms of behavior—body language, the importance of "face," norms regarding punctuality, norms regarding team representation, and so forth. Behavioral diversity causes differences in how people communicate what they believe in—rather than in the content of the beliefs themselves. Consider, for example, a cross-border business team in a Franco-American company such as Alcatel-Lucent or Accor. The typical norm in most American teams is that the most senior member will present the team's perspective. In contrast, in most French teams, the typical norm is exactly the opposite—it is often the most junior member who presents the team's perspective. Thus, unless the members of the Franco-American team are sensitized to these differences, misunderstandings can easily emerge, blocking and distorting current and future communication.

We believe that behavioral diversity is best regarded as a necessary evil—something that you cannot avoid per se but whose effects you must attempt to minimize or even eliminate through language training and cultural sensitization. There is no merit whatsoever in accepting or sustaining communication barriers that do nothing but foster misunderstanding.

Creating a GBT often poses a dilemma. On many occasions, in order to secure needed substantive knowledge and skills, a GBT may need to include one or more individuals whose behavioral skills and attitudes fall short of the ideal. In this case, the team composition generally should be driven by substantive considerations; process mechanisms should then be designed to deal with the consequent challenge of team integration. This issue is discussed later in this chapter.

The Question of Team Size

What is the optimal size of a team? As a guideline, we would argue that the ideal size of a GBT is one that can ensure the required knowledge and skill base with the smallest number of people.

There is an inherent dilemma in deciding on the optimal team size. On one hand, the need to represent every required knowledge and skill would call for a very large team. On the other hand, the need to work smoothly and develop mutual trust would call for a small one—very large teams can be cumbersome and dysfunctional. It is not only difficult to foster broad participation and bring out diverse viewpoints in a very large group, it is also hard to unify the group in determining a meaningful course of action.[13] An effective solution to this dilemma is to establish a core team and supplement it as needed with other individuals, thereby creating an extended team. Membership in the core team would be limited to a relatively manageable number, say, up to about ten members. Then, if the core team requires input from other individuals, they could be brought into the team on an ad hoc basis. In this way, the extended team could include all relevant knowledge-holders and stakeholders, both within and outside the organization. For example, many global customer account teams include even the corporate CEO on an ad hoc basis. This becomes necessary if, for instance, the team needs to renew its contract with the customer and it is deemed important for the company's CEO to meet with the CEO of the customer organization.

If, for some reason, the core team itself must be very large, then it is best to break the team into subteams, each assigned to tackle specific aspects of the overall team objectives. This is the approach adopted by companies such as Microsoft when creating teams for major product development projects. Given the need to integrate multiple technologies and market requirements, having a large team is often unavoidable. However, the large team is then disaggregated into a number of subteams, each of which focuses on a specific product feature, component, or market adaptation.

Selection of Team Leadership

Structuring the leadership of a GBT involves decisions on three roles: team leader, external coach, and sponsor.

Choice of an effective team leader. Despite increasing emphasis on self-management by teams, in the case of cross-border teams, self-management is often problematic. The organizational, linguistic, cultural, and physical distances that separate members of a typical GBT can create severe communication barriers, impede the development of trust, and contribute to the misalignment of team members' goals. These are just some of the reasons why the role of the team leader in a GBT can be pivotal.

An effective GBT leader is likely to be one who has a big stake in the outcome of the project. Other important qualities of an effective GBT leader would include credibility as a result of proven track record; conflict resolution and integration skills; and expertise in process management (diagnosis, situation assessment, option generation, and option evaluation).

Need for an external coach. By *external coach*, we refer to someone who serves as an ad hoc member of the team and who is an expert on process, as opposed to content. The more complex and challenging the process to be managed, the greater the need for and value added by an external coach. It is precisely these considerations that led GE Capital to recognize the value of using an "integration manager" to help ensure rapid and effective post-merger integration. By design, this integration manager is someone other than the business leader and comes from outside the particular business.

Figure 7.2 provides a framework that depicts the conditions under which a GBT is likely to find using an external coach beneficial. The need for such a coach is likely to be particularly high when the process management task is complex and the team leader's own process management skills are inadequate. This framework would have been useful in the case of a global financial services firm that set up a cross-border task force to rationalize the number of its offices spread across three continents. The appointed leader, a team member with a major stake in the project's outcome, turned out to be rigid, inflexible, and overbearing to the point that alternative views and ideas were stifled. The team was able to make progress only when an external coach was brought in.

Role of the GBT sponsor. The sponsor of a GBT is typically a senior executive who has a credible interest in, even a passion for, the success of the team. A sponsor who performs this role well can

Figure 7.2. Conditions Under Which GBTs Need an External Coach

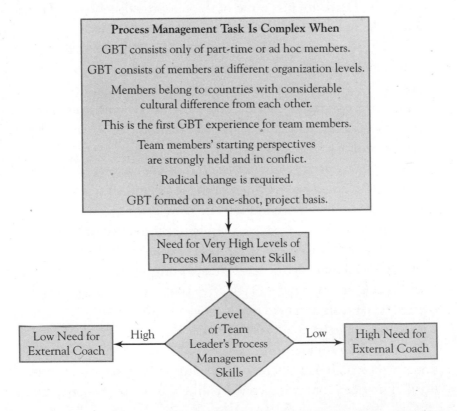

indirectly encourage open and candid conversations among team members drawn from different countries and cultures. Among the responsibilities of the sponsor are to clarify and interpret the charter; clarify performance expectations and deliverables; provide ongoing guidelines, input, and support; facilitate access to needed resources; manage political roadblocks on behalf of the team; be an intellectual sounding board on content; review team progress; and hold the team accountable.

Managing Team Process

Team charter, team composition, and team process work as a system to determine team effectiveness. Having a clearly and correctly defined charter and an optimally constituted team is merely the foundation. Without skillful management of the team process, even a well-constructed team is more than likely to fail in accomplishing its objectives.

In the case of a global business team, the primary goals of an effective team process would be to facilitate open and rich communication among the team members and to cultivate a culture of trust among them. Accomplishing these goals is essential in order to exploit the full potential of the diverse knowledge and skill base represented in the team, to integrate these diverse perspectives into creative, meaningful, and implementable solutions, and to further develop team members' knowledge, skills, and mindsets so that their participation in the GBT enriches them intellectually.

The following sections discuss the primary process levers that can be used to overcome communication barriers and to cultivate a culture of trust.

Overcoming Communication Barriers

We have argued earlier that global teams are particularly prone to communication barriers. Several process mechanisms can be used to overcome communication issues.

Language and cross-cultural training. To overcome barriers to communication created by the obvious linguistic and cultural distances separating members of the typical GBT, companies need to invest in language and cross-cultural training. Investments in language training reduce the need for third-party mediators such as translators and thus foster communication that is more direct, spontaneous, and free-form. The ABB Group provides a good example of how even halfway progress on linguistic skills can go far toward reducing communication barriers. Goran Lindahl, ABB's former CEO, was explicit in referring to his company's official language as "poor English"—to drive home the point that no one should be embarrassed to express an idea simply because their English is not perfect.

Investments in cross-cultural skills help GBT members in several other ways. A better understanding of team members' disparate cultures can be expected to improve the richness of communication; people would pick up the signals in each other's verbal and nonverbal communications more comprehensively and more accurately. Also, investment in cross-cultural skills can be expected to improve team members' ability to understand and respect diversity and turn it into competitive advantage.

Agreement on norms of behavior. Establishing ground rules that reflect the desired norms of behavior can serve as a powerful self-policing mechanism to overcome communication barriers, enrich the content of team discussions, and keep the team operating as an integrated network.

A global customer account management team created by a European industrial packaging company illustrates how explicit agreement on certain ground rules can facilitate a team's smooth functioning. This team established two ground rules: whenever a member of the account team had any meeting with the customer, that member would send a briefing to every other member of the team, and the customer's primary contact would be with one or more of the members of the global account team—no other employee of the firm was authorized to discuss or decide policy and strategy issues with the customer. These ground rules proved beneficial especially in circumstances when the customer tested the relationship. Occasionally, the customer would contact employees other than those on the account team, but the employees would always refer them to someone on the team. In cases where the global customer would contact different members on the account team about such issues as prices and delivery times, the ground rules ensured that the customer always got the same answer from each member.

Bias for data-driven discussions. In the absence of facts, people tend to resort to opinions. As everyone knows, discussions based solely or largely on opinions can easily degenerate into personal attacks. On the other hand, if the opinions are accompanied by factual data, conflicting ideas can be evaluated more objectively and are less likely to be viewed as personal attacks. Fact-based discussions encourage team members to be more forthcoming in sharing their viewpoints even if their views may be at odds with the prevailing wisdom.[14]

A global consumer products firm formed a cross-border team to recommend ways to improve the profitability of one of its global businesses. The team, with the help of a consulting firm, assembled a detailed fact base including the fundamental shifts in the industry, competitors' moves, and the company's current positioning. The concrete factual data helped elevate the team's level of discourse. Instead of denying the problem, shifting the blame to uncontrollable external factors, or focusing on individual personalities, the team was able to brainstorm and come to terms with the critical vulnerabilities in the company's competitive positioning. A clear agreement emerged that these vulnerabilities required immediate, decisive, and visible action.

Developing multiple alternatives to enrich the debate. Explicitly surfacing multiple alternatives is often very useful in ensuring the expression of diverse views within a GBT. The "dialectical inquiry" and the "devil's advocate" approaches are two of the well-recognized formal mechanisms aimed at the uncovering of multiple alternatives.[15] In a dialectical inquiry, for every potential solution, the team is instructed to develop a full-fledged counter idea based on different assumptions; then a debate ensues on the merits of the plan and the counter plan. In the devil's advocate approach, the team is told to critique a potential solution (but not necessarily to develop a full-blown counter plan). Both of these approaches can benefit the process as well as the outcome of team discussions by adding a sense of creativity while giving license to members to express different views.

The industrial products firm team (described earlier) used the approach of explicitly seeking multiple alternatives to draw out the intellectual diversity represented within the team. Their mission was to make recommendations on the optimal worldwide organization for the five major global businesses. For each global business, the team collectively generated three distinct organizational forms and assigned subsets of the team to develop the best set of arguments for each form. The resulting recommendations reflected the comprehensive discussions that followed each subteam's presentation of its approach to solving the problem.

Rotating the location for meetings. Rotating the geographic location of team meetings to different parts of the world is yet another mechanism to enrich the cognitive base of the team and also legitimize the expression of divergent viewpoints. In Chapter Five, we discussed the case of VeriFone, a market leader in the automation and delivery of secure payment and payment-related transactions. VeriFone used this approach to keep the top management team well informed about the global environment. The team, consisting of the CEO and his direct reports, would meet for five days every six weeks at different locations around the globe.[16]

Cultivating a Culture of Trust

As discussed earlier, global business teams are also particularly prone to perennially low levels of trust. Firms can engage in several process mechanisms to cultivate trust among team members.

Face-to-face meetings. It is critical that the first few meetings of a GBT occur in a face-to-face context. Other things being equal, the more deeply the members of any GBT know each other and understand each other, the greater the likelihood that they will trust one another. It is well known that different modes of communication vary in terms of the richness (or bandwidth, to use the current popular term) of communication that they permit. Face-to-face interaction enables the richest form of communication and can help develop a solid social foundation and mutual trust that can be subsequently leveraged through distance technologies.

In our interviews, the CEO of a global consumer products company underscored the importance of early face-to-face meetings in cultivating trust: "There is an enormous premium on good, clean non-bureaucratic communication and that depends enormously on a high level of trust. That's why at the start of the team process, you have to be together personally. You can't start them with memos or telephone calls or things like that. You've got to get the group together to know each other and get a level of comfort and trust with one another. After that you can resort to the phone calls and videoconferences."

Rotation and diffusion of team leadership. Rotating team leadership across the various decisions that a GBT may have to make is beneficial but it is even more important to diffuse team leadership for different GBTs across different countries. By rotating and diffusing team leadership across countries, managers in several subsidiaries learn to appreciate the need for cross-border coordination. Moreover, diffusion of team leadership creates mutual interdependencies across countries because typically a country manager will lead one GBT while acting as a contributing member in another. Mutual dependence does not eliminate all conflicts, but it certainly minimizes politicking and harmful conflicts, as managers are forced to iron out and resolve conflicts en route to achieving their objectives and outcomes.

To quote John Pepper, former chairman of the board of Procter & Gamble: "We felt that if each subsidiary manager also led a team, they would come to understand the value and challenge of working on a regional basis. We set up a brand team on Lenor, another on Pampers, another on Pantene, and so on. We assigned different country managers to lead these. Really wanting to get everybody into the fire so to speak in experiencing it. What made the teams work was the mutual interdependency that grew."[17]

Linking rewards to team performance. Consider two scenarios. In the first, the subsidiary manager's incentive bonus is based solely on country-level performance, even though part of the manager's time is devoted to being a member of a GBT. In the second scenario, this manager's bonus is partly linked also to the attainment of the expected outcomes of the GBT.

In the second scenario, the motivation of the team members to resolve conflicts and reach an effective solution would be higher since their incentive bonus depends on team outcomes as well. Thus in the second scenario, as compared to the first, there will be less incentive for team members to behave in a distrusting manner since such behavior would work against self-interest in terms of rewards. These considerations lie behind Procter & Gamble's policy to give explicit weight to both country and team performance in computing annual incentive payments to its country managers.[18]

Investments in building social capital. At any given time, a global firm typically has many GBTs working on different cross-border coordination issues. It therefore makes abundant sense for the firm to undertake corporate-wide initiatives to create interpersonal familiarity and trust among key managers of different subsidiaries. Such corporate-wide initiatives could take many forms: bringing managers from different subsidiaries together in executive development programs, horizontal rotation of managers across locations, and building language skills among these managers so that these "get to know each other" encounters have high value.

Unilever, the Dutch-British multinational, has used several mechanisms to build social capital among its employees. In each country, the company uses sophisticated recruitment techniques to attract the best and brightest local nationals to come and work for its subsidiaries in that country. Unilever then couples this foundation of local recruitment with a strategic expatriate program. This involves rotating high-potential executives across countries, across different tasks in a given function (such as advertising, selling, and brand management within the marketing function), and across different businesses (such as exposure to diverse businesses such as ice cream, tea, and detergents). These job rotations help build strong social networks. To quote Floris Maljers, the former cochairman and CEO of Unilever: "Exposure to another environment not only gives them [the expats] more know-how but also improves their 'know-who.' In addition, cross-postings between companies are very important for establishing unity, a common sense of purpose, and an understanding of different national cultures and attitudes."[19]

Unilever started its management development center, Four Acres, in the mid-1950s. Every year about four hundred executives from all over the world are selected and sent by the headquarters to Four Acres for learning and development. Each executive program typically consists of about thirty participants drawn from different subsidiaries and countries. One of the objectives of these courses is to help participants get reacquainted with old friends and make new friends.

Through careful attention to global human resource management—selection, training, and development of global managers—Unilever has attempted to build social capital. Such human resource initiatives build strong personal networks that can facilitate the smooth functioning of multiple GBTs.

Conclusion

GBTs have become a ubiquitous phenomenon among global firms. Yet making such teams achieve their intended outcomes is far from easy. The unique factors that cause GBTs to fail are communication barriers and difficulties in cultivating trust among team members. Correct choices in team charter, team composition, and team process can increase a GBT's likelihood of achieving its objectives. Our framework for designing high-performing GBTs is summarized in Figure 7.3.

When the GBT is composed of members with unique and distinct knowledge and skill bases drawn from different subsidiaries in

Figure 7.3. Effective Team Process

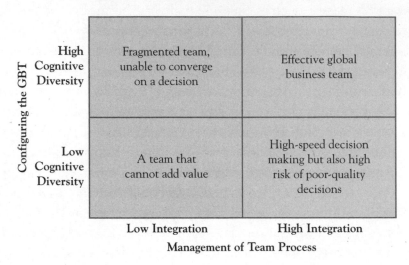

different countries, the potential for cognitive diversity is high. Since no individual has a monopoly on wisdom, such intellectual diversity constitutes a source of strength. However, intellectual diversity within a GBT almost always brings with it some degree of interpersonal incompatibility and communication barriers due to cultural and linguistic differences. Recognizing and anticipating these pitfalls, a company should put process mechanisms in place to enable the team to reconcile diverse perspectives and arrive at better, more novel solutions by integrating the best of individual members' ideas and contributions.

8

Globalizing the Young Venture

Bangalore, Singapore, Tokyo, Tel Aviv. These days,
they're not just vacation spots, they're home to
your clients, partners, and staff.[1]

—*Business 2.0*

As barriers to cross-border trade and investment come down and as people become more aware of customers, suppliers, and talent in foreign lands, an increasing number of young ventures are starting to go global early in their lives. A growing subset is even "born global" right from day one. It is important to note that this is true not just for information and online service businesses (such as Internet portals and search solution providers) but also for businesses that sell physical products (such as candles, bedroom furnishings, and even bulky furniture). Do these developments suggest that distance is dead? Would most young ventures now be better off if globalization were high on their strategic agenda? If not, what can go wrong? How should entrepreneurs decide if early globalization is right for their venture and, if so, how might they mitigate the hazards and increase the odds of benefiting from it? We address these and related questions in this chapter.[2] We start with a few examples that illustrate sharply the emerging global context within which today's entrepreneurs create and nurture new ventures.

In January 1996, two PhD students at Stanford (Larry Page, an American, and Sergei Brin, a Russian immigrant) began collaborating on a search engine called BackRub, so-named because of its unique ability to analyze the "back links" pointing to a given Web site. Two years later, in September 1998, their newly formed company, Google, opened its first office in Menlo Park, California. Another two years later, in 2000, Google was available in ten languages to enable users worldwide to conduct searches in their own native languages. The company went public in 2004. By 2007, Google was the world's largest Internet search and advertising company, with revenues exceeding $13 billion and a stock market value exceeding $160 billion.[3]

In 2003, two Scandinavian geeks (Niklas Zennstrom, a Swede, and Janus Friis, a Dane) created a little piece of software that would enable people anywhere in the world to communicate with each other easily and, if both parties were connected to the Internet, at zero cost. By 2007, their software and service, Skype, was available in twenty-eight languages and was used in almost every country in the world. Acquired by eBay, a Silicon Valley company headquartered in San Jose, California, Skype was run largely as an autonomous business from its own headquarters in Luxembourg, Europe.[4]

In 2005, three foreigners living in China (Irishman Ken Carroll, Canadian Hank Horkoff, and Briton Steve Williams) pooled their expertise in language training and technology to create ChinesePod, a Web and iPod-based Chinese language learning service. By 2007, millions of people in 110 countries were reported to be downloading free ChinesePod broadcasts. Several thousand of these were paying customers who subscribed to the company's premium service. The founders' parent company, Praxis, had already started a parallel service to teach people Spanish.[5]

In November 2005, Krishnan Ganesh, an Indian technology entrepreneur based in Bangalore, founded TutorVista with the goal of combining content, scientific pedagogy, and online teaching to bring high-quality content and personalized tutoring to schoolchildren around the world. Priced at $19.99 per hour ($99.99 per month for unlimited monthly tutoring), TutorVista provided personalized one-to-one tutoring in a variety of subjects. Voice-over-

IP and a digital writing pad enabled the tutor and student to engage in real-time conversation and to write, type, or draw with both of them able to see what was being written or drawn. By 2007, the company had attracted $15 million in venture capital funding and was serving paying students in the United States, United Kingdom, and India.[6]

In May 2007, Joe Burke, the owner of Extreme Outdoors, a Florida-based company specializing in elaborate outdoor kitchens, decided to make his eBay listings available worldwide. eBay had encouraged Burke to expand his market reach noting that the company's PayPal online payments service made it feasible and easy for merchants to collect payments in many currencies. Just two months later, Burke was getting 15 percent of his new orders from abroad. His customers included a happy Norwegian attorney who paid only $1,400 plus $500 in shipping for a grill that would have cost him $3,600 at his local retailer.[7]

In July 2007, two education and media entrepreneurs (Chris Whittle, an American, and Sunny Varkey, a Dubai-based Indian) teamed up to announce the formation of Nations Academy, a global network of sixty multimillion-dollar schools to be located in leading cities across the world. The network of high-end schools would have identical syllabi and would cater to the children of mobile executives who may need to uproot their families and move across borders—often. In addition to serving the unique needs of mobile parents, the schools would also emphasize the cultivation of an international outlook. All students would be expected to do four stints in sister schools in different countries.[8]

These examples provide vivid testimony in support of Tom Friedman's thesis that the world is indeed becoming flatter and that the barriers to cross-border business transactions are declining not just for large established companies but also for young ventures.[9] The next box highlights the multitude of factors that are increasing the upside and reducing the risks, costs, and hassles associated with globalizing the young venture.

Enablers of Early Globalization

- *Explosion of growth in emerging markets.* The much higher growth rates of emerging markets (more than double that of the developing economies) has resulted in a near-global acceptance of the notion that potential buyers and potential suppliers can exist anywhere in the world, not just in developed countries. This new reality has expanded the potential for early globalization for new ventures in both developed as well as developing economies.

- *Rapidly growing power and declining cost of Internet and communications technologies.* High-speed broadband connections are rapidly becoming the norm in not just developed but also many developing countries. China already has over 70 million broadband subscribers, equal to almost 50 percent of the total with Internet connections. Other complementary technologies already in use or just around the corner include mobile telephony (there are over 500 million mobile phone users in China and over 150 million in India), voice-over-IP and video-over-IP (as in Skype), broadband connections over the mobile phone, wide area networks, and fiber optic connections to the home and workplace.

- *Rapid spread of fluency in the English language.* Notwithstanding strong nationalist sentiments, English has now become the language of instruction at some of the best business schools in many countries where it is not the native language, including France, South Korea, and Japan. Developing English language fluency across the entire country has even become part of national policy in a country with more than 20 percent of the world's population— China. Fluency in a common language speeds up communication, fosters the cultivation of informal social ties, increases transparency, and thus reduces friction in cross-border collaborations.

- *Increasing speed and declining cost of transportation for goods as well as personal travel.* Shipping a full forty-foot-long container from Shanghai to Los Angeles now takes less than two weeks and costs only $2,800. The costs of shipping a container-load from Los Angeles to Shanghai are even lower because exports from China to the United States far exceed those from the United States to China. Thus containers returning back from the United

States to China have empty space ready to be sold at prices only marginally above variable costs.

- *Broader usage of global trading platforms such as eBay and Alibaba.* As illustrated by the case of Extreme Outdoors, the outdoor kitchen equipment company discussed above, these global trading platforms provide a complete marketing and sales infrastructure for the young venture at almost zero fixed costs and a ramp-up to cross-border sales measured in days rather than weeks or months.

- *Adoption of global online payment systems such as PayPal.* These payment systems radically speed up the time that it would take many young ventures to collect payments from customers while also significantly reducing the risks of nonpayment.

- *Rapid globalization of media.* The emergence of global media (such as CNN, CNBC World, Google AdWords) has made it easier, faster, and less expensive for a young venture to target advertising and promotional efforts to specific customer segments in a particular country.

- *Greater information transparency among potential buyers and sellers.* As almost every business, small or large, now has a Web page, search engines permit potential buyers and sellers to collect significant chunks of information about each other before deciding whether to explore the potential for a business transaction. This transparency vastly reduces the cost of search and the wasted time and effort that might otherwise get spent in talking with an inappropriate buyer or seller.

Early Globalization—a Double-Edged Sword

Even though the enabling conditions for globalizing the young venture are becoming more friendly, it is crucial to remember that doing so is full of not only promises but also perils. We focus first on the potential benefits that a young venture can reap from early globalization.

Potential benefits from early globalization. One of the most important benefits from early globalization can be rapid growth or even the transformation of an interesting but economically nonviable business idea into a viable one. The potential for rapid growth is illustrated well by the examples of ChinesePod and Extreme Outdoors cited earlier. The global market for lessons in Mandarin or high-end outdoor kitchens is much larger than in any single country, be it China or the United States. Because of scale effects, early globalization can also transform potentially nonviable ideas into viable ones. Imagine, for example, a product or service tailored to a micro-segment of the population which suffers from a rare type of illness. The market size for this product or service even within a large country such as the United States may number only in the thousands. However, on a global basis, the market size may be ten to twenty times larger, making the business venture much more economically viable.

A second important benefit from early globalization can be the rapid accumulation of competitive advantage in those situations where most potential customers are themselves multinational and would have a strong preference for a single global provider of the product or service across countries. This is clearly so in the case of new ventures designed to provide an enterprise application software or online service to large global companies. We discuss one such company, Approva Corporation, in some depth later in this chapter. Often, though not always, the business processes of large global companies tend to be globally standardized and globally integrated. Thus the software or online service may need to work globally in order for it to be of serious and sustained interest to potential customers.

A third important benefit from early globalization can be access to lower-cost human, capital, or physical resources without any sacrifice in quality. As is well known, virtually every new venture suffers from limited resources. Locating a high-cost activity in a relatively low-cost location can make a dramatic difference to the new venture's burn rate. This can not only enable the venture to be more price competitive but also reduce the risk of running out of capital prematurely. Given the growing power and declining cost of digital technologies, the range of activities that can be located in lower-cost locations is growing rapidly to include not only such routine tasks as data entry but also highly specialized tasks, such as data mining and strategic analysis. The case of TutorVista discussed earlier provides an apt example. Young ventures may also be able to reduce costs of capital by locating research and development activities within designated science parks in selected countries. Depending on the specific context, this may enable the young venture to obtain interest-free or low-cost loans from the local government.

Last but not least, early globalization can also serve as a potential source of learning for the new venture. Diversity across markets and cultures can encourage the young venture to absorb or create a wider array of technological, product, and process innovations as compared with staying within the relatively more homogeneous domestic market.

Notwithstanding the potential benefits of early globalization, one should never forget that it also has the potential to weaken the venture and even increase the risk that it may not survive. Nurturing a venture to success is in many ways analogous to nurturing a child. As with a child, the entrepreneur needs to guide the venture, to help it learn step-by-step, and to help it build the capabilities needed to go after big opportunities and to withstand tough competition. Doing so effectively is a balancing act. If you expect little, you are likely to get little. And if you overextend or push too hard, you run the risk of alienating customers and business partners and frustrating key employees, thus rapidly increasing the odds of an early failure. We identify below some of the major challenges associated with early globalization.

Challenges associated with early globalization. First, the young venture typically has little slack in terms of managerial, organizational, and financial resources. Cross-border expansion will almost always expose the new venture to greater market and cultural diversity and increase the complexity of the business. Often, setting up offices and operations in multiple locations will also increase the venture's fixed costs ahead of any economic benefits in terms of higher revenues or lower costs. As it is, young ventures often find themselves to be desperately short of managerial, organizational, and financial resources. Early globalization has the potential to deplete these resources at an even faster pace.

Second, the young venture often lacks market knowledge, channel access, and market relationships in foreign markets. As the experience of Wal-Mart's moves toward globalization illustrate (see Chapter Three), in the early stages, even large companies suffer from lack of local knowledge and established local relationships. For a young venture that may be struggling to build such knowledge, channel access, and relationships in the home country, the challenge of having to do so simultaneously in several countries can be overwhelming.

Third, the young venture may be unable to build the needed local capabilities in foreign locations. The fact that there exists a large potential market for your company's products or services on other continents in no way implies that you will be able to attract experienced local marketing and sales people to work for you. Young companies are known to be high-risk employers. That you are a young company located thousands of miles away may increase the perceived risks even further. Similarly, the fact that, between them, India and China produce almost a million scientists and engineers each year in no way implies that, if you set up a development center in either country, you will succeed in attracting or retaining the type of talent that you need. Given rapid growth in India and China, even major companies such as IBM and Microsoft face annual staff turnover in the double digits. As a young company, you may find yourself with a staff turnover so high as to render the potential of China or India to reduce your cost structure little better than a fantasy.

Fourth, the young venture may have limited or no experience in preventing or managing cross-cultural conflicts. In situations where your key personnel are separated not just by physical distance but also cultural, language, and time differences (and, lest one forget, egos), the risk of high internal conflict is real. If you are not able to mitigate the potential for such conflicts or to resolve them effectively and speedily when they occur, you may find that your venture is saddled with slow and poor decision making and even gridlock.

Last but not least, the young venture may find the direct and indirect costs of cross-border coordination to be unsustainable. Direct costs include time and money spent on travel and conference calls. Indirect costs include the cost of misalignment between elements of the value chain (such as customers, manufacturing operations, design and development centers, and suppliers) that are dispersed across multiple countries and locations. Misalignments can result in not only missed opportunities but also wasted time, resources, and effort.

Empirical research has already established that there is such a thing as *the liability of newness*—that is, given multiple sources of risk and uncertainty, the survival rate of new ventures tends to be quite low.[10] Empirical research has also established that, when they spread their wings across borders, even large companies suffer from *the liability of foreignness*.[11] As the above discussion points out, young ventures that globalize early in their lives face a double whammy—the liability of foreignness on top of the liability of newness.

To Globalize or Not to Globalize—Early?

Taking into account the potential opportunities as well as the potential challenges associated with early globalization, Figure 8.1 presents the key factors that should drive the speed and extent of global expansion by young ventures. These are: industry imperatives, industry constraints, and organizational capability. The stronger the industry imperatives for globalization, the weaker the industry constraints against it, and the higher the young venture's organizational capability at managing cross-border operations, the more likely it is to benefit from early globalization.

Industry imperatives in favor of early globalization. These tend to be stronger when the industry exhibits one or more of the following features: high R&D intensity, high-scale economies, and the dominating presence of customers who are themselves multinational. High

Figure 8.1. Drivers of Early Globalization

R&D intensity (as in the case of biotech or software products) implies that young ventures that globalize early may be able to spend larger sums on R&D than competitors who do not globalize and stay smaller. Early globalization may also enable such a venture to reduce the cost of R&D by locating all or part of it in a low-cost, high-talent location, such as India or China. High-scale economies, while obvious in the case of high R&D intensity industries, may also exist in activities such as manufacturing or service operations. Praxis, the Shanghai-based company which sells Web- and iPod-based language training services to teach people Mandarin and Spanish anywhere in the world, is an example of a company with high-scale economies. Given almost zero variable costs, the larger the customer base that Praxis can build, the greater the amount of money it can spend on better training material, faster and more user-friendly operations, and more extensive marketing. Finally, if the industry is dominated by multinational customers, the young venture must be able to deliver its products and services across countries, or it may have a difficult time being taken seriously by potential customers.

Industry constraints against early globalization. These tend to be stronger when the industry exhibits one or more of the following features: the venture's product or service requires a high degree of local adaptation, creating and delivering the product or service requires local infrastructure, or regulatory barriers prevent or seriously inhibit doing business in foreign countries. Take a look at need for local adaptation. Products and services targeted at individual consumers often require more local adaptation than do those targeted at businesses. This is why B2B ventures often globalize much earlier than do B2C ventures. Consider now the need for local infrastructure. A comparative analysis of the speed with which Yahoo!, eBay, and Amazon globalized in the first five to six years of their lives illustrates powerfully the constraining effects of the need for local infrastructure. All three companies were founded in 1994–1995, and all three would emerge as winning survivors from the brutal dot-com collapse that ensued in 2000–2001. Within five years of its founding—that is, by early 2000—Yahoo! already had operations and portals in twenty-two countries. The five-year number for eBay is seven countries. In contrast, the five-year number for Amazon is only three countries.[12] There is just one explanation for the big difference in the speed of globalization between Yahoo! and Amazon. Because the only product Yahoo! offers is information services, the only infrastructure it needs is that its customers have access to the Internet. In contrast, most of what Amazon sells are physical products. Thus its operations depend on establishing sourcing, warehousing, and distribution operations in every country that it enters. Setting up physical infrastructure of this type requires significant capital investment, takes time, and is quite risky. All of these factors imply that, notwithstanding an aggressive and ambitious leadership team, Amazon had little choice but to globalize at a much slower rate than Yahoo! or eBay.

Organizational capability. The young venture's organizational capability to manage cross-border operations is likely to be greater when the leadership team includes people with considerable cross-border experience, when they overinvest in building cross-border coordination capabilities within the organization, and when they help the venture to co-opt the resources and competencies of other organizations via cross-border alliances and acquisitions. Unlike industry characteristics which are external to the venture and largely a given, the venture's leaders do have considerable leeway in the extent to which they help the venture accumulate the necessary organizational capabilities. The case of Approva Corporation, discussed next, illustrates vividly how a young venture's leaders can help it build such capabilities.

Disciplined Pursuit of Early Globalization: The Case of Approva Corporation

In 2007, Approva Corporation was a privately held venture-capital-backed software company headquartered in Reston, Virginia, a suburb of Washington DC.[13] Approva is an excellent example of a company that globalized soon after it was founded in 2001, did so by design, and where the company's leaders have been systematic in building organizational capabilities to manage globally dispersed operations. Within six months of founding, Approva had set up its primary software development center in Pune, India. On the marketing front, the company began targeting customers in North America, Europe, and Asia right from the very beginning. By 2007, Approva had attracted over $30 million in venture capital funding. The company's staff of over three hundred professionals was spread across several continents: the United States, India, Australia, and Europe. Approva's customer list included well-established companies in many parts of the world including Procter & Gamble in the United States, Siemens in Germany, Sony in Hong Kong, Lucent in China, Amcor in Australia, Saudi Aramco in Saudi Arabia, SAPPI in South Africa, and Reliance Industries in India.

Approva was founded in late 2001 in the aftermath of financial scandals such as Enron and Worldcom. These scandals cost investors dearly, shook their confidence in capital markets, and appeared to demonstrate that investors lacked adequate protection against (and

public disclosure of) conflict-ridden actions by the officers and directors of publicly listed companies. They also served as the trigger
for the 2002 enactment of the Sarbanes-Oxley Act (SOX). SOX
required tougher governance from the board of directors and gave
investors more visibility into the actions of public companies. It also
required CEOs and CFOs to personally vouch for the accuracy of
revenue and other financial data. If they were found to have falsi-
fied information, the penalties were stiff—up to twenty years in jail,
not to mention fallout in terms of ruined careers, negative public-
ity, and loss in shareholder value. Importantly, SOX rapidly became
the template for similarly tough corporate governance regulations
in many of the major economies outside the United States, including much of Europe, Australia, Japan, and even some developing
economies such as India.

Approva's business mission was to provide internal and external auditors with software solutions that would continuously monitor and automatically probe the client company's ERP systems and
internal controls of key business processes. The value added would
be more thorough, faster, and better quality audits and continuous
business improvement. An important by-product would also be reduced likelihood of fraudulent behavior. As Prashanth V. Boccasam
("PV"), the company's founder and CEO, noted in a 2004 article
for the Association for Financial Professionals: "The ability to look
deep into the ERP system helps to keep individuals' responsibilities
segregated, restricts access when needed to decrease the potential
for unscrupulous activities, and enables a smoother compliance effort because [of] the continuous testing of [key] processes."

Impetus for early globalization. The impetus for Approva to globalize from the get-go came from a combination of strong industry
imperatives (such as the "Big Four" accounting firms' need for globally consistent audits), low industry constraints, and the founder's
proven capability at managing a global venture.

PV, the company's founder, was born in India, held computer
science degrees from India and the United States, and had served
as an executive for Microsoft's business software division for several

years before launching his first B2B software company, Entevo, in 1995. Entevo was created as a born global company with product development work centered in India. PV sold Entevo to a NASDAQ-listed company in 2000, helped manage the post-merger integration for several months, and then left to start Approva, his second entrepreneurial venture. In an interview with the authors, PV recounted the driving forces behind Approva's early globalization:

> Approva received $3 million in first-round funding from a syndicate of three VCs: New Enterprise Associates (NEA), Novak Biddle, and Columbia Capital. The VCs liked the fact that there was a global market for our product and that our business was globally scalable. Even if you have a U.S.-based customer such as Procter & Gamble, you cannot say that your software will not work in a subsidiary outside the U.S. It also helps that virtually all providers of ERP and other enterprise systems are global companies such as SAP, Oracle, and the like. Thus, in our business, either you go global or you die. The VCs also knew that our staying power would be much greater if we could execute on our vision by doing the development work in India rather than the U.S. It is particularly risky to have a 10,000-mile separation between where you do product development and where your customers sit. Two of the VCs—NEA and Novak Biddle—had been investors in my previous company Entevo. They knew me and had confidence that I knew what it took to get a product done, with quality, 10,000 miles away.

Globalizing the search for customers. Approva released its flagship product suite, Bizrights, at SAP America's Annual User Group Conference in May 2003. Consistent with its original business plan and discussions with first-round investors, the company's leadership immediately went global in the search for customers. In 2003, PV himself would visit Europe on four different occasions to meet with potential customers.

In the worldwide search for customers, Approva's leaders were deliberate in leveraging the strengths of partner organizations. In

March 2003, the company appointed Philip B. Livingston, CEO of Financial Executives International (FEI), to its Board of Directors. Serving fifteen thousand members, FEI was the preeminent membership association for senior financial executives. In September 2003, Approva announced a marketing and implementation alliance with Ernst & Young LLP. In April 2004, it appointed Richard Steinberg, former senior partner and founder of PwC's corporate governance program to the board of advisers. In June 2004, Approva became a founding member of Compliance Consortium, an industry group dedicated to promoting corporate governance and risk and compliance management. In March 2005, the company set up an agreement with Consider Solutions, a U.K.-based systems integrator. Consider Solutions had very good access to the top one hundred European companies. As PV recounted, "They'd set up meetings with CFOs and then we'd go in to demonstrate our software and product expertise." One month later, in April 2005, Approva appointed Harvey Pitt, former Chairman of the United States Securities and Exchange Commission, to join its board of directors. In November 2005, the company expanded its advisory board to also include Suhas Deshpande, managing partner of one of India's largest accounting firms, and Julie McLellan, Australia's leading expert on government sector governance and a former partner at KPMG.

As a positive surprise, the company discovered that cracking the European market was somewhat easier than cracking the U.S. market. Because their home markets were relatively small, most European multinationals had become sensitized to the risks of globalization much earlier than their counterparts in the United States. Thus, in Europe, the company's marketing staff did not have to do as much educational work as in the United States. Most CFOs already appeared to be interested in automating internal audit and Approva only had to show that its solutions could do this more cheaply, more effectively, and more efficiently. By contrast, in the United States, the company had to spend more time in educating CFOs on the need for automation—and not just a checkbox item to be "good enough."

In mid-2007, along with his board of directors, PV was exploring an unconventional approach to cracking the Japanese market: "We're now looking to get a Japanese Partner (or a VC) to strategically invest in Approva. It's not that we need more funding at this stage. However, having a prominent Japanese partner to acquire a stake in Approva would give us a highly motivated and well-connected ally in cracking the Japanese market at a faster pace."

Building the organization's capability at cross-border coordination. The following observations by PV illustrate very concretely the mechanisms that the company's leadership utilized in order to systematically build the organization's capability at ensuring effective and efficient cross-border coordination:

> Every three months, we have a quarterly kick-off meeting in Reston and also one in India. The president of India operations attends every kick-off meeting in Reston. Similarly, I make sure that one of my direct reports from the U.S. and I travel to India for the quarterly kick-off meeting there. With business class travel, these visits do get expensive. However, in my judgment, the travel cost is nothing compared with the value that we generate in terms of better intellectual understanding and greater interpersonal cohesion and trust. Besides, who wouldn't love a good curry!
>
> Every October, we have our annual planning session where we work on next year's plans, budgets, forecasts and so forth. Our India director is intimately involved in this process. He comes here and spends 45–60 days working with the CFO on all aspects, not just those pertaining to activities in India. Without this intimate involvement, he would be out of the loop with regards to what's happening globally and how best the Indian operations can leverage and complement or take over what the company is doing in other locations. Now we have started to rely on India for not just software development and customer support but also many administrative tasks. As an example, take the case of a 500-person user conference that we recently organized in the U.S. We had a project manager from

India come here for several weeks and she directed an India-based event management team from here. . . .

One of our mandatory requirements is that, after every visit to a client, every person including the CEO must complete a Client Visit Report (CVR). The CVR asks for data on a number of items such as what the customer liked and did not like, what systems are already being implemented by the customer, and so forth. We generate over 2,000 CVRs every year, all of them accessible over the intranet. We have a dedicated Field Support Specialist whose sole job is to keep track of the CVRs and make sure that the dots get connected across departments. This is one of the channels through which we try to make sure that high touch data from the customer side becomes useful information to product developers and designers sitting 10,000 miles away. Every quarter, product managers are required to revise the product roadmaps and product priorities. Details such as enhancement requests and bugs reported in the CVRs become a critical input to the product managers in this process. . . .

Every Thursday morning from 7.30 A.M. to 9.00 A.M. EST, we have a world-wide "synch-up call" where the heads of all our offices and key functions call in to review any major new developments of the previous week and to plan mid-course corrective actions. . . .

In my e-mail signature, below my name, I provide contact information for two headquarters—the India headquarters and the U.S. headquarters. Even though India is converting from cost center to a full P&L center, it is important for me to keep reinforcing the fact that our India operations are as crucial to the company's success as the ones in the U.S. This is particularly important with our U.S.-based staff.

Conclusion

In closing, we put forward the following guidelines that can help entrepreneurs in deciding if they should pursue early globalization and, if the answer is yes, how they can increase the odds of success.

Industry Matters

The imperatives for globalization and the constraints against globalization vary across industries. The entrepreneur must look hard at these industry characteristics when deciding how rapidly to pursue globalization and how extensive such globalization should be. As we noted earlier, Amazon, which needs physical infrastructure, has globalized much more slowly than Yahoo! and eBay, which do not have this need. We also noted earlier that B2B businesses often globalize much faster than B2C businesses. This is because, on average, B2B ventures have less need for local adaptation than do B2C ventures.

Never Neglect Position in Strategic Markets

A strong position in strategically important markets ("home bases") provides the young venture cash flow, external and internal credibility, and the managerial resources to support expansion into new markets. The venture's leaders should never let global expansion distract them from maintaining and strengthening the venture's position in the strategic markets. To quote a veteran Silicon Valley entrepreneur in the information technology sector: "We've said from the very beginning that we'll not go overseas unless we're confident of a very secure position in the U.S. If globalization distracts you from building a secure position in the most strategic market—and, for us, that's the U.S.—then it's a liability, not an asset. In our industry, overseas buyers look at what the U.S. customers are buying, what the U.S. analysts are saying and, if you're not successful in the U.S., they'll stop buying from you overseas."

Leverage Existing Relationships

The young venture should actively leverage opportunities to tag along with existing customers and to collaborate with existing suppliers and complementors who are globalizing or are already global.

Leveraging existing relationships in new markets significantly reduces the risks associated with early globalization. Having secured a foothold via existing relationships, the young venture can then leverage these beachhead positions to go deeper into the new markets.

Resist the Temptation to Globalize Too Many Activities at One Time

Globalizing multiple activities in the value chain simultaneously creates a serious risk that the young venture may take on too much complexity at one time. It is crucial that the complexity not exceed the venture's organizational capability to deal with it. Otherwise, the most likely result will be missed opportunities to follow up on customer leads, poor service to existing customers, and internal conflicts and inefficiency. A much smarter approach is to globalize only one activity at a time so that the organization builds additional capabilities before moving on to the next step.

Overinvest in Integration Capabilities

As we saw clearly in the case of Approva Corporation, entrepreneurs who choose the path of rapid globalization should deliberately establish formal processes early in the new venture's life. Relying on informal, ad hoc processes could work in a single location business. However, when employees are separated by time zones and language differences, an ad hoc approach can lead to a rapid escalation in coordination costs. Think about the consequences of waking up one day to learn that two of your key salespeople in Frankfurt (or two of your key developers in India) have left the company. Without formal processes, it would take the organization much longer to replace the lost institutional memory. Formal processes make the venture's information infrastructure more robust. As a by-product, they also give the venture's leaders greater flexibility in switching people from one role to another without undue concern about the ability of new appointees to ramp up quickly.

Besides formal processes, a venture's integration capabilities also depend on how much time the key people located in different countries spend in face-to-face communication with each other, in developing personal and social ties outside of the work environment, and in cultivating mutual trust. The direct costs of these capability-building measures pale in comparison with the indirect costs of misalignment in poorly coordinated activities that are dispersed across countries.

Co-Opt and Leverage the Experience of Veteran Globalizers

Given scarcity of resources and limited slack, the new venture can ill afford serious missteps. One way for the venture's leaders to accelerate the learning process without fatal mistakes is to leverage the experience of others who have already gone down the globalization learning curve. They can do this in one or more ways. They can hire liberally from larger, more experienced, and more global companies. On a very selective basis, they can add the needed expertise to the company's board of directors. Seasoned entrepreneurs have also discovered that a very effective and low-cost mechanism to leverage the experience and the relationship network of global veterans is to invite them to join the venture's board of advisers. Unlike the board of directors, members of an advisory board have no fiduciary responsibilities. Thus an advisory board can be expanded (or contracted) at will without diluting the formal power and responsibilities of the board of directors.

9

Leveraging China and India for Global Dominance

> The likely emergence of China and India, as well as others, as new major global players—similar to the advent of a united Germany in the 19th century and a powerful United States in the early 20th century—will transform the geopolitical landscape, with impacts potentially as dramatic as those in the previous two centuries.[1]
>
> —U.S. *National Intelligence Council*

China and India are changing the rules of the global game. Not only are they two of the world's ten largest economies by size of GDP, China and India also have been the two fastest-growing economies of the last two decades. By the end of 2007, China will have surpassed Germany to become the world's third largest economy behind the United States and Japan. India's economy is about ten to fifteen years behind China's but is also growing at a steady rate, exceeding 9 percent a year. According to most projections, China will overtake the United States to become the world's largest economy by around 2035. India's GDP too is projected to overtake that of the United States by around 2045. It is very likely that by 2050, the world's three largest economies will be China, India, and the United States—in that order.[2] No wonder that in its 2005 report to the White House, titled "Mapping the Global Future," the U.S. National Intelligence Council identified the rise of China and India as among the most profound developments transforming the economic and political landscape of the world.[3]

In this chapter, we examine the opportunities and challenges that the rapid growth of the Chinese and Indian economies poses for companies everywhere, not just those that are based outside China and India but also those with roots within these two countries. Building on this analysis, we outline how companies can leverage the market and the resource opportunities proffered by the China and India phenomenon to achieve global dominance within their particular industries.[4]

The Reemergence of China and India

For much of the last two millennia, China and India were the two largest and, by the standards of those times, among the most scientifically and technologically advanced societies in the world.[5] China is believed to have invented paper, gunpowder, and the compass. In turn, India is believed to have brought to the world abstract mathematical concepts, such as the number zero, negative numbers, decimals, and fractions. As recently as 1820, China and India together accounted for almost 50 percent of world's GDP (see Table 9.1). Barely a hundred years later, the tables had turned. By the early part of the twentieth century, China and India added up to only about 16 percent of the world's GDP.

Table 9.1. China and India: A Look Back

	Percentage of World GDP			
Year	U.S. plus Other Western Offshoots	Europe (including former USSR)	China	India
1000	0.7	13.4	22.7	28.9
1500	0.5	23.9	25.0	24.5
1700	0.2	29.7	22.3	24.4
1820	1.9	32.3	32.9	16.0
1913	21.7	46.6	8.9	7.6
1950	30.6	39.3	4.5	4.2

Source: Angus Maddison, The World Economy: Historical Statistics. OECD, 2003.

The primary explanation for the relative eclipse of China and India lies in the fact that the industrial revolution of the nineteenth century that made first Europe and then America rich almost completely bypassed China and India. When the British became India's de facto rulers in the late eighteenth century, India's economy was much larger than that of Britain's. However, the British had the benefit of good timing. India's emperor was weak and the country was politically divided, creating a very opportune time for a smart foreign colonial ruler. China's was a roughly similar story of internal misrule coupled with control by foreign powers. What is happening now in both China and India is the delayed industrial and technological revolution. Technology and capital move much faster now than they did two centuries ago. Thus it is not surprising that the economic growth that took one hundred years to make Europe and America rich may now take only thirty to fifty years.

Table 9.2 includes data on the size of the world's twelve largest economies as of 2005–06 and their growth rates over the recent fifteen-plus years. Tables 9.3 and 9.4 include projections regarding the structure of the world economy over the next forty years. These projections are based on generally conservative assumptions. Recent growth rates in all four of the BRIC countries (Brazil, Russia, India, and China) have been faster than the original projections. Considering also the robustness of the underlying econometric models, we regard these long-term projections as credible. To abstract from and summarize these projections, we can think of the world economy in 2050 as consisting of four major economic blocks—China, India, the United States, and the European Union—each accounting for about 15–25 percent of world GDP, with all other countries accounting for the remaining 15–25 percent. The decision makers and the decision shapers in both China and India are well aware of these projections. When they look at the history of the last thousand years and the fact that the delayed industrial and technological revolution is propelling current growth, they believe firmly that the rise of their countries is inevitable and that it is their destiny to be superpowers again.

Table 9.2. World's Twelve Largest Economies

Country	2005 GDP (US$ billions)	GDP Growth Rate (%) 1990–2000	2000–2005	2005–2006	2005 GDP/ Capita (US$)
United States	12,417	3.5	2.6	3.3	41,530
Japan	4,534	1.1	1.4	2.2	35,420
Germany	2,795	1.8	0.7	2.8	34,090
China	2,234	10.6	9.6	10.7	1,700
United Kingdom	2,199	2.7	2.4	2.8	36,650
France	2,127	1.9	1.5	2.0	34,870
Italy	1,763	1.5	0.6	1.9	29,830
Spain	1,125	2.7	3.1	3.9	25,570
Canada	1,114	3.1	2.5	2.8	33,760
India	806	6.0	7.0	9.2	726
Brazil	796	2.9	2.2	3.7	4,260
Russia	764	−4.7	6.2	6.7	5,380

Source: World Bank, *World Development Indicators 2007*.

Table 9.3. Projected World Economic Structure

Country	Percentage of World GDP 2004	2025	2050
United States	28	27	26
EU	34	25	15
Japan	12	7	4
China	4	15	28
India	2	5	17
Other Countries	20	21	10

Note: During 2005, 2006, and 2007, the Chinese and Indian economies have grown at a much faster rate than predicted. This acceleration has led most observers to make upwards revisions in the projected size of these two economies in 2025 and 2050.

Source: "Reshaping the World Economy," *BusinessWeek*, Aug. 22, 2005.

**Table 9.4. The Rise of the BRIC Economies
(Year When Each BRIC Country's GDP Is
Projected to Exceed That of the G6's)**

	Italy	France/United Kingdom	Germany	Japan	United States
China	2004	2005	2007	~ 2013	~ 2035
India	~ 2012	~ 2015	~ 2020	~ 2025	2040–45
Russia	~ 2020	~ 2030	2035–40		
Brazil	2025–30	~ 2035	~ 2040		

Note: Coined by Goldman Sachs, the term *BRIC* refers to Brazil, Russia, India, and China. Goldman Sachs focused its analysis on these four countries because they are the four largest of all emerging economies and, even on the basis of nominal GDP, are already among the twelve largest economies in the world.

Source: D. Wilson and R. Purushothaman, "Dreaming with BRICs: The Path to 2050," *Goldman Sachs Global Economics Paper No. 99*, Oct. 2003; and T. Poddar and Eva Yi, "India's Rising Growth Potential," *Goldman Sachs Global Economics Paper No. 152*, Jan. 2007.

China and India share many similarities, but there also are important differences between the two economies. The following box summarizes some of the important differences.

China Versus India

- *China's twelve-year lead:* In 1980, China and India had roughly the same, albeit very low, per capita incomes. Since then, China's economy has grown to become almost three times as large as that of India's. Deng Xiao Ping kick-started the economic revolution in China around 1979. In contrast, India started on the path of domestic liberalization and global integration in 1991, fully twelve years later. That twelve-year gap remains alive and well today. Most of the key economic indicators for India in 2006 look strikingly similar to the figures for China in 1994 or 1995.

- *India's demographic dividend:* The median age of India's population is 24.3 years as compared with 32.6 years for China. Because of the one-child policy, China's population is not only eight years older than that of India's, it is also aging faster. As a result, by 2020, China's dependency ratio (that is, dependents as a proportion of working age population) will be significantly higher than that of India's. Given this demographic dividend, most analysts expect that, from around 2020 onwards, India's economic growth is likely to exceed that of China's.[6]

- *Manufacturing sector:* In 2006, manufacturing accounted for 47 percent of China's GDP but only 28 percent of India's. Taking into account China's much higher GDP, this implies that China's manufacturing sector is five times as large as that of India's. China's lead over India in the manufacturing sector is formidable and rests on several sources of comparative advantage: larger scale at the plant level, greater experience, significantly better infrastructure, and more compliant labor.

- *Services sector:* In 2006, services accounted for 41 percent of China's GDP but 55 percent of India's. In particular, India is far ahead of China in software services as well as most other types of services that can be delivered remotely via information technology. Examples of the latter range from low-end commodity services (such as call centers) to high-end knowledge-intensive services (such as design of Web sites, search engine optimization, market research, marketing analytics, legal research, securities analysis, drug discovery services, and so forth). India's lead over China in these types of IT-enabled services rests on several sources of comparative advantage: native fluency in the English language, economies of scale, over twenty years of experience in serving global customers, incorporation of Toyota-like process discipline and rigor into the creation and delivery of services, and deep domain knowledge of key customer industries.

- *Infrastructure:* China's physical infrastructure (such as highways and paved roads, rail lines devoted to goods transport, and seaports) is significantly more developed than India's.[7] This is due in part to more effective policy making and implementation in China and in part to the fact that China started to invest heavily in infrastructure in the mid-1990s, something that India is only beginning to do now.

- *Foreign direct investment:* Over the past ten years, China has attracted about ten times as much foreign direct investment as has India.[8] Some of the major reasons for this difference are: major tax breaks given by the Chinese government to foreign-invested enterprises,[9] the attraction of a larger domestic market within China, better infrastructure, and more compliant labor within China—thereby making the country a much more attractive location for global manufacturing.

- *Health and primary education:* China ranks ahead of India in health and primary education. The 2006–07 Global Competitiveness Report by the World Economic Forum ranks China at 55 and India at 93 (out of a total of 125 countries) on measures of health and primary education.

- *Innovation drivers:* The 2006–07 Global Competitiveness Report ranks India ahead of China in higher education and training (49 versus 77), technological readiness (55 versus 75), business sophistication (25 versus 65), innovation (26 versus 46), and company operations and strategy (25 versus 69).

- *Political institutions:* Last but not least, China and India differ greatly in the structure of their political institutions. China is a command and control economy. Senior political leaders are selected and appointed by the Communist Party of China and the media is expected to help implement national policies. In contrast, India is a free-wheeling democracy modeled after that of the United Kingdom. Political leaders are elected by the citizens and the media remains free from government censorship.

In understanding the rise of China and India, it is also crucially important to look at two other factors besides the size and growth rates of the two countries' GDPs. First, both are still extremely poor countries. The last column in Table 9.2 illustrates this vividly. Even though China is on the verge of becoming the world's third largest economy, its per capita income is less than one-twentieth that of the United States. India's per capita income is even lower, less than one-fortieth of that of the United States. Measured on a purchasing power parity basis, the differences in per capita incomes would be lower but still very large. As we examine later in this chapter, the very low per capita incomes have major strategic implications for companies. They call into question the extent to which most of the potential customers in China and India are ready for current or merely "de-featured" versions of Western products and services. Second, the integration of China and India into the world economy has not only brought 2.4 billion new customers to the global marketplace but also added almost 1.5 billion eager and very inexpensive workers to the global labor pool. The resulting globalization of the job market poses major opportunities as well as major challenges for established multinationals.

China and India as Four Game-Changing Realities

China and India are the only two countries in the world that simultaneously constitute four game-changing realities: (1) megamarkets for almost every product and service, (2) platforms to dramatically reduce a company's global cost structure, (3) platforms to significantly boost a company's global technology and innovation base, and (4) springboards for the emergence of new fearsome global competitors. Many countries feature one or two of these realities, but only China and India feature all four. Each of these new realities is strategically crucial for most medium to large companies worldwide. The fact that all four have emerged simultaneously makes China and India particularly central to the future of most companies. We discuss each of the four realities in turn.

Mega-markets. Within any country, the size of the market for a particular product or service (shampoo, clothing, fast food, cars, tractors, computers, mobile phones, you name it) depends on a number of factors: population size, buying power, demographics, cultural norms and habits, geography, stage of economic development, and so forth. Consider two of the most important factors—population size and buying power. Between them, China and India currently account for 40 percent of the world's population, 7 percent of the world's GDP in nominal terms, and 20 percent of the world's GDP when adjusted for purchasing power parity. As these numbers would suggest, for most products and services, China and India already account for between 10 to 40 percent of the global demand. Further, in line with GDP growth rates, demand is growing at an annual rate of about 10 percent in real terms. Given long-term economic projections that we saw earlier in Tables 9.3 and 9.4, there is good reason to anticipate that, by 2040–50, China and India together may account for 40 percent of the world's market for almost every product or service imaginable. Given below are some illustrative examples of the large market that China and India currently represent:

- In 2007, China's car market will be the second largest in the world. Between 2015 and 2020, it is projected to become even larger than that of the United States. At that time, India's car market is projected to be the third largest after China and the United States.

- In 2007, China and India are respectively the first and second largest markets for Nokia Corporation. Each country is adding about six million new subscribers every month!

- India is currently the primary battleground between Hewlett-Packard, Dell, and Lenovo in their fight for global dominance in the PC industry. H-P and Dell have commanding market shares in Europe and the United States. In turn, Lenovo has a commanding market share in China. India still represents a rapidly growing open field. Whichever of these companies establishes a dominant position within India would be able to leverage scale in two or three of the world's mega-markets to achieve global dominance.

- Wal-Mart executives have noted that China (and, over a longer term, India) may be the only countries where they can build a revenue base as large as that in the United States.

- Between 2007 and 2020, airlines in China and India are projected to be the two largest buyers of commercial airplanes from the likes of Boeing and Airbus.

Given the current and potential market size of China and India, it should be clear that a suboptimal China and India strategy is no longer a matter of merely leaving some money on the table. Any medium to large company that does not develop well-thought-out strategies for China and India could face severe threats to its very existence in as little as ten years' time. If you are not leveraging the market and the resource opportunities that China and India represent, rest assured that somebody else is. That somebody could be your well-known archrival. Equally likely, however, that somebody could be a new homegrown competitor from within China or India that may have your entire company marked with a bull's-eye for acquisition or annihilation.

Platforms for global cost reduction. Table 9.5 compares the average hourly compensation (including benefits) for production workers in China, India, and several other countries. As these and other data indicate, although there are some countries (including Indonesia, Vietnam, and Bangladesh) that have an even lower cost base, China and India continue to provide some of the lowest labor costs in the world. Our own field interviews during 2007 confirm that, even in relatively high-cost locations within both China and India (such as the Suzhou Industrial Park near Shanghai, and the province of Haryana near New Delhi), the total cost of blue-collar workers runs at about $1/hour. Labor costs in the countryside are even lower. In comparison, labor costs exceed $3 per hour in Brazil, $4 per hour in Hungary, $18 per hour in the United Kingdom, and $20 per hour in both Japan and the United States. In short, the cost of production workers in China and India remains a tiny fraction of that in the developed countries and considerably less than the figure for even many of the emerging economies of Central Europe and Latin America.

Large cost differences also exist in white-collar jobs between China and India on one side and the developed economies on the other. In 2007, the total annual compensation for fresh software engineers just out of college in India was about $5,000, and the national average for all software professionals was around $15,000.[10]

**Table 9.5. Labor Cost Comparisons
(Average Hourly Compensation Including
Benefits for Production Workers, in US$)**

	2003	2009 (projected)
Indonesia	0.30	0.70
China	0.80	1.27
India	1.12	1.68
Russia	1.50	2.38
Mexico	2.45	3.28
Poland	2.70	3.83
Brazil	2.75	3.90
Hungary	3.53	5.30
South Korea	9.99	13.01
United Kingdom	17.87	20.14
Japan	20.68	22.61
United States	21.86	25.34
Germany	30.60	34.46

Source: Abstracted from the Economist Intelligence Unit, Euromonitor, U.S. Department of Labor, and Boston Consulting Group

Compensation levels in China were similar. To sum up, despite significant salary jumps in recent years as well as currency appreciation in both the yuan and the rupee, the cost of engineering talent in China and India remains at around 10–15 percent of that in the developed countries.

These cost differences suggest that both China and India offer global companies major opportunities for dramatically reducing the cost structure in many activities of the value chain pertaining to both physical as well as information work.

Platforms to boost the company's global technology and innovation base. The potential of China and India to boost a company's global technology and innovation base is rooted in two opportunities. The first opportunity pertains to the large, well-trained, and low-cost pool of scientific and engineering talent within China and India that is eager for challenge, career advancement, and better creature comforts. Leveraging this talent pool can dramatically extend the R&D capabilities of most companies. The second opportunity pertains to the innovation demanded by the unique needs of the Chinese and Indian markets, such as low buying power, energy and raw material scarcity, environmental degradation, large populations, and high population densities. Designing new products, services, and even entire business models to cater to these unique needs can yield innovations that can serve as cutting-edge sources of competitive advantage not just in other emerging economies but also back home in the developed economies.

Consider first the pool of the available scientific and engineering talent within China and India. In 2005, the estimated number of people who received master's and PhD degrees in engineering, technology, and computer science was about sixty thousand for the United States, about seventy-five thousand for China, and about sixty thousand for India.[11] Further, over 50 percent of the PhD degrees in engineering awarded in the United States were earned by foreign nationals. Among these, students from China and India constituted the dominant foreign groups and a significant proportion of them chose to return to their home countries. In short, the pool of available research and development talent in China and India is among the largest in the world, growing rapidly, and relatively low cost. A company that can tap into this talent effectively and efficiently can boost the productivity of its R&D expenditures by several multiples.

Consider now the potential for innovation offered by a company's decision to invent new products, services, and business models to serve the unique needs of Chinese and Indian markets. Given low per capita incomes, the vast majority of the inhabitants in China and India cannot afford to buy cars that cost $20,000, PCs that cost $1,000, or cell phone services that cost ten cents per minute. This is true not just in B2C contexts but also in many B2B contexts. Take, for example, the market for hospital equipment, such as CT scanners and MRI machines. Yes, there are a growing number of well-financed hospitals in the major cities that can afford to buy the same equipment as can be found at hospitals such as Massachusetts General or Johns Hopkins. However, think about the potential market that can be unleashed if companies such as GE and Siemens could develop imaging machines that are high-caliber in terms of core functionality, cost a fraction of their existing high-end models, but may lack many of the sophisticated yet nonessential features. Low buying power is only one feature of what makes the Chinese and Indian markets unique. Consider also the scarcity of water, shortage of space, dependence on energy imports, and ongoing environmental degradation. In an integrated global economy (and the fact that we live on a small planet), these are challenges not just for China and India but for the entire world. These challenges are also economic opportunities. As we noted above, China and India possess vast and relatively low-cost scientific and engineering capabilities. Companies that can leverage these resources (on top of the existing global R&D network and historical stock of technical knowledge) to address the unique needs of China and India have the potential to emerge as the globally dominant players of tomorrow.

Springboards for the emergence of fearsome new competitors. Unlike the emergence of global competitors from Japan and South Korea during 1970–2000, the more recent emergence of global champions from China and India is taking place at a much faster and more fearsome pace. As we discussed in Chapter One, virtually all Japanese and Korean giants (look at Toyota, Sony, Samsung, and Hyundai) grew organically. In contrast, the globalization of Indian and Chinese companies already shows signs of being much more acquisitions-driven. Capital markets, both public and private, are significantly more global today than they were two decades ago. Thus, globalizing companies from China and India can access equity and debt capital from the global capital markets much more freely and easily than was possible twenty years ago. Also, Chinese and Indian companies now have easy access to global investment banks as well as global consulting firms, most of them with well-staffed offices in

both countries. Finally, the large size of Chinese and Indian economies means that many domestic companies from both countries are
able to accumulate global scale before venturing abroad.

Illustrative examples of emerging global champions from China
across a diverse set of industries include Huawei Technologies,
Lenovo, Haier Group, and Chery Automobile.

- Huawei is China's leading telecommunications equipment
  company and perhaps the toughest long-term competitor to
  Cisco Systems. Its 2006 sales were $11 billion, a 34 percent
  growth over 2005. Huawei derived well over 50 percent and a
  growing proportion of these revenues from customers outside
  China in developing as well as developed economies.

- Lenovo is China's leading company in personal computers. Its
  2005 acquisition of IBM Corporation's PC business made
  Lenovo the third largest PC company in the world behind
  H-P and Dell. Lenovo had its official global headquarters in
  North Carolina, its American CEO (William Amelio) lived
  in and worked out of Singapore, and its Chief Marketing Officer (Deepak Advani) was an Indian-American.

- Haier Group is China's leading home appliance manufacturer
  with a growing manufacturing and market presence and market
  share in the United States, Europe, India, and other countries.
  In 2005, Haier made an aborted acquisition attempt to buy the
  U.S.-based Maytag Corporation. With revenues exceeding $14
  billion in 2006, Haier was the fourth largest white goods manufacturer in the world.

- Founded in 1997, Chery Automobile is one of China's most
  ambitious and most global car companies. In 2006, Chery sold
  over three hundred thousand cars, an increase of 62 percent
  over the previous year. Chery's 7.2 percent market share
  made it China's fourth largest car company. In 2007, Chery
  announced a global strategic alliance with Chrysler Corporation to manufacture small cars that would be sold by Chrysler
  under the Dodge brand.

Illustrative examples of emerging global champions from India across a diverse set of industries include Infosys, Tata Steel, Bharat Forge, and Suzlon Energy.

- Infosys is one of India's homegrown giants in information technology. Founded in 1981, Infosys became a NASDAQ-listed company in 1999. In mid-2007, Infosys had a market capitalization of over $26 billion, twelve-month trailing revenues of $3.3 billion, and was growing at over 40 percent per year. In mid-2007, rumors circulated that Infosys had considered a bid for France-headquartered Capgemini, a company three times bigger in terms of revenues but with a market capitalization of only $10 billion.

- Founded in 1907, Tata Steel is Asia's first and India's largest private sector steel company. Tata Steel was widely regarded as one of the world's lowest cost steel producers. In early 2007, Tata Steel acquired the Anglo-Dutch steel giant Corus for US$11 billion, a company three times its size. After this acquisition, Tata Steel became the sixth largest steel company in the world.

- Bharat Forge was one of the world's five largest (and India's leading) manufacturers of forgings (such as parts for engines, axles, and similar automotive subsystems). Its revenues for 2006–07 exceeded $1 billion, representing a 38 percent growth over the previous year. Bharat Forge operated across Europe, North America, and Asia. During 2003–07, it acquired two companies in Germany, one in Sweden, and one in the United States. Bharat Forge also held a majority stake in a Changchun-based joint venture with First Auto Works, one of China's biggest car companies.

- Founded in 1995, Suzlon Energy was the world's fifth largest (and Asia's and India's leading) manufacturer of wind turbines. Suzlon's 2006–07 revenues were $2 billion representing a 100 percent growth over the previous year. In mid-2007, Suzlon acquired Germany's REpower Systems at a price exceeding EUR 1.3 billion.

Major Challenges and Common Mistakes

For established companies from the developed countries, China and India represent a double-edged sword. Each country is rich in promises but also thick with perils. The challenges can be both external (that is, rooted in features of each country) and internal (that is, rooted in some companies' parochial mindsets or a penchant for short-term profit maximization). We examine first the external challenges.

Some of the common challenges that cut across both China and India pertain to the vastness, the diversity, the internal complexity, and the multi-layered political structure in each country. Each country is large not just in terms of population but also geographically. China's surface area is as large as that of the United States. India's is smaller but still larger than that of the European Monetary Union. In short, both China and India could be viewed as continents rather than just countries. As a direct result, both countries also feature very high levels of internal diversity along multiple dimensions: wealth, language, culture, and particularly in the case of India, religion. China and India have some of the highest levels of income inequalities in the world.[12] Consider now language diversity. In China, even if we leave aside minority languages (such as Tibetan, Mongolian, Miao, and Tai), the Chinese languages include many vastly different dialects (such as Mandarin and Cantonese). In India, linguistic diversity is even greater with twenty-two officially recognized national languages. Relative to the United States or Europe, China and India also feature greater cultural and religious diversity. Given the ongoing liberalization of religious practice within the country, China has a rapidly growing number of Buddhists and the estimated number of Chinese Muslims is greater than twenty million. India has an estimated 140 million Muslims, followed by a sizable minority of Christians, Sikhs, Buddhists, Jains, and followers of other faiths. The strategic implication of all of this multidimensional diversity is that developing a single homogenous strategy for China or India will rarely be optimal or even barely satisfactory.

Politically, too, China and India represent a complex structure. Of course, given India's democratic system, it is all too common that the central government may be composed of uneasy alliances between coalition partners and that the ruling parties in various states may be different from that (or those) at the center. However, even in seemingly monolithic China, political power is distributed widely—across various ministries at the center who do not always see eye to eye, and across the provinces, counties, and cities where the governing premise for centuries has been that "the mountains are high and the emperor is far away." Thus, in both China and India, a company may find that an agreement with one branch or one level of government does not necessarily mean that they will not run afoul of some other branch or level of government.

Aside from common challenges that bedevil both China and India, each country also offers its unique difficulties. In China, some of the most common challenges pertain to unexpected and sudden changes in laws and regulations, a media that is expected to serve national policy rather than be objective or neutral, a legal system that is still being developed after its decimation during the Cultural Revolution, and barriers imposed by vast cultural and language differences between Western countries and China. In India, some of the unique challenges pertain to a still quite poor infrastructure, bureaucratic red tape, and potential for unexpected opposition from local politicians, nongovernmental organizations, and local media that may be sympathetic to the latter.

In developing robust strategies for China and India, many established companies face not just the external challenges noted above but also internal challenges rooted in ignorance (and possible misinformation) about China and India. There are at least three reasons why this is so. One, these two countries are very different from the developed countries on multiple dimensions: per capita incomes, languages, cultural beliefs and norms, and political systems (especially in the case of China). The more different a social system is from what managers are used to, the more "alien" it will appear and the poorer the understanding that people will have about the new system's internal structure and dynamics. Two, these countries are very large, internally diverse, and complex. These features compound the cognitive challenge faced by corporate executives in understanding

China and India well. Three, both China and India are changing rapidly at a pace that's three to four times faster than that of the United States, Europe, or Japan. Thus, past knowledge about China and India becomes obsolete at a rapid rate and increases the risk that your strategies for tomorrow are designed for the realities of yesterday.

Added to ignorance about China and India, many companies also suffer from internal challenges rooted in a penchant for short-term profit maximization. As a result, some of the most common mistakes that companies make include (1) viewing China and India solely through the lens of off-shoring and cost reduction, (2) building marketing strategies that are centered around just the rich cities and the top 5–10 percent of the population, (3) looking primarily at other multinationals as their relevant competition while pooh-poohing domestic players that often control the bulk of the market, (4) naiveté regarding the choice of local partners and management of the partnership, and (5) treating these two countries as peripheral rather than core to the company's global strategy.

Like the development of a new line of business, China and India are long-term stories. A company may be fortunate and find that it can generate profits and a positive cash flow from its Chinese or Indian operations right from the early years. However, companies need to be mindful of the possibility that, if this is the case, perhaps they are just skimming the surface and preparing the ground for others to take over and nudge them aside. At the very least, companies need to develop near-term strategies for China and India with the long term firmly at the top of their agendas.

Designing Robust Strategies for China and India

Taking into account the mega-opportunities as well as the mega-challenges offered by the rise of China and India, we present below some of the key ideas that should guide companies in designing robust strategies for these two economies. The three key premises that underlie these strategic guidelines are: (1) companies must be proactive in capturing the growing market opportunities that China and India represent, (2) companies must be proactive in leveraging the human resources of these two countries to transform the competitiveness of their global operations, and (3) companies must think of China and India as core to their global strategies and as their permanent homes.

Think China and India, Not China or India

Companies should design and pursue an integrated China and India strategy rather than waste time and energy in debating whether to pursue China or India. There are three reasons why. First, for many industries, both China and India present some of the highest growth rates in the world and are emerging as mega-markets. Take cell phones. The number of cell phone users in China exceeds 500 million. The estimated figure for India is 150 million, a number that is growing by 6 million new subscribers per month. Not surprisingly, China and India represent the first and the second largest markets worldwide for Nokia Corporation.

Second, China and India offer complementary strengths that can be leveraged in a synergistic manner. As we discussed earlier, China is much stronger than India in mass manufacturing and logistics; in contrast, India is much stronger than China in software and IT services. IBM Corporation provides a perfect example of how a company can leverage the differing strengths of China and India as part of creating a globally integrated enterprise. Outside the United States, IBM has relied on China as its primary procurement source to support the hardware business. In 2006, the company even decided to relocate its global procurement headquarters to Shenzhen. Complementing these moves, IBM has made its Indian operations one of the most important global hubs for the delivery of IT services to clients worldwide. Nearly one-sixth and a growing proportion of IBM's global workforce is now based in India.

Another possible benefit of developing an integrated China and India strategy is that companies could significantly reduce risks of intellectual-property leakage by disaggregating and distributing core

R&D and core component production across China and India as well as other countries. Consider the case of a European manufacturer that sells machinery to construction contractors. Burned by the experience of seeing its former Chinese partner produce copycat versions of an earlier model, this company is now planning to consolidate the production of some subsystems in India and some other subsystems in China, while keeping assembly operations localized within each country. Such an approach will still permit the company to benefit from the low manufacturing costs in each country. At the same time, however, it could significantly reduce the extent to which the totality of the company's design blueprints and manufacturing processes are exposed to local partners or job-hopping local employees.

Pursue a Two-Track Strategy for Each Market

Companies should design strategies for China and India along two complementary strategic tracks: how to leverage the company's capabilities from other markets for success within China and India, and how to leverage the strengths of China and India for global advantage.

Because you will not always know which track may yield faster results, it is often better to keep both in mind and let unfolding events dictate which may be given higher priority at any particular time. GE's initial entry into India was motivated by perceived market opportunities in such businesses as lighting, appliances, power generation, and medical systems. However, the company discovered that leveraging Indian R&D and IT services for its global business was in some ways an even more promising opportunity at that stage. Two examples of such leveraging are a highly successful joint venture with India's Wipro for lower-end, low-cost medical systems products and the Bangalore-based John F. Welch Technology Centre, one of GE's four corporate-level research centers worldwide.

In its early forays in China, Microsoft wasted years in futile efforts to generate meaningful revenue from sales of its operating systems and software applications. In recent years, however, the company has done an about-face and started to place much greater emphasis on leveraging Chinese universities for leading-edge technology development. Examples of such efforts include setting up research labs at some of China's top universities, the creation of Microsoft Fellowships for China's best computer science PhD students, and expansion in the scope of Microsoft's research center in Beijing, recently lauded by MIT's Technology Review as one of the hottest computer labs in the world. Interestingly, this shift in strategy has also made it easier for Microsoft to get the government's cooperation in enforcing intellectual property protection laws in the software sector. Obviously, in the long run, the two tracks are totally synergistic and will serve as stepping stones for each other.

Start with a Beachhead

Each of the two markets is too big and too complex for broad attack. Such an approach runs a high risk of costly failure, economically as well as in terms of damage to the company's reputation. A much smarter approach is to identify and occupy a beachhead that offers the best potential for early success and which can serve as a launching pad for deeper market penetration. As examples, look at McCormick Foods' entry into China and the German retailer Metro's entry into India.

In the early stages of its entry into China, McCormick targeted Western fast-food chains (such as McDonald's) that were already its institutional customers in the United States and Europe. Targeting this segment in China meant that McCormick had a ready-made market with very low market or financial risk. Much of what these global customers needed in China (including spices, herbs, ketchup, mustard sauce, and so on) was very similar to what McCormick had a long history of supplying in markets outside China. Using this customer segment as a beachhead gave McCormick an operational base from which to broaden its marketing efforts to include local institutional customers as well as the retail consumer.

Metro entered India in the wholesaling business by setting up cash-and-carry distribution centers targeted for B2B sales to such customers as hotels, restaurants, caterers, and small retailers. Although Indian regulations do not permit foreign multibrand retailers to operate within the country, there are no such restrictions on B2B wholesaling. As the world's third largest trading and retailing company, Metro also has one of the world's largest procurement and wholesaling operations. Although Metro has yet to state its ambitions in the retailing sector in India, it is clear that by setting up B2B distribution centers as a beachhead, the company has positioned itself well to start retail operations through either local partners or, if the regulations change, its own operations.

A well-chosen beachhead reduces up-front cash burn, serves as an excellent learning vehicle, and can let a company attack other market segments while being well protected in its own nest.

Create a Business Model from the Ground Up

China and India are the only two poor countries among the world's ten largest economies. As noted earlier, per capita incomes in China and India are a tiny fraction of those in the other large economies (one-twentieth of the United States in the case of China, and one-fortieth in the case of India). In essence, China and India constitute mega-markets with micro-customers. Thus, unlike the case of a U.S. firm entering Japan or vice versa, mere adaptation of the business model to China or India will generally do little more than scratch the surface of the vast market opportunity in each country. While leveraging the company's core competencies, you will have to invent the business model from the ground up. This is how you can align your product and service offerings, your distribution channels, and your prices with the buying power, buyer behavior, and buyer needs of some of the largest market segments in China and India. Almost always, this reinvention will require designing products and services that can be manufactured and delivered at ultra-low prices while still yielding satisfactory profit margins.

Toyota's newly launched program to develop from scratch an ultra-low-cost car for China, India and other emerging markets is illustrative of such an approach. With a targeted sales price of less than $6,500, Toyota is rethinking all aspects of the car from design to materials to production methods. In our judgment, such an approach is imperative if Toyota is to avoid ceding long-term market leadership in China and India to ambitious competitors, such as Chery Automobiles from China and Tata Motors from India, both of which are working aggressively on their own ultra-low-cost auto projects. We should add that, whereas an ultra-low-cost car would be crucial to Toyota's prospects for leadership in the largest and fastest growing market segments, the company needs to continue with a multi-segment strategy that includes cars at all levels, including Lexus at the very top.

When developing a strategy to achieve market success in China and India, you need to think like Southwest Airlines. Southwest saw itself competing not with United, American, or Delta but with the bus or a self-driven car. Sidestepping almost every convention in the airline industry other than safety, Southwest designed and implemented a radically low-cost business model that was novel in almost every respect, such as elimination of travel agents, choice of secondary airports, use of a single type of aircraft, no assigned seating, no meals on board, and a very harmonious relationship with a young and cooperative workforce. It is this kind of mindset that most companies need if they are to compete for the biggest market segments in China and India.

Focus on Market Development

Given the combination of low per-capita incomes and rapid growth rates, Chinese and Indian markets for most products and services (insurance, nursing homes, wine, rock-crushing machines, you name it) are at a very early stage of development. Companies that focus on market development and not just market-share development can create the potential to realize two important advantages: a bigger market opportunity and a brand name that's almost synonymous with the market space.

Consider the case of Adidas Group, the sports-products company headquartered in Germany. As one of the world's leading manufacturers of soccer shoes, Adidas is engaged in developing soccer camps, soccer stadiums, and other components of the soccer ecosystem in China—not only to develop the market but also to make its brand image synonymous with soccer.

Another example is Sandvik, which is headquartered in Sweden and is one of the world's leaders in metal-cutting tools. After its entry into China, Sandvik realized early on that Chinese customers were unwilling to pay the premium prices for the company's cutting tools because they simply did not see any objective benefits that these tools offered over cheaper domestic alternatives. Sandvik started solving this problem only when it invested resources in educating distributors (and, through them, end customers) on such technical issues as what machines to use for different applications and how to use Sandvik's advanced tools to derive the maximum benefits from their superior design, material properties, and manufacturing.

Segment, Segment, Segment

China and India have the world's two largest populations, two of the world's six largest geographic areas, greater linguistic and sociocultural diversity than any other country, and among the highest levels of income disparity in the world. According to *Forbes* magazine,[13] India has not only the largest number of billionaires in Asia but also the world's largest number of the really poor—that is, people who live on less than one dollar a day. Given this size and diversity, one should abandon any notion that there is such a thing as "an average Chinese customer" or "an average Indian customer."

Even though average per-capita income is low in both countries, it is important to remember that these are large countries with huge variations in buying power, needs, and preferences. In each country, even the middle of the income pyramid consists of over three hundred million people, encompassing significant diversity in incomes, geographic climates, cultural habits—even language and religious beliefs. Thus, whether you're selling beer, cars, or e-commerce services, success in China and India will come only to those companies that are extremely market-centric.

This requires a company to be conscious and competent in segmenting the Chinese and Indian markets, developing a strategy tailored to the needs of the targeted segments, and leveraging a strong position in one segment to enter and occupy other adjacent segments. China and India provide highly rewarding opportunities to those companies that want to create and apply the world's leading-edge practices to identifying and serving different segments effectively and efficiently. Examples of such practices include mass customization, a standardized core with customizable peripherals, appropriate variations in packaging and advertising execution, and perhaps the use of different distribution channels for different segments.

Don't Obsess over Intellectual Property Issues

The fact that, historically, China and India have been lackadaisical at enforcing laws to protect intellectual property (IP) has become almost a cliché. However, in our judgment, arguing that IP issues constrain you from having aggressive and vibrant China and India strategies is nothing but a cop-out.

Although it is almost certainly true that more than 80 percent of the software and music consumed in China and India is pirated, people forget that estimated piracy rates in the United States, the bastion of IP protection, run upward of 30 percent. In any case, imitation by competitors that leads to rapid erosion of competitive advantage is an increasing everyday reality even in the developed markets. Thus, instead of obsessing about IP issues in China and India, the central agenda for companies should be maintaining a rapid rate of innovation that makes life difficult for imitators and pirates in developed and developing markets alike. Rapid innovation may not reduce piracy; however, it will help ensure that pirates' products are viewed by local customers as consistently inferior to yours, thereby reducing their desirability. Also, piracy can be reduced by making your products or services more affordable. This is what Microsoft is now attempting with the introduction of Windows XP Starter Edition, a no-frills and very low-priced version of its Windows operating system for China, India, Brazil, and other emerging markets.

As noted earlier, another important mechanism to reduce the risk of IP leakage includes dispersing core R&D and core component production across China, India, and other locations so that competitors in any given location have access to only a limited set of IP development activities.

On the IP front, it is also important to remember that governments in both China and India are finally becoming much more serious about enforcement of IP protection laws. In each country, what's driving this new trend is the ambition to beef up the country's science, technology, and innovation base coupled with the realization that weak IP regimes inhibit technological innovation by not just foreign companies but also domestic scientists and engineers.

Minimize Partner Risk

Every company relies on a network of partners (such as suppliers, channel partners, logistics companies, and customers) in the countries they serve. However, in China and India, companies often find that they may need to rely on strategic partners even for their core operations. The need for such strategic partners may be driven by regulatory requirements (for example, in the auto sector in China and the retailing sector in India where the respective governments do not yet permit 100 percent foreign-owned operations) or by the need to bridge gaps in local knowledge, local capabilities, and local relationships. Far too many companies act naively (often blindly) when deciding whether to partner, with whom to partner, and how to manage the relationship.

To minimize partner risk, companies need to follow the logic of smart partnering. Key elements of this logic are:

1. Look for partners that bring the highest set of complementary capabilities but the lowest level of business overlap, thereby reducing the potential for conflict.

2. Minimize overdependence on any single partner by assigning a narrow scope to each alliance.

3. To the extent possible, maintain advantage in, or control over, complementary activities (such as R&D, component production, and distribution channels).

The risk of being denied access to these complementary activities is likely to make your partner wary of abandoning you in order to steal your business.

Honda in India, which uses different partnering strategies for different product lines and activities, represents an example of smart partnering. Honda has a motorcycle joint venture with Hero Group, India's largest bicycle manufacturer, an automotive joint venture with Siel, a chemicals and vegetable oil products company, and 100 percent owned subsidiaries for R&D, auto components, logistics, and trading.

In contrast, notwithstanding General Motors' claims of success in China, it appears that it may have made itself overly dependent on Shanghai Automotive (SAIC). The web of alliances that support Shanghai-GM (the joint venture between GM and SAIC) are controlled by SAIC rather than GM. Also, as one of China's largest and oldest car companies, SAIC has explicitly declared that it aims to become one of the world's ten largest auto companies within the next five to ten years. Tellingly, in mid-2006, SAIC even hired Philip Murtaugh, former chairman of GM China, to run its own subsidiary SAIC Motor.[14]

China and India as Global Hubs

No matter how large the opportunities and how brilliant your strategies, success in China and India is impossible without winning the local war for talent. One of the by-products of explosive growth in each market is that top-quality scientists, engineers, and managers are scarce, and job-hopping is far too common. Salaries are going up by over 10 percent a year and, even for blue-chip companies such as IBM and Microsoft, turnover rates can run in the 15–20 percent range. Although companies have little choice but to be market-competitive in terms of compensation, winning (as opposed to just playing) the war for local talent requires a fundamental shift in mindset about the future role for your Chinese and Indian stars.

They need to see and believe that the capabilities they are trying to build are central rather than peripheral to the parent company's global agenda, that these operations are global hubs rather than merely peripheral nodes, that they have a career track in the company's global operations, and that the flow of knowledge, capabilities, and people runs both ways, not just from the United States, Europe, or Japan to China or India but also the other way around. China and India are emerging as economic superpowers. It should come as no surprise that the top talent in China and India will want to join and stay with your company only if they see these ambitions realized within your company rather than in your fast-rising competitor with a home base or a global hub in China or India.

To date, many companies have had at least partial success in reducing their cost structure by moving manufacturing or business support activities to China and India. However, the future belongs to those companies that look at these countries holistically and treat them as central hubs in their global strategies. Cisco Systems presents an interesting case of a deliberate attempt to create tomorrow's company today. In December 2006, Cisco appointed Wim Elfrink as the company's Chief Globalization Officer, reporting directly to CEO John Chambers. With his primary home and office base in India, Elfrink's central mission is to help Cisco and its top executive team become more Asia- and India-centric.[15] Among major corporations, to date, Cisco has been a leader in more ways than one (for example, as a pioneer in leveraging external R&D, and in running the company's operations on the Internet to the maximum extent possible). We believe that this is just one more instance of Cisco paving the way for the rest of the Fortune 500.

Given the rapidly changing economic topography of the world, we take it as given that the Fortune 500 company of tomorrow will be much more China- and India-centric in every respect than at present. The only open question is whether this will be your company or your competitor's after you have been swallowed or annihilated.

Notes

Chapter One

1. Thomas A. Stewart, "A Way to Measure Worldwide Success," *Fortune*, Mar. 15, 1999, p. 196.
2. We would like to thank Michael Knetter and Anant Sundaram for helpful comments on this chapter. In developing our thinking on this chapter, we have also benefited from the pioneering work of R. E. Caves, *Multinational Enterprise and Economic Analysis*, Cambridge: Cambridge University Press, 1982; P. J. Buckley and M. Casson, *The Future of the Multinational Enterprise*, New York: Holmes & Meier, 1976; S. H. Hymer, "The International Operations of National Firms: A Study of Direct Foreign Investment," PhD dissertation, Massachusetts Institute of Technology, 1960; and R. Vernon, *Storm over the Multinationals*, Cambridge: Harvard University Press, 1977.
3. International Monetary Fund, *World Economic Outlook 1997*.
4. UNCTAD, *World Investment Report 1999*.
5. OECD, *Globalization of Industry: Overview and Sector Reports*, 1996.
6. "Marks & Spencer: Black Marks," *Economist*, Nov. 6, 1999, p. 66.
7. UNCTAD, *World Investment Report 1996*.
8. Thomas A. Stewart, "See Jack. See Jack Run Europe," *Fortune*, Sept. 27, 1999, pp. 124–136; "The House That Jack Built," *Economist*, Sept. 18, 1999, pp. 23–26.
9. World Bank, *From Plan to Market: World Development Report 1996*; and UNCTAD, *World Investment Report 2006*.
10. World Bank, "Global Economic Prospects and the Developing Countries: Beyond Financial Crisis," 1998-99; Ted Bardacke, "Thailand Quietly Eases Rules Governing Foreign Ownership," *Financial Times*, June 23, 1998, p. 6; John Burton, "Korea Returns to Privatisation," *Financial Times*, June 23, 1998, p. 6; Ted Bardacke, "GE Capital Acquisitions Build on Thai Operational Platform," *Financial Times*, Sept. 29,1998, p. 22; Gillian Tett, "GE Capital Creates a Stir Becoming Big in Japan," *Financial Times*, Feb. 23, 1999, p. 20.
11. Dominic Wilson and Roopa Purushothamn, "Dreaming with BRICS: The Path to 2050," *Goldman Sachs Global Economics Paper No. 99*, Oct. 1, 2003.

12. Tushar Poddar and Eva Yi, "India's Rising Growth Potential," *Goldman Sachs, Global Economics Paper No. 152*, Jan. 22, 2007.
13. Quoted in G. Pascal Zachary, "Let's Play Oligopoly! Why Giants Like Having Other Giants Around," *Wall Street Journal*, Mar. 8, 1999, p. B1.
14. "Globalization in Historical Perspective," *World Economic Outlook*, May 1997, International Monetary Fund.
15. F. Warren McFarlan, William C. Kirby, and Tracy Yuen Manty, "Li & Fung 2006," *Harvard Business School Publishing Case No. 9-301-077*, Revised version May 10, 2007.
16. Quoted in Paul Hofheinz, "What Now?" *Wall Street Journal Reports: A Survey of World Business*, Sept. 27, 1999, p. R25.
17. "FT 500," *Financial Times*, May 4, 2000.
18. "FT 500," *Financial Times*, June 29, 2007.

Chapter Two

1. Daniel Barnard, *Financial Times*, Dec. 12, 1998, p. 14.
2. In developing the conceptual framework for this chapter, we have benefited from the research of many scholars, including F. R. Root, *Entry Strategies for International Markets*, Lexington, Mass.: Lexington Books, 1987; S. Zaheer, "Overcoming the Liability of Foreignness," *Academy of Management Journal*, 1995, 38(2): 341–363; S. J. Chang, "International Expansion Strategy of Japanese Firms: Capability Building Through Sequential Entry," *Academy of Management Journal*, 1995, 38(2): 383–407; J.-F. Hennart and Y.-R. Park, "Greenfield vs. Acquisitions: The Strategy of Japanese Investors in the United States," *Management Science*, 1993, 39, 1054–1070; J. Li, "Foreign Entry and Survival: Effects of Strategic Choices on Performance in International Markets," *Strategic Management Journal*, 1995, 16, 333–352; X. Martin, A. Swaminathan, and W. Mitchell, "Organizational Evolution in the Interorganizational Environment: Incentives and Constraints on International Expansion Strategy," *Administrative Science Quarterly*, 1998, 43(3), 533–601; H. G. Barkema and F. Vermeulen, "International Expansion Through Start-Up or Acquisition: A Learning Perspective," *Academy of Management Journal*, 1998, 41(1), 7–26; and A. Delios and W. J. Henisz, "Japanese Firms' Investment Strategies in Emerging Economies," *Academy of Management Journal*, 2000, 43(3), 305–323.
3. Marriott annual reports.
4. Authors who have discussed globalization imperatives include J. P. Jeannet and H. D. Hennessy, *Global Marketing Strategies*, Boston: Houghton Mifflin, 1998; S. Ghoshal, "Global Strategy: A Conceptual Framework," *Strategic Management Journal*, 1987; G. Hamel and C. K. Prahalad, "Do You Really Have a Global Strategy?" *Harvard Business Review*, July-Aug. 1985; and George S. Yip, *Total Global Strategy*, Upper Saddle River, N.J.: Prentice Hall, 1995.

5. Vijay Govindarajan, "Note on the Global Paper Industry," Tuck School of Business Administration, Dartmouth College, 1999.

6. T. Khanna, R. Gulati, and N. Nohria, "Alliances as Learning Races," *Proceedings, Academy of Management Annual Meetings*, 1994, pp. 42–46.

7. Benjamin Gomes-Casseres, "Xerox and Fuji Xerox," *Harvard Business School Case No. 9-391-156*.

8. Ken Iverson and T. Varian, *Plain Talk: Lessons from a Business Maverick*, New York: Wiley, 1997.

9. Sandra Sugawara, "Japanese Shaken by Business U.S.-Style," *Washington Post*, Feb. 9, 1999, p. E4.

10. Robert Anthony, "Euro Disney: The First 100 Days," *Harvard Business School Case No. 9-693-013*, p. 12.

11. Donna Everatt, "Managing Performance at Haier (A)," *IMD Case No. IMD-3-1332*, 2004.

12. Anthony St. George, "Mercedes-Benz in Alabama: Lessons from the Field," *Harvard Business School Case No. 9-199-028*, p. 2.

13. Krzysztof Obloj and Howard Thomas, "Transforming Former State-Owned Companies into Market Competitors in Poland: The ABB Experience," *European Management Journal*, Aug. 1998, 16(4), 391.

14. Douglas A. Blackmon, "A Factory in Alabama Is the Merger in Microcosm," *Wall Street Journal*, May 8, 1998, p. B1.

15. "In Global Drive, Nike Finds Its Brash Ways Don't Always Pay Off," *Wall Street Journal*, May 5, 1997, p. A1.

16. "Whirlpool Expected Easy Going in Europe, and It Got a Big Shock," *Wall Street Journal*, Oct. 4, 1998, p. A1.

17. "Anheuser-Busch Brews Battle with SABMiller," *Modern Brewery Age*, May 31, 2004.

18. Richard Lambert, "An Essential Component," *Financial Times*, Oct. 29, 1998, p. 3.

19. David Kirpatrick, "How Microsoft Conquered China," *Fortune*, July 23, 2007.

20. "TCL, Thomson Alliance to Lead Global TV Production," *China Daily*, Nov. 4, 2003.

Chapter Three

1. Sam Walton's comments upon receiving the Medal of Freedom in 1992, quoted in Ali Farhoomand, "Wal-Mart Stores: Everyday Low Prices," in *China, Case No. HKU590*, Asia Case Research Center, University of Hong Kong, 2006.

2. Unless otherwise indicated, data for this chapter have been derived primarily from the annual reports of Wal-Mart Stores, Inc., and the company's Web site (www.walmart.com).

3. These observations are based on *The Wal-Mart Encyclopedia, Volume III*, Salomon Brothers, Oct. 1995, p. 32; and Merrill Lynch, pp. 18–19.

4. William J. Holstein, "Why Wal-Mart Can't Find Happiness in Japan," *Fortune*, July 27, 2007.
5. GE annual reports.
6. Procter & Gamble annual reports.
7. Carrefour Group annual reports.
8. Metro Group annual reports.

Chapter Four

1. Tony Jackson, "Keep the Home Fires Burning," *Financial Times*, Jan. 9, 1998, p. 25.
2. Robert A. Burgelman and Philip Meza, "The De-Globalization of Marks & Spencer in 2001: An Update," *Case No. SM-87*, Stanford University Graduate School of Business, Revised Mar. 16, 2007.
3. For some of the pioneering ideas on the sources of global competitive advantage, see B. Kogut, "Designing Global Strategies: Comparative and Competitive Value Chains," *Sloan Management Review*, 1985; M. E. Porter, *Competition in Global Industries*, Cambridge: Harvard Business School Press, 1986; C. A. Bartlett and S. Ghoshal, *Managing Across Borders*, Cambridge: Harvard Business School Press, 1989; and C. K. Prahalad and Y. L. Doz, *The Multinational Mission*, New York: Free Press, 1987.
4. "As Business Goes Global, So Does Business Week," *Business Week*, July 1, 1996.
5. Remarks by John Pepper, chairman and CEO of Procter & Gamble, to MBA class at Tuck School, Dartmouth College, May 1995.
6. Microsoft's Web site at www.microsoft.com.
7. "Tata Steel Wins Corus with $12 Billion Deal," *New York Times*, Jan. 31, 2007.
8. For an excellent example of the tensions created by the simultaneous need for central coordination as well as local autonomy, see Jay Lorsch and Alexis Chernak, "DLA Piper: Becoming a Global Law Firm," *Harvard Business School Publishing Case No. 9-407-057*, Oct. 31, 2006.
9. Manjeet Kriplani, "IBM: Star of India," *Business Week*, Aug. 23, 2007.
10. "Texas Instruments' Global Chip Payoff," *Business Week*, Aug. 7, 1995.
11. Paul Ingrassia, "Industry Is Shopping Abroad for Good Ideas to Apply to Products," *Wall Street Journal*, Apr. 29, 1985, p. 1.
12. Susan MacKenzie, "Procter & Gamble: Accounting for Organization 2005," *Case No. A-183*, *Graduate School of Business*, Stanford University, Feb. 2002.
13. Dan Nystedt, "Dell Launches Low-Cost PC in China," *InfoWorld*, Mar. 21, 2007.
14. "Furnishing the World," *Economist*, Nov. 19, 1994, pp. 79–80.
15. Remarks by John Pepper.
16. William Taylor, "The Logic of Global Business: An Interview with ABB's Percy Barnevik," *Harvard Business Review*, Mar.-Apr. 1991, pp. 93–105.

17. Remarks by John Pepper.

18. Rebecca Chung and Katrina Paddack, "CEMEX: Global Growth Through Superior Information Capabilities," *IMD Case No. IMD-3-0953*, 2003.

19. Disguised names. This example comes from the consulting engagement of one of the authors. Some data elements have been altered in order to preserve the confidentiality of the companies.

Chapter Five

1. Nayan Chanda's interview with Infosys founder N. R. Narayana Murthy, conducted Apr. 28, 2006, at Yale University and published in *YaleGlobal*.

2. Quoted in Joseph B. White, "Global Mall," *Wall Street Journal*, May 7, 1998, p. A1.

3. See C. Argyris and D. A. Schön, *Organizational Learning*, Reading, Mass.: Addison-Wesley, 1978; A. Newell, *Unified Theories of Cognition*, Cambridge: Harvard University Press, 1990; H. A. Simon, "A Behavioral Model of Rational Choice," *Quarterly Journal of Economics*, 1955, 69, 99–118.

4. Speech by Samuel J. Palmisano, CEO, IBM Corporation, at INSEAD Business School, Fontainebleau, France, Oct. 3, 2006.

5. Reported in B. Dumaine, "Don't Be an Ugly-American Manager," *Fortune*, Oct. 16, 1995, p. 225.

6. See J. P. Walsh, "Managerial and Organizational Cognition: Notes from a Trip Down Memory Lane," *Organization Science*, 1995, 6(3), 280–321, for a comprehensive review of the literature on managerial and organizational cognition that builds on the work of such pioneers as F. C. Bartlett, *Remembering*, Cambridge: Harvard University Press, 1932; L. Festinger, *A Theory of Cognitive Dissonance*, Evanston, Ill.: Row Peterson, 1957; and U. Neisser, *Cognitive Psychology*, New York: Appleton-Century-Crofts, 1967.

7. See Simon, "A Behavioral Model of Rational Choice"; and W. H. Starbuck and F. J. Milliken, "Executives' Perceptual Filters: What They Notice and How They Make Sense," in D. C. Hambrick (ed.), *The Executive Effect: Concepts and Methods for Studying Top Managers*, Greenwich, Conn.: JAI Press, 1988.

8. See R. Nisbet and L. Ross, *Human Inference: Strategies and Shortcomings of Social Judgment*, Upper Saddle River, N.J.: Prentice Hall, 1980; and R. P. Schank and R. P. Abelson, *Scripts, Plans, Goals, and Understanding*, Hillsdale, N.J.: Erlbaum, 1977.

9. See J. P. Walsh and L. C. Charalambides, "Individual and Social Origins of Belief Structure Change," *Journal of Social Psychology*, 1990, 130, 517–532.

10. Walsh, "Managerial and Organizational Cognition," p. 282.

11. As quoted in "The Past, Imperfect," *Time*, July 15, 1996, p. 54.

12. See Coca-Cola Company annual report, 1995.

13. See, for example, F. H. Allport, *Social Psychology*, Boston: Houghton Mifflin, 1924; M. Douglas, *How Institutions Think*, Syracuse, N.Y.: Syracuse

University Press, 1986; and E. Durkheim, *The Rules of Sociological Method*, New York: Free Press, 1938.

14. Walsh, "Managerial and Organizational Cognition," p. 291.

15. For research on how organizational-level cognitive schemas can change, see J. M. Bartunek, "Changing Interpretive Schemes and Organizational Restructuring," *Administrative Science Quarterly*, 1984, *29*, 355–372; R. Greenwood and C. R. Hinings, "Organizational Design Types, Tracks, and Dynamics of Strategic Change," *Organization Studies*, 1988, *9*, 293–316; H. Hopfl, *Judgment and Choice: The Psychology of Decision*, New York: Wiley, 1992; and M. A. Lyles and C. R. Schwenk, "Top Management, Strategy, and Organizational Knowledge Structures," *Journal of Management Studies*, 1992, *29*, 155–174.

16. Our dual emphasis on cognitive diversity as well as integrative ability is fully consistent with the perspectives reflected in the papers by T. P. Murtha, S. A. Lenway, and R. P. Bagozzi, "Global Mind-Sets and Cognitive Shifts in a Multinational Corporation," *Strategic Management Journal*, 1998, *19*(2), 97–114; S. J. Kobrin, "Is There a Relationship Between a Geocentric Mind-Set and Multinational Strategy?" *Journal of International Business Studies*, 1994, *25*(3), 493; R. Clapp-Smith, F. Luthans, and B. J. Avolio, "The Role of Psychological Capital in Global Mindset Development," *The Global Mindset: Advances in International Management*, Vol. 19, pp. 105–130, New York: Elsevier, 2007; S. Beechler and M. Javidan, "Leading with a Global Mindset," *The Global Mindset: Advances in International Management*, Vol. 19, pp. 131–169, New York: Elsevier, 2007.

17. W. E. Taylor, "The Logic of Global Business: An Interview with ABB's Percy Barnevik," *Harvard Business Review*, Mar.-Apr. 1991, pp. 93–105.

18. These classifications parallel Perlmutter's notion of geocentric, ethnocentric, and polycentric organizations. See H. V. Perlmutter, "The Tortuous Evolution of the Multinational Corporation," *Columbia Journal of World Business*, 1969, pp. 9–18.

19. As quoted in J. L. Johnson, "Sears Questions Global Quest," *Discount Merchandiser*, Feb. 1995, *35*(2), 10.

20. Letter to shareholders, Wal-Mart Stores, Inc., annual report, 1994.

21. Letter to shareholders, Wal-Mart Stores, Inc., annual report, 1998.

22. As quoted in "GE Capital in Asia," *Economist*, June 6, 1998, pp. 72–73.

23. See B. Newman, "Dutch Are Invading JFK Arrivals Building and None Too Soon," *Wall Street Journal*, May 13, 1997, p. A1.

24. Procter & Gamble annual reports 1998–2006; and company Web site, 2007 (www.pg.com).

25. See J. S. Black and H. B. Gregersen, "The Right Way to Manage Expats," *Harvard Business Review*, Mar.-Apr. 1999, pp. 52–63.

26. See Alison Maitland, "New Paths to Global Thinking," *Financial Times*, Dec. 3, 1998, p. 23.

27. Authors' interviews with SABMiller executives, 2005.

28. See J. Ball, "DaimlerChrysler's Renschler Holds Job of Melding Officials into Cohesive Team," *Financial Times*, Jan. 12, 1999, p. B7.

29. This conclusion is consistent with research findings by, among others, C. Eden, "On the Nature of Cognitive Maps," *Journal of Management Studies*, 1992, *29*, 261–265; R. Mitchell, "Team Building by Disclosure of Internal Frames of Reference," *Journal of Applied Behavioral Science*, 1986, *22*, 15–28; and Walsh and Charalambides, "Individual and Social Origins of Belief Structure Change."

30. For more details, see D. B. Stoppard, A. Donnellon, and R. I. Nolan, "VeriFone," *Harvard Business School Case No. 9-398-030*.

31. See V. Govindarajan and A. K. Gupta, "Global Mindset of Samsung," *Tuck School Case Study*; and A. Dragoon, "Samsung Electronics: Not Accidental Tourists," *CIO*, Aug. 1996, p. 62.

32. Gurcharan Das, "Local Memoirs of a Global Manager," *Harvard Business Review*, Mar.-Apr. 1993, pp. 38–47.

33. IBM annual report, 2006.

34. See Procter & Gamble's Web site: www.pg.com.

35. See Microsoft's Web site: www.microsoft.com.

Chapter Six

1. Letter to shareholders dated February 12, 1999, GE annual report, 1998.

2. "Strategies from the Bottom of the Pyramid," presentation by John Ripley, senior vice president–corporate strategy, Unilever Ltd., annual meeting, Academy of Management, Chicago, Aug. 1999; and communication with Unilever executives in India and Brazil.

3. Authors' interviews with Dr. Yong Rui, director of strategy, Microsoft China Research & Development Group, Beijing, July 2007.

4. For a scholarly development of some of the ideas in this chapter, see also A. K. Gupta and V. Govindarajan, "Knowledge Flows and the Structure of Control Within Multinational Corporations," *Academy of Management Review*, 1991, *16*(4), 768–792; A. K. Gupta and V. Govindarajan, "Knowledge Flows Within Multinational Corporations," *Strategic Management Journal*, 2000, *21*(4), 473–496; Nitin Nohria and Sumantra Ghoshal, *The Differentiated Network: Organizing Multinational Corporations for Value Creation*, San Francisco: Jossey-Bass, 1997; J. Birkinshaw, N. Hood, and S. Jonsson, "Building Firm-Specific Advantages in Multinational Corporations: The Role of Subsidiary Initiative," *Strategic Management Journal*, 1998, *19*(3), 221–242; B. Kogut and U. Zander, "Knowledge of the Firm, Combinative Capabilities, and the Replication of Technology," *Organization Science*, 1992, *3*(2), 383–397; W. M. Cohen and D. A. Levinthal, "Absorptive Capacity: A New Perspective on Learning and Innovation," *Administrative Science Quarterly*, 1990, *35*, 128–152; R. L. Daft and R. H. Lengel, "Organizational Information Requirements, Media Richness, and Structural

Design," *Management Science*, 1986, *32*, 554–571; M. Polanyi, *The Tacit Dimension*, London: Routledge & Kegan Paul, 1966; and D. J. Teece, "Technology Transfer by Multinational Firms: The Resource Cost of Transferring Technological Know-How," *Economic Journal*, 1977, 87, 242–261.

5. Rebecca Chung and Katrina Paddack, "CEMEX: Global Growth Through Superior Information Capabilities," *Case No. IMD-3-3953, IMD International*, Lausanne, Switzerland, p. 7.

6. For an extensive discussion of the pathologies that beset companies attempting to use knowledge existing within or outside their corporate boundaries, see also Jeffrey Pfeffer and Robert I. Sutton, *The Knowing-Doing Gap: How Smart Companies Turn Knowledge into Action*, Cambridge: Harvard Business School Press, 2000.

7. "Otis Pacific Asia Operations (A): National Challenges," *Harvard Business School Case No. 9-393-009*, 1992.

8. This analysis of Nucor Corporation is based predominantly on the period 1965–1999 when Ken Iverson served as the CEO (1965–1996) and chairman (1996–1999) of the company. Data for this analysis are drawn primarily from Vijay Govindarajan and Anil K. Gupta, "Nucor Corporation: A Case Study," Tuck School of Business, Dartmouth College, 1998.

9. Ken Iverson, cited in P. Ghemawat and H. J. Stander III, "Nucor at a Crossroads," *Harvard Business School Publishing Case No. 9-793-039*, 1992, p. 8; and K. Iverson and T. Varian, *Plain Talk*, New York: Wiley, 1997, p. 96.

10. Letter to shareholders, GE annual report, 1998.

11. "The 70 Percent Solution: Google CEO Eric Schmidt Gives Us His Golden Rules for Managing Innovation," *Business 2.0*, Nov. 28, 2005.

12. Marriott annual report, 2006.

Chapter Seven

1. As quoted by John A. Byrne, "21 Ideas for the 21st Century: Management," *BusinessWeek*, Aug. 30, 1999, p. 88.

2. See "Arcelor Agrees to Mittal Takeover," *International Herald Tribune*, July 7, 2006; and ArcelorMittal's Web site at www.arcelormittal.com.

3. W. E. Taylor, "The Logic of Global Business: An Interview with ABB's Percy Barnevik," *Harvard Business Review*, Mar.-Apr. 1991, pp. 93–105.

4. For an excellent treatise on designing the right organizational structure for a global corporation, see Jay A. Galbraith, *Designing the Global Corporation*, San Francisco: Jossey-Bass, 2000.

5. In a broader treatment of the international dimensions of organizational behavior, Adler suggested that, notwithstanding such teams' necessity, the challenge of managing diversity would often render cross-cultural teams highly ineffective in achieving their goals. See Nancy Adler, *International Dimensions of Organizational Behavior*, Boston: Kent, 1986. More recently, Early and Mosakowski have reported that, at least in the early stages, culturally heterogeneous teams demonstrate poorer performance than do

homogeneous ones. See P. Christopher Early and Elaine Mosakowski, "Creating Hybrid Team Cultures: An Empirical Test of Transnational Team Functioning," *Academy of Management Journal*, 2000, *43*(1), 26–49.

6. M. Becerra and A. K. Gupta, "Perceived Trustworthiness Within the Organization: Moderating Impact of Communication Frequency on Trustor and Trustee Effects," *Organization Science*, 2003, *14*(1), 33–44; and R. C. Mayer, J. H. Davis, and F. D. Schoorman, "An Integrative Model of Organizational Trust," *Academy of Management Review*, 1995, *20*, 712.

7. D. J. McAllister, "Affect- and Cognition-Based Trust as the Foundations for Interpersonal Cooperation in Organizations," *Academy of Management Journal*, 1995, *38*, 24–59.

8. See R. M. Kramer and T. R. Tyler (eds.), *Trust in Organizations: Frontiers of Theory and Research*, Thousand Oaks, Calif.: Sage, 1996.

9. G. Hofstede, "Motivation, Leadership, and Organization: Do American Theories Apply Abroad?" *Organizational Dynamics*, Summer 1980, pp. 42–63. According to Hofstede, cultures can differ across four dimensions: power distance, the extent to which power is centralized; individualism/collectivism, the extent to which people view themselves as individuals as opposed to belonging to a larger entity; uncertainty avoidance, the difficulty people have in coping with uncertainty and ambiguity; and masculinity/femininity, the extent to which people value materialism as opposed to concern for others. Although it is unlikely that a current writer would use the latter terms in this sense, the management literature still associates concern with things and concern with people with male and female approaches to business life.

10. Amos Tversky and Daniel Kahneman, "The Framing of Decisions and the Psychology of Choice," *Science*, Jan. 30, 1981, *211*, 453–458.

11. These ideas are consistent with many scholarly studies on group effectiveness in general and on top management teams and multicultural teams in particular. See D. Ancona and D. Caldwell, "Demography and Design: Predictors of New Product Team Performance," *Organization Science*, 1992, *3*, 342–355; K. Bantel and S. Jackson, "Top Management and Innovations in Banking: Does the Composition of the Top Management Team Make a Difference?" *Strategic Management Journal*, 1989, *10*, 107–124; J. R. Hackman and Associates, *Groups That Work and Groups That Don't*, San Francisco: Jossey-Bass, 1990; D. Hambrick, T. Cho, and M-J Chen, "The Influence of Top Management Team Heterogeneity on Firms' Competitive Moves," *Administrative Science Quarterly*, 1996, *41*, 659–684; L. H. Pelled, "Demographic Diversity, Conflict, and Work Group Outcomes: An Intervening Process Theory," *Organization Science*, 1996, *7*, 615–631; S. Finkelstein and D. Hambrick, *Strategic Leadership*, San Francisco: Jossey-Bass, 1996; J. R. Katzenbach and D. K. Smith, "The Discipline of Teams," *Harvard Business Review*, Mar.-Apr. 1993, pp. 111–120; P. Hinds and M. Mortensen, "Understanding Conflict in Geographically Distributed Teams," *Organization Science*, 2005, *16*(3), 290–307; and J. A. Espinosa, S. A. Slaughter,

R. E. Kraut, and J. D. Herbsleb, "Familiarity, Complexity, and Team Performance in Geographically Distributed Software Development," *Organization Science*, 2007, *18*(4), 613–630.

12. Carlos Ghosn, "Saving the Business Without Losing the Company," *Harvard Business Review*, Jan. 2002, p. 43.

13. K. G. Smith, K. A. Smith, J. D. Olian, D. P. O'Bannon, and J. A. Scully, "Top Management Team Demography and Process: The Role of Social Integration and Communication," *Administrative Science Quarterly*, 1994, *39*, 412–438.

14. K. M. Eisenhardt, J. L. Kahwajy, and L. J. Bourgeois, "How Management Teams Can Have a Good Fight," *Harvard Business Review*, July-Aug. 1997, pp. 77–85.

15. M. N. Chaniu and H. J. Shapiro, "Dialectical and Devil's Advocate Problem Solving," *Asia Pacific Journal of Management*, May 1984, pp. 159–168.

16. D. B. Stoppard, A. Donnellon, and R. I. Nolan, "VeriFone," *Harvard Business School Case No. 9-398-030*.

17. John Pepper, chairman of the board, Procter & Gamble, remarks to an MBA class at the Tuck School, Dartmouth College, May 1995.

18. John Pepper, remarks to an MBA class.

19. These comments are based on our study of thirty-nine country heads in Unilever and on Floris A. Maljers, "Inside Unilever: The Evolving Transnational Company," *Harvard Business Review*, 1992, pp. 46–51.

Chapter Eight

1. Davinna Attar, Anuradha Kher, and Michal Lev-Ram, "The Road Warrior's Guide to Travel," *Business 2.0*, Sept. 2007.

2. This chapter builds on our own field research as well as a growing body of academic literature on international expansion by young companies. Some of the key articles in this stream of research include Erkko Autio, Harry J. Sapienza, and James G. Almeida, "Effects of Age at Entry, Knowledge Intensity, and Imitability on International Growth," *Academy of Management Journal*, 2000, *43*(5), 909; Shaker A. Zahra, R. Duane Ireland, and A. Hitt Michael, "International Expansion by New Venture Firms: International Diversity, Mode of Market Entry, Technological Learning, and Performance," *Academy of Management Journal*, 2000, *43*(5), 925; Suresh Kotha, Violina P. Rindova, and Frank T. Rothaermel, "Assets and Actions: Firm-Specific Factors in the Internationalization of U.S. Internet Firms," *Journal of International Business Studies*, 2001, *32*(4), 769; Gary A. Knight and S. Tamar Cavusgil, "Innovation, Organizational Capabilities, and the Born-Global Firm," *Journal of International Business Studies*, 2004, *35*(2), 124; Benjamin M. Oviatt and P. McDougall Patricia, "The Internationalization of Entrepreneurship," *Journal of International Business Studies*, 2005, *36*(1), 2; Shaker A. Zahra, "A Theory of International New Ventures: A Decade of Research,"

Journal of International Business Studies, 2005, 36(1), 20; Nicole E. Coviello, "The Network Dynamics of International New Ventures," *Journal of International Business Studies*, 2006, 37(5), 713; Harry J. Sapienza, Erkko Autio, Gerard George, and Shaker A. Zahra, "A Capabilities Perspective on the Effects of Early Internationalization on Firm Survival and Growth," *Academy of Management Review*, 2006, 31(4), 914; and Lianxi Zhou, Wei-ping Wu, and Xueming Luo, "Internationalization and the Performance of Born-Global SMEs: The Mediating Role of Social Networks," *Journal of International Business Studies*, 2007, 38(4), 673.

3. See www.google.com and www.yahoo.com.

4. See www.skype.com.

5. "Mandarin 2.0," *Economist*, June 7, 2007, and www.chinesepod.com.

6. See www.tutorvista.com and "Face Value: The Outsourcer," *Economist*, June 23, 2007, p. 76.

7. Riva Richmond, "More Small Firms Expand Abroad," *Wall Street Journal*, July 3, 2007, p. A12.

8. Jon Boone, "Global Network of Schools Planned," *Financial Times*, June 23-24, 2007, p. 3.

9. Thomas L. Friedman, *The World Is Flat*. New York: Farrar, Strauss & Giroux, 2005.

10. See J. Bruderl and R. Schussler, "Organizational Mortality: The Liability of Newness and Adolescence," *Administrative Science Quarterly*, 1990, 35(3), 530–547; and J. Bruderl, P. Preisendorfer, and R. Ziegler, "Survival Chances of Newly Founded Business Organizations," *American Sociological Review*, 1992, 57(2), 227–242.

11. See Srilata Zaheer, "Overcoming the Liability of Foreignness," *Academy of Management Journal*, 1995, 38(2), 341–363.

12. See www.yahoo.com, www.ebay.com, and www.Amazon.com.

13. See www.approva.net.

Chapter Nine

1. "Mapping the Global Future," *Report of the U.S. National Intelligence Council's 2020 Project*, Dec. 2004 (see www.dni.gov/nic/NIC_globaltrend2020.html).

2. D. Wilson and R. Purushothaman, "Dreaming with BRICs: The Path to 2050," *Goldman Sachs Global Economics Paper No. 99*, Oct. 2003; and T. Poddar and Eva Yi, "India's Rising Growth Potential," *Goldman Sachs Global Economics Paper No. 152*, Jan. 2007.

3. See "Mapping the Global Future."

4. A condensed version of the ideas in this chapter was published as an invited article by Anil K. Gupta and Haiyan Wang, "Getting China and India Right," *Wall Street Journal*, Apr. 28, 2007.

5. See Angus Maddison, *The World Economy: Historical Statistics*. OECD, 2003. Maddison is perhaps the most renowned scholar of world economic

history and has published a series of books for the OECD on the changing structure of the world economy over the last two thousand years.

6. See "Dreaming with BRICs."

7. In 2004, the percentage of paved roads to total was 81 percent in China versus 47 percent in India; rail lines hauled five times as much goods tonnage in China as in India; and, China's port container traffic was eighteen times that of India's. See World Bank, *World Development Indicators 2007*.

8. In 2006, China and India attracted $79 billion and $7 billion respectively in inbound FDI. See World Bank, *World Development Indicators 2007*.

9. In March 2007, China enacted a new enterprise income tax law due to take effect from January 1, 2008. Under this law, the corporate tax rates would be equal for foreign as well as domestic enterprises. In effect, for domestic enterprises, the tax rates would come down from 33 percent to 25 percent; and, for foreign enterprises, they would go up from the current average of 15 percent to 25 percent.

10. Authors' field interviews plus an IDC India survey as reported in Amy Yee, "Soaring Salaries to Hit India IT Group Margins," *Financial Times*, Sept. 12, 2007, p. 18.

11. See V. Wadhwa, G. Greffi, B. Rissing, and R. Ong, "Where the Engineers Are," *Issues in Science and Technology*, National Academy of Sciences, Spring 2007.

12. See "Inequality in Asia," report by Asian Development Bank, Aug. 8, 2007.

13. See Luisa Kroll and Allison Fass, "The World's Billionaires," *Forbes*, Mar. 8, 2007.

14. In September 2007, Philip Murtaugh would leave SAIC to join Chrysler LLC as the chief executive of its Asian operations. From all evidence including our interviews with SAIC executives, it appears that Murtaugh's one-year tenure at SAIC was viewed as positive and productive by both sides.

15. "Wim Elfrink Discusses Globalization and the Decision by Cisco Systems Inc to Focus on India," Cisco Systems, July 12, 2007 (http://newsroom.cisco.com.dlls/2007/ts_071207.html).

The Authors

Anil K. Gupta (agupta@rhsmith.umd.edu) is the Ralph J. Tyser Professor of Strategy and Organization, Research Director–Dingman Center for Entrepreneurship, and Research Director–Center for International Business Education & Research at the Robert H. Smith School of Business, The University of Maryland–College Park. He earned his doctorate from the Harvard Business School. He has been recognized by *Business Week* as an Outstanding Faculty in its *Guide to the Best B-Schools* and honored with inclusion in the *Academy of Management Journals' Hall of Fame*. The recipient of numerous research and teaching awards, Dr. Gupta has authored over sixty articles in major journals as well as three books including *Global Strategy and Organization* (John Wiley, 2003), and *Smart Globalization* (Jossey-Bass, 2003). His next book on *The Battle for China and India* (coauthored with Haiyan Wang) will be published in 2008. He is a regular speaker at major industry and academic conferences and serves as an adviser, consultant, and director for corporations in the United States, Europe, and Asia.

Vijay Govindarajan (vijay.govindarajan@tuck.dartmouth.edu) is the Earl C. Daum 1924 Professor of International Business at the Tuck School of Business. His areas of expertise are strategy, globalization, innovation, and execution. He has been recognized by *BusinessWeek*, *Forbes*, and the *London Times* as a top thought leader in the field of strategy. He works with CEOs and top management teams in Fortune 1000 corporations to discuss, challenge, and escalate their thinking about strategy. He is the coauthor of the best-selling book, *Ten Rules for Strategic Innovators: From Idea to Execution*, which has been rated by the *Wall Street Journal* as a Top 10 Recommended Read. He is on a one-year leave from Tuck to join General Electric (GE) in a new role as "professor in residence and chief innovation consultant" to advance GE's growth and innovation agenda.

Haiyan Wang (hwang@chinaindiainstitute.com) is Managing Partner of China India Institute, a Bethesda, Maryland–based research and consulting organization dedicated to helping companies develop more effective global business strategies regarding China and India. A native of China, she has spent the last twenty years consulting for and managing multinational business operations in China and the United States in several different industry sectors. Her experience includes managing steel imports for one of China's largest conglomerates and serving as a consultant for Kepner-Tregoe, as director of business development for E-Steel, and as director of marketing & operations for PTI Inc. Drawing on her broad international experience, she consults with clients and speaks at conferences on building and exploiting global presence, especially in China. Her coauthored article titled "Getting China and India Right" was published recently by the *Wall Street Journal*.

Index